Writing Handbook

for COMPUTER PROFESSIONALS

Writing
Handbook
for COMPUTER
PROFESSIONALS

William D. Skees

LIFETIME LEARNING PUBLICATIONS
BELMONT, CALIFORNIA
A division of Wadsworth, Inc.

London, Singapore, Sydney, Toronto, Mexico City

Jacket and Text Designer: Richard Kharibian

Editor: Gail Todd

Illustrator: Carl Brown

Composition: Bi-Comp

Printed in the United States of America

1 2 3 4 5 6 7 8 9 10—86 85 84 83 82

Library of Congress Cataloging in Publication Data

Skees, William D., 1939–
    Writing handbook for computer professionals.

    Bibliography: p.
    Includes index.
    1. Electronic data processing—Authorship.
I. Title.
QA76.165.S53   808'.066001021   82-190
ISBN 0-534-97946-7   AACR2

Contents

PART D Promotional Writing 243

*To Elizabeth Riddle, tireless typist and
irreplaceable resource; to Carol, perpetual rallier-round; to Shannon and Edward,
long past being surprised by their Dad;
to John Sayer, quintessential consultant.*

ACKNOWLEDGMENTS

We are grateful to the following publishers and organizations for permission to reprint material used in this book.

Acropolis Books for the material from *Writing with Precision* by Jefferson D. Bates used in section 4.4.3.

Petrocelli/Charter for the forms from *Systems and Programming Standards* by Susan Wooldridge used in figures 8-14 through 8-17.

American Management Associations for the forms from *Management Standards for Developing Information Systems* by Norman L. Enger used in figures 8-18 through 8-20.

Van Nostrand Reinhold for the diagrams of the HIPO method from *Systems Design and Documentation* by Harry Katzan, Jr., used in figures 9-5 through 9-7.

IBM for the Flowcharting Worksheet (figure 9-11) and for the extracts (figures 11-1, 11-4, and 11-5) from the "Information Management System/360, Version 2, General Information Manual."

Creative Computing magazine for the excerpt from "Landing Simulator" by Jake Jacobs used in figure 9-13.

Wang Laboratories for the examples of abbreviated and detailed error messages from the *Wang BASIC Language Reference Manual* used in figures 11-6 and 11-7.

McDonnell Douglas Automation Company for the McDonnell Automation Directive from "Control Procedure CP 14.501-K" used in figures 12-10a and 12-10b.

Prentice-Hall for the quotation from *Software Reliability Guidebook* by Robert L. Glass used in section 14.1.3.

The University of Kentucky Computer Center for the excerpts from *The Kentucky Register* used in figures 15-2a, 15-2b, and 15-3.

Preface

WHO THIS BOOK IS FOR

This book is intended for anyone in the computing field who needs to communicate in writing. This includes programmers, systems analysts, managers, documentation writers, technical writers, procedure writers, operators, administrators, clerical support personnel and anyone else who has a need to "write it down and send it out."

WHY IT IS USEFUL

This work is a *practical, complete* and *comprehensive* tool, to be used in all types of data processing and computer-related writing:

Correspondence Shows how to write economically, clearly, and persuasively and how to get results.

Vendor surveys and requirement studies Teaches how to conduct surveys and requirements studies on time and within budget.

User documentation Explains how to write documents that teach non-technical people exactly what they need to know in order to use computer systems confidently and effectively.

Systems analysis and design documents   Shows how to use structured top-down techniques to guarantee a thorough job of analysis and logical development; how to explain the results of logical analysis using straightforward, expositional writing; how to present findings and recommendations so as to generate interest and motivate the reader.

Promotional documents   Shows how to present and describe products and ideas, how to develop and present budgets, and how to sell people through carefully worded résumés.

Presentations   Teaches how technically-oriented computer professionals can reach non-technically oriented top level managers through well-chosen and informative graphic techniques and fast-moving presentations.

HOW IT IS ORGANIZED

This book consists of four main parts. *Part A* presents the *general background* for skills and techniques needed in all kinds of computer writing. *Part B* focuses on *writing technical documentation and project development communication. Part C* concentrates on *writing of a managerial and administrative nature. Part D* covers *marketing and promotional writing,* such as proposals, résumés and brochures.

This work is organized for quick reference by busy professionals. Both the table of contents and the detailed index list topics by page and by section numbers, thus making the reference task easy.

I believe that you will find this text to be a helpful and practical tool in all your written communication.

William D. Skees

Writing Handbook
for COMPUTER PROFESSIONALS

PART A

Fundamentals of DP Writing

This section provides rules and techniques essential to success in every kind of DP writing.

1

The Computer Professional's Writing Challenge

1.1 THE ROOTS OF THE PROBLEM

Programmers, systems analysts, and managers spend the majority of their time writing, yet they give surprisingly little attention to improving the writing skills that keep them in business. Programmers are paid to write programs and specifications. Systems analysts are paid to write studies and specifications. Managers are paid to write proposals, budgets, and procedures.

When not actually engaged in writing, the computer professional spends time attending meetings, the purpose of which is to initiate and produce writing. A conference to establish the contents of a new manual is an example of such a meeting.

Other meetings may be called to modify existing written material—perhaps to change the specifications for software products. Still other meetings extend writing that is in progress by adding new material. Such meetings occur when DP managers meet for the purpose of improving the general appearance of documentation by adding either more detail or more summary information to that documentation. (A note on terminology: I have found the phrase "computer professional" to be the best phrase for identifying the audience for this book. Since this phrase does not adapt well to an adjective form, I have used an older term, "data processing," usually employing the initials DP, as in "a DP study." This use avoids such awkward phrases as "a computer professional's study" and the obviously ambiguous form "a computer study.")

Despite all these writing responsibilities, computer professionals get little or no formal training in writing. In fact, for members of a profession whose livelihood depends on communication, *data processing people are often quite poor at written communication.*

1.1.1 Programmers with Writing Problems

The computer industry is about thirty years old. After all this time programmer-to-computer communication is still so ineffective that more money is spent on repairing errant programs than on writing programs in the first place.

Part of the fault lies with poor programming techniques. However, another significant part of the system reliability problem results from each programmer's inability to communicate design ideas to other programmers who must develop and maintain the code. This book deals with this person-to-person side of a programmer's writing.

1.1.2 Systems Analysts with Writing Problems

Many systems analysts have a similar communications problem. Often the systems analyst-to-programmer communication is so ineffective that the programmers end up building the system to their own liking. This is a sure guarantee that a company-wide trauma will follow when people try to use the new system.

Sometimes users and systems analysts communicate so poorly that no final agreement is ever reached on system specifications. Then the analysts must make arbitrary decisions to keep systems from being abandoned. These hasty decisions have detrimental consequences.

1.1.3 Managers with Writing Problems

In both government and industry, I have seen managers flounder again and again when trying to sell proposals acceptable to customers and top management. I have known computer center managers who seem unable to produce or obtain a cogent written statement of users' needs. This book was written for people who have experienced or who have been concerned about such problems.

1.2   WHAT COMPUTER PROFESSIONALS WRITE

A data processing person does not normally think of himself as a professional writer, yet he is paid to spend his time writing. What exactly do computer professionals write?

1.2.1   Programmers

Programmers write the *programs* which computers will execute. They write the *specifications*, both general and detailed, from which the programs are created. They write *reports*—status reports, performance reports, testing reports. They write *manuals*—manuals for operators to follow in running the programs and manuals for users to follow in using code.

Programmers write *procedures* for people to follow—for users to follow when utilizing programs, for other programmers to follow when linking common modules together, and for computer center employees to follow when handling decks, listings, or library modules. Programmers write *correspondence*—from memoranda to detailed installation guides—answering inquiries about programs, ordering information, or advising other installations about how to make use of programs.

1.2.2   Systems Analysts

Systems analysts also spend their time writing. They produce *study reports* and *specifications*—systems specifications, external specifications, program specifications, performance specifications, and a myriad of other reports which contain the products of systems analysis activities.

Systems analysts also write documents connected with the administrative and human side of things. Such writing includes *correspondence*—seeking, giving, and revising information. They write *manuals of instruction* so that other people can use programs and follow procedures, and they write the *procedures* for others to follow.

1.2.3 Managers

Managers also spend much of their time writing. Managers who have profit and loss responsibility or cost center responsibility must spend time developing *budgets,* a process that calls for creative work as well as painstaking crossfooting and reconciliation with other documents.

Managers also write *letters* to one another and to other organizations. Managers have the responsibility of setting policies and for carrying them out; consequently, they must write *directives* incorporating the procedures which implement those policies. Managers also write *reports* to other managers.

Any of these professionals—programmers, analysts, and managers—may be called away from their regular writing activities and asked to write, or to join with a team of others in writing, *proposals* for new business contracts. They may be called upon to give *presentations* to top management and to prospective clients.

1.3 WHY IMPROVE DP WRITING SKILLS?

The primary benefit of improving written communication is to make that communication more effective, that is, to achieve results. Effective communication is so important that today data processing professionals must have top-quality writing skills in order to be competitive and successful.

1.3.1 Time Saving and Productivity

An improvement in writing skill has two implications—less time is spent in writing an individual document, and documents are of better quality. Of course spending less time with each document means that there is more time to turn out more documents. Hence, there is also a payoff in improved productivity.

1.3.2 Easier Writing + Easier Reading = Greater Effectiveness

Writing better means using techniques that make it *easier to write,* that make the written products *easier to read,* and that make the documents *more effective.*

Documents are easier to write when you know ahead of time how to organize your material and put the words together. For some, the major hurdle is learning what to do first—how to make that first step—so that the ice is broken, and the words begin to flow. I call this problem the "blank page syndrome" (see section 3.1).

Making a document easier to read requires that the document be short and convincing. The document should make its point in a straight-forward way, so that the reader does not have to spend too much time puzzling over what you are trying to say.

The combination of these two things, easier writing and easier reading, makes for a more effective document. The less time it takes to write something, to read it, and to understand it, the sooner the reader can get down to action. A directive that is written quickly and is readily understood becomes a directly implementable procedure.

1.3.3   Better Management

Effective writing means better management of your own time and better use of the reader's time. This translates directly into increased productivity, that is, more communication yield per man-hour.

1.3.4   More Effective Management

Effective writing means more effective management of the systems development process. It is inefficient, for example, to have a computer programmer spend part of his time programming something—that is, communicating his thoughts to a computer—and then spend the rest of his time documenting it—that is, communicating those same thoughts to a human being.

It is much more efficient to have the programmer develop his logic first, using a written logic analysis tool such as HIPO diagrams (see section 9.1.2). Then he can publish those diagrams as a deliverable document such as a programming specification. If a document serves the programmer as a tool for working out his logic and at the same time serves the manager as a deliverable, then I call such a document a *double-duty document*. Double-duty documents are discussed fully in section 2.5.

1.4   WHAT THIS BOOK DOES

Each of the documents discussed earlier in this chapter has a particular audience and a specific objective. In order to produce the unique document required by each combination of audience and objective, you must employ a unique set of tools. Each combination calls for planning, organizing, and wording skills.

This book provides guidlines for planning these documents. It shows through rules and examples how to organize the material, and it discusses the style of wording appropriate to each document.

This book covers all types of data processing writing:

- *correspondence that gets results.* It investigates how to write economically and how to get action.
- *vendor surveys and requirements studies.* It shows how to conduct surveys and requirements studies in a thoroughly professional way. That is, it shows how to do these studies on time and within budget.
- *systems analysis and design documents.* It shows how to use structured top-down techniques in order to guarantee a thorough job of analysis and logical development. It shows how to explain the results of logical analysis using straightforward, motivational writing. It shows how to present findings and recommendations in a convincing manner to the reading audience.
- *promotional documents.* It shows how to present and describe products and ideas, how to reveal and describe budgets, and how to sell people through resumes.
- *presentations.* It shows how technically oriented data processing professionals can reach non-technically oriented top level managers through well-chosen and informative graphic techniques and fast-moving presentations.

1.5   HIGHLIGHTS

- Whether they realize it or not, data processing people are professional writers, yet they pay little attention to their writing skills.

- Programmers, systems analysts, and managers turn out a large number of different documents, each with a specific audience and objective, and each requiring appropriate planning, organizing, and wording.
- Improved writing skills will result in increased productivity, more effective use of time, and better management.

2

Writing Basics for the Computer Profession

2.1 THE PRINCIPLES OF EFFECTIVE WRITING

There are three ingredients which are essential to every successful writing endeavor. These ingredients are the same whether you are writing for a technical audience or for a newspaper audience, whether you are writing works of fact or works of fiction. You must know your subject. You must know your audience. You must know your objective.

In my writing experience, I have found that managing the writing process means limiting the document. You limit the document so that the writing does, after all, get finished. You also limit the document so that you cover all that has to be presented but only that which has to be presented. This leads to the formula:

$$1 \text{ OBJECTIVE} + 1 \text{ AUDIENCE} + 1 \text{ SUBJECT} = 1 \text{ DOCUMENT}$$

Each combination of the three ingredients produces one unique document. Change any one term in the formula and you must write a different document. Let us look at the ingredients in the subject-audience-objective formula a little more closely.

2.1.1   Know Your Subject

You are responsible. Someone else's facts are o.k. but they must be verified.
There is nothing more embarrassing than realizing that the person you
are talking to knows you don't know what you are talking about. In
order to be successful as a writer of data processing documents, you
must know your subject. You must understand what you are trying to
say so that you can get that understanding across to the audience.

Authorship responsibility. With systems studies—feasibility studies,
requirements studies, systems analysis reports—you are primarily engaged in presenting facts. As author of one of these documents, or as the
team leader of a group writing one of these documents, you are responsible for all the facts that appear in that document.

They may be somebody else's facts. That is, you may have gotten
the facts from someone, or one of your subordinates may have gotten
the facts for you. The point is that you are responsible for the accuracy of
whatever facts you use in your writing.

Verification. Obviously it is not possible to verify each and every
fact, yet each fact must nonetheless be verified. What I have found
works is to require each of my subordinates to record the source for each
of his facts, then I *verify a random sample of those facts to make sure that
the recording is accurate.* This gives me a statistical basis of confidence
when I turn the report over to my client or to my boss.

2.1.2   Know Your Audience

If you want your written documents to be effective, you must be well
aware of the nature, the background, the education, and the interests of
the audience for which you are writing. You must write in the language
that your audience uses every day.

Suppose you are describing a nationwide communications system
with distributive computers. Suppose, further, that the audience consists of bankers whose banks will be interlinked by this computer network. In this case you must try to use terms from the banking community such as debits, credits, and transactions, rather than computer
terms such as characters, bytes, records, and blocks.

Unfamiliar terms, acronyms, and abbreviations. If it is necessary to
introduce a term that is unfamiliar to your audience, then you must
define that term. How you define the term is a matter of style.

In my company, writers prefer to introduce a new term by setting it off in quotation marks, and then giving a one or two sentence definition of that term. The definition is not repeated in the same document.

If a document is complex or there are many new terms introduced throughout the document, writers sometimes find it useful to attach an *index to terms used* in the document or to attach a *glossary* in which the terms are redefined.

An audience should be familiar with any acronyms or abbreviations you use in the writing. (An acronym is a word formed from the initial letters of a name.) In my company, whenever anyone mentions the name of the company in writing, he writes out the company's name and then follows the name with the leading capital letters in parentheses. Subsequent appearances on the same page require only the initials of the company.

Reading the readers' minds. When writing for a particular audience, try to think as the members of that audience would think. When you raise an issue that is sure to suggest a certain question in your reader's mind, anticipate that question and answer it immediately in the text. That way your presentation will be parallel to and slightly ahead of the audience's thinking as they read through the document. You will have established an author-audience rapport.

It is also important to tie your writing to the audience's own experience and business background. Suppose that you are describing a warehouse inventory control system, and you want to discuss a particular function that the new automated system is going to perform. You can show how the present manual inventory control system depends on that particular function or how the present system suffers because the function is not present. For example, you might show how the proposed inventory control system would locate a particular item of stock on the shelf or how it would calculate the economic order quantity (EOQ) for that particular item.

2.1.3 Know Your Objective

Whatever document you write must be a means to a specific end. The document must reflect and support your objective. It must provide exactly what is needed to make that end achievable:

- *investigative documents.* The document must explain the advantages and disadvantages of each approach, and be self-sufficient in helping management to reach a decision.

- *instructive, analytic, and developmental documents.* The document must reveal the underlying logic and the particulars of whatever process you are describing.
- *directive documents.* The document must clearly, unambiguously, and in sufficient detail, provide instructions for carrying out a particular policy of the organization.
- *archival documents.* The document must faithfully, succinctly, and unambiguously describe what has happened.
- *promotional documents.* The document must be able to sell what it is intended to sell without being dependent on an oral presentation to accompany it.

2.2 THE AXIOMS OF DP WRITING

2.2.1 Writing Need Not Be Difficult

Several years ago my boss told me something which I have found very useful in all business activities—writing, speaking, and decision making. It was equally applicable to proposals and to programs. His advice was this:

> You don't have to be creative to be successful.
> You only have to be resourceful.

I have taken this advice to mean that when you have an intellectual problem to solve, like the problem of writing a study or a specification or a letter, you need not look around for inspiration. Indeed, you may find no inspiration.

However, you *can* always be resourceful. Suppose you are at least faintly acquainted with the subject matter. Then in order to get started, it is necessary only to write down what you know about that subject even if this is little more than where to find information on that subject. If so, then you should write down all the places where you expect to find that information. Then you simply proceed to dig up the information out of those places.

You can also be resourceful by generating and using previously written material. If the material is well-written, and if you have the right to use it, why not do so? Suppose you had a project which you had taken from the conception stage through the design stage to the programming stage. The system concept in the study would become the system overview in the specification (see figure 2-1).

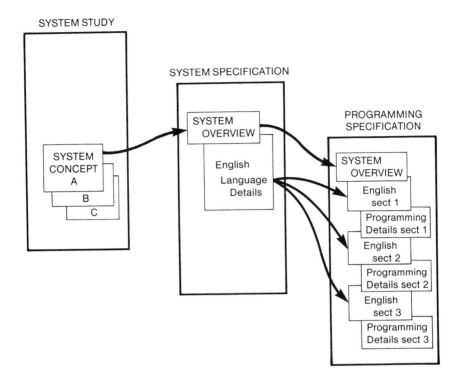

Figure 2-1. Old Material Can Be Reused

2.2.2   There Is a Format for Everything

Another aspect of this resourcefulness business is that you need not even dream up from your creative intellect the format that you are going to use for a particular document. Throughout the industry there are formats which are standards of one sort or another. These formats tell you how to write a document and how to organize the material that goes into it.

Some formats are formal. That is, they are standards. Of these, some are published standards; others are merely precedents that you can follow from one document to the next or from one generation of documents to the next (see figure 2-2, part A).

Some formats are informal. That is, they are traditional ways of doing things in a particular setting (see figure 2-2, part B). For example, one consulting company that I know traditionally uses an executive summary with every report. (An executive summary is a recapitulation of the entire report, condensed for the busy executive reader.)

A. *formal format*—an official standard, e.g.,

THE SYSTEM SPECIFICATION STANDARD
for A. B. Cdef Corporation

I. *Introduction*
The introduction will contain a statement of purpose and a brief summary of the system concept.

I.1 ---

I.1a --

I.1b --

I.2 ---

B. *informal format* using the traditional form, i.e., by example

```
┌──────────────────┐     ┌──────────────────┐
│      WICS        │     │      ABC         │
│     SYSTEM       │     │     SYSTEM       │
│  SPECIFICATION   │     │  SPECIFICATION   │
│     MANUAL       │     │     REPORT       │
└──────────────────┘     └──────────────────┘
```

Figure 2-2. Formats

Some formats are like newspaper formats. When there is no standard or traditional way to lay out a document, the newspaper format is your fall-back position. The newspaper format says "Tell them right away— tell them who, what, where, and when. Fill in the details later."

2.3 GOLDEN RULE OF AUTHORSHIP

The golden rule goes back further than my research can determine. It dates at least from the first years of this century where I have seen it in manuals dealing with writing. The rule is *write unto others as you would have others write unto you.*

2.3.1 Information Content

The rule means to write in such a way that you would be interested in reading your own writing. For example, what would you yourself like to know about database management if you were new to database technology? What you would want to know is what you should write.

2.3.2   Organization and Access

The golden rule also applies to organizing the material that goes into the document. How much time would you be willing to spend to find a particular item in that document? More than likely you would want to be able to locate the item quickly. This ability is especially valuable in user manuals and operator's manuals. It calls for such features as carefully-prepared indexes and informative tables of contents.

A quick reference user manual also contains lists of error messages. In systems analysis documents "quick reference" may mean a visual table of contents (VTOC) in the HIPO structured design methodology (see section 9.1.2). How you organize a manual should reflect the way you would prefer to find your way around in it if you were the reader.

What tone would you expect to find in the document you are reading? Generally, you would expect a completely atonal report in anything dealing with technical matters. Emotion has no place in technical writing.

2.4   MANAGING BY DELIVERABLES

There is a close correlation between good programming management and good documentation. The effective DP manager gets things done through documentation. The documents which his subordinates prepare are an extension of his own management activities, controlling the day to day programming development tasks.

2.4.1   Keeping in Touch

Except in the very smallest shops, it is not possible for the DP manager to be right on top of the development work that his programmers are doing. Frequently, DP managers tend to rely on an occasional exchange of small talk to find out what their programmers are doing. Unfortunately this approach hides some of the real problems associated with software development.

2.4.2   Writing Things Down

The truly effective manager insists that his programmers put things on paper. He insists that they do this in a straightforward, understandable way, following certain rules. In other words, he requires a form of structured documentation. The structure should be a flexible one which is directed toward the production of code rather than toward making a record for a project archive. Properly done, this documentation not only helps the programmer write good code but it helps the manager control the project. It is double-duty documentation (see section 2.5).

2.4.3   Communication Gaps

Data processing is a highly technical field, and frequently only the person writing a program really understands it. As a result, there is a natural communication gulf between a programmer or systems analyst and his manager.

Through informal conversation the manager can obtain at best only the vaguest idea of where a programmer or an analyst is in his current project at that particular time. In fact, such casually-obtained information is demonstrably unreliable.

Consider the following scenario:

A manager walks by his programmer's desk. "How are things going, Joe?" asks the manager.

"Very, very well," answers the programmer. The manager goes away with a good feeling that the project is right on target. He is blissfully unaware of the real reason why the programmer is so happy today. The reason is that today, for the first time in this project, the programmer has gotten three-hour computer turnaround. All during the previous six weeks, he had been lucky to achieve forty-eight hour turnaround.

Actually the project, instead of being on target, is already one and a half months behind schedule. The prognostication is that it is probably going to be a whole lot further behind schedule very soon unless something can be done about the computer room.

With good documentation at frequent intervals the manager would have long since been aware of the degenerating computer-turnaround time problem. He would not experience the shock that is in store for him on the program's due date to find that the goal is nowhere in sight.

2.4.4   What If Something Happens?

Consider also the *runaway truck syndrome*. Assume that Joe is really doing a very good job of coding. Even though he's not doing much documentation, he is writing fantastic code. Assume further that things go along well for a time. Then something unfortunate happens. Late one night a runaway truck hits Joe on his way home from the computer center and Joe is hospitalized indefinitely.

What about the state of the project at the moment Joe was hit by the truck? If yesterday was the last time Joe wrote documentation for his program, then the project is twenty-four hours behind schedule. If, on the other hand, it has been six months since Joe made an earnest effort to explain in writing what he is doing, then the project is guaranteed to be six months behind at the instant the tragedy struck.

Just as the U.S. Army runs on its stomach, a programming project moves on its documentation. Through the documentation that he receives, a manager can tell precisely where the programmer or analyst is in his work at any time.

2.4.5   The Importance of Documentation

Too often people consider the deliverables of a programming project to consist solely of the program, or the program supplemented by a user manual. Without further documentation it is hardly feasible to hope to maintain such a program. In fact, without documentation, it is optimistic to expect to get the program working at all.

An effective manager will insist on deliverables—physical deliverables that he can touch, examine, read, and understand. These deliverables need not be extensive, but they do need to be understandable to be effective.

2.5   DOUBLE-DUTY DOCUMENTS

Too often an author looks at the production of a document as a burden. The way to get around this problem is to arrange things so that the programmer gets just as much out of the document as the manager does. Hence the double-duty document concept.

2.5.1   Complementary Uses of Documentation

Every programmer, even the very brightest, must write *some* things down on paper while he thinks out his program logic. Sometimes these things look just like doodles on a page. Sometimes they are snatches of code. By showing the programmer how to give structure to his doodles, such as with HIPO diagrams or with modular decomposition (see chapter 8), the manager can obtain the deliverable that he needs. At the same time the programmer can get on with his doodling as he works out his program logic. The two ends are complementary.

2.5.2   Discipline and Reliability

Disciplined problem analysis, disciplined program design, and disciplined program development tend to create more reliable code. The documents of any structured approach are tools which help the programmer to use that structured approach.

2.5.3   Advantage to Management

Programming is more effectively managed when the programming activities are divided into discrete steps. The completion of each step should be marked by the delivery of a particular document. If the document satisfies its documentation goals—clarity, straightforwardness, content, organization—and the document is on time, then the manager has reasonable assurance that the project is moving along properly. Also, by reading the document, he is able to spot the deficiencies in the methodology or scope of a particular sub-task. He can make corrections early, when they count.

2.5.4   Advantage to the Writer

The double-duty document avoids extra writing by making the writer's developmental worksheet and the manager's report one and the same thing. Earlier I mentioned the rule for document production—one objective + one audience + one subject = one document. The double-duty document does not violate this rule. The technical objective is still the same—to produce the developmental worksheet. Double-duty documentation satisfies management's objective at the same time by putting the document on a time schedule, where it should have been anyway.

2.6 DOCUMENT MODULARITY

Managing a programming project by deliverables requires a schedule with a very fine mesh. That is, the schedule should work with very short increments of time, each as small as a week or less. The individual documents delivered under such a schedule should be limited in scope and size. It is unrealistic to expect a programmer or an analyst to produce a 200-page specification in a week's time or less. However, the programmer or analyst *can* readily deliver a *modest* specification such as the general logic of a program module or the pseudo code of a program module in that span of time. *Modular work requires modular documents.*

2.7 HIGHLIGHTS

- To produce an effective document, you must know your subject, your audience, and your objective.
- You need not be creative to produce successful DP writing; you do need to know how to use available resources.
- Write the kind of documents you, yourself, would like to read.
- Through documentation, the effective manager keeps abreast of his programmers' activities.
- With "double-duty" documentation the programmer's developmental worksheet and the manager's report can be the same document.

3

Writing Correctly

When I teach effective writing for data processing professionals, in at least every other class one of my students will ask me how to get over stage fright in writing. In other words, how to get started writing a document—how to make the words start to flow.

I recommend that the student tackle the problem head on, taking a blank piece of paper and getting a pencil in hand. A blank sheet of paper is what scares most people, and my solution is to get things written down on that blank sheet of paper right away.

The writing instrument should be a pencil, not a pen, because there will be things to scratch out and erase.

3.1.1 Generating Ideas

I start off by asking myself what I want to put into the document. Then I just start writing down the thoughts that occur to me. I use bullets (small, round dots) to mark each item as shown in figure 3-1. There is a certain satisfaction in using the bullet—as if I were saying to myself, "There. That's another idea written down!"

It is too soon to attempt to organize material at this stage. Rather

Network Requirements Study Charter

- Current Costs

- Communications Media We Use in Maintaining Manufacturing & Marketing Activities

- Special Telephone Systems

- Computer Interfaces

- Travel

- Team

- Resources

Figure 3-1. Random Ideas for a Charter to Study Network Requirements (Note: The black dot preceding each item is called a bullet. The bullet identifies individual items.)

you should simply write down the thoughts as they occur to you. It is very tempting to say, "This item is really a sub-item of an earlier item." It is also tempting to try to combine items and say, "Oh, I have actually mentioned that already under a slightly different name."

These attempts at organization, while meritorious, are misplaced. They lead you into trying to do two contradictory things at the same time. One thing is to generate ideas; another thing is to organize those ideas and to put them into relationships with one another. The brain is less effective when it tries to do two things at once, so leave the organizing activities till the second stage.

Very soon you will see the blank piece of paper begin to fill up. In fact, you may cover page after page before exhausting your imagination. This is the time to stop and have a cup of coffee. Then come back and go to the second step—organization.

3.1.2 Organizing Your Ideas

Here is where you will appreciate the unique capabilities of pencils. Begin to move things around, putting some items under others, combining some, and changing the spelling, terminology, and phrasing of others to achieve parallel ideas and to get themes developed in a straightforward way.

The first sub-task of this step is to do the marking up on the original sheet of paper (see figure 3-2). Only after it becomes too messy to make any further improvements by marking up, do I attempt to recopy (see figure 3-3). In recopying I like to regenerate something that is neat, so I delay this step until I find it counterproductive to try to improve further what I have been marking up. Often, after this third step, the recopying step, I make further improvements. It is best to recopy first, producing something like figure 3-3, then to make strike outs and improvements (see figure 3-4).

The next step is to flesh out the outline. This is easy. Once the general outline is there, once the ice has been broken, it is always easy to add ideas. First, break up the ideas by doing a refined outline (see figure 3-5). The result can be immediately put into a rough draft as shown in figure 3-6.

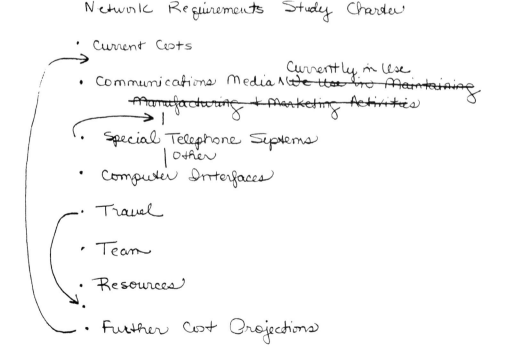

Figure 3-2. Marked Up List of Ideas

Network Requirements Study Charter

- Current Costs

- Future Cost Projections

- Communications Media Currently in Use
  - Telephone Systems
  - Other

- Computer Interfaces

- Team

- Resources

- Travel

Figure 3-3. Recopied List of Ideas

The realization that it is much easier to add to an existing outline than to begin writing on a blank page was brought home to me years ago by a fellow worker at a university computer center.

Before I came to understand his situation, I was puzzled by his reaction when we were given assignments by our boss. We would be assigned to do the work together, but he would defer making any contribution until I had produced a first draft. Then, it seemed to me, he would tear it to shreds.

Later I came to realize that he was actually improving what I had written by critiquing and making additions. At the time I was too involved in writing the document, and had too much pride of authorship, to appreciate that contribution.

I have subsequently found that it seems to be easier for everyone, not just that person, to add to an existing document rather than to create a new document.

The fleshed out outline leads very naturally into a text. It only needs to have the thoughts wrought into complete sentences, the ideas

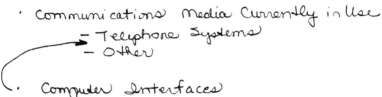

Network Requirements Study Charter

- Current Costs

- Future Cost Projections

- Communications Media Currently in Use
  - Telephone Systems
  - Other

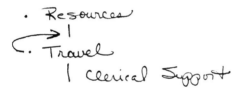

- Computer Interfaces

- Team

- Resources
- Travel
  | Clerical Support

Figure 3-4. Improved Copy

checked for logical development, and the words and sentences reviewed for readability. It has become a finished document!

3.2 GRAMMAR

Incorrect grammar and poorly constructed sentences lead to ambiguity. In the following example, the double negative leads to total confusion:

> Never execute file merge when none of the file checking routines have been linked.

Because of the double negatives "never" and "none," the above sentence might cause one reader to assume that the file merge programs were to be run only with file checking, and another reader to assume

Network Requirements Study Charter

- Authorization
- Current Costs
- Future Cost Projections (5 years)
- Interviews
- Current Communications Systems
    - Telephone
    - Computer
    - Mail
    - Other
- Ootential Communications Technologies
- Team
    - Organization
    - Individuals
- Resources
    - Facilities
    - Clerical Support
    - Travel

Figure 3-5. Refined Outline

that they were to be run without file checking. If the former were meant, you should say:

Run file merge with the file checking routines.

If the latter were intended, you should write:

Never run file merge with file checking routines.

3.2.1 Correct Usage

There are some ungrammatical usages in data processing that cause the purist to grit his teeth when he encounters them in the text. One example is the word *input*. The word *input* is a noun, not a verb. It should *not* be used in the following manner: "Input the data". The proper usage is "Enter the data." Unfortunately, the verb usage is becoming more prev-

Network Requirements Study Charter

The Vice President – Marketing has authorized the establishment of a study team to determine our company's requirements for a communications network or networks. The team will identify current costs of communications and ~~future~~ project costs ~~for~~ a 5-year planning horizon. ~~By~~ Primarily through interviews with the managers involved, they will investigate our current telephone, computer, mail and other communications systems.

The team will ~~perform limited~~ attempt to identify the communications technologies that will be available in ~~the~~ planning time frame.

The ~~study~~ team will consist of . . .

Figure 3-6. First Draft from Refined Outline

alent and eventually the computer industry will probably come to accept *input* as a verb.

The word *data* is also misused. *Data* is a plural noun, not a singular one. If you intend to put a single element of information into the system, you should use the phrase "Enter the datum," not "Enter the data." The latter form is correct only if you mean more than one element. Unfortunately, *data* as a singular noun is becoming acceptable usage, probably because so few people are familiar with Latin. Latin students know that *datum* is singular and *data* is plural.

A more serious problem caused by a lack of knowledge of Latin shows up frequently in computer documents. The problem is the confusion between the terms "e.g.," *exempli gratia*, and "i.e.," *id est*. "E.g." means *for example* and "i.e." means *that is*. A typical misuse of these Latin abbreviations occurs in the following sentence:

> There are several large-scale computers, i.e., the IBM 3033, which will do the job.

It is obvious that the author is talking about a class of computers, not a single computer. It is appropriate instead to use "e.g." as in the following:

> There are several large-scale computers, e.g., the IBM 3033, which will do the job.

The proper use of "i.e." is illustrated in the following sentence:

> We used our other computer, i.e. the IBM 3033, to do the job.

3.2.2 Passive Voice

A practice which leads to a multitude of problems in technical writing is the practice of using the passive voice. In an active-voice sentence, the subject of the sentence *does* the action. In a passive-voice sentence, something *is done* to the subject of the sentence. For example, "The boy throws the ball" is an active-voice sentence. "The ball is thrown by the boy" is a passive-voice sentence.

The first problem with the passive voice is that it is wordier than the active voice. "The report was written by the project team" (passive) takes two more words than "The project team wrote the report" (active).

The passive voice tends to make extra work for the writer and hence extra work for the reader. Suppose that you are writing a manual giving instructions for a user to follow. The passive voice leads us to sentence groups such as the following:

> The employee number should be entered. Then the employee name should be entered. Then the date of birth should be entered. This should be done by the shift supervisor and his initials should be entered and his account number should be validated.

The extra, final sentence is needed to identify the responsible party. It is much more succinct to use the active voice and say:

> The shift supervisor should enter his initials and his password. Then he should enter employee number, employee name, and date of birth.

Here the responsible party appears as the subject of the first sentence. In order to be as precise as the active voice, the passive voice has to be more wordy.

The passive voice is useful for an occasional change of pace from the active voice. Other than that, there is not much to be said for it in the business environment. Today's technical world is an action oriented world and the passive voice is, after all, well, passive.

3.2.3 Transition Words

Ideas can be linked together by using words which are transitional in nature, that is by using words which point back to a preceding idea as having an obvious relationship to its successor. A good example is the following:

> We have a heavy workload, but we continue to meet our deadlines.

The word *but* here is a transitional word and it shows that the first idea has an important relationship to the second idea.

At first, it might seem that the use of transitionals will cause your sentences to get longer and your writing to become confusing. Such is not the case. Two thoughts linked by a transitional are two sequential and distinct thoughts which can be digested one at a time, in the order in which they are encountered. Ideas linked by transitionals are as easily processed as those set off by periods.

The complicated way to link ideas is to bury one thought within the other. An example of the wrong way to do it is the following:

> We continue, although we have a heavy workload, to meet our deadlines.

The second thought is buried within the first one, and the sentence is very hard to read and understand the first time around. A better version would be

> Although we have a heavy workload, we continue to meet our deadlines.

It is best to keep transitionals simple. For example, use the word *yet* or the word *but* rather than *however*. Likewise, the word *so* is preferable to *therefore*.

3.2.4 Parallel Sentence Elements

Using parallel elements is a very effective technique for tying thoughts together in a way that preserves their relationships and, in fact, emphasizes their relationships. The following sentence illustrates the use of parallel elements:

> We chose this compiler because it is fast, has good diagnostics, and implements advanced language features.

The parallel elements are well illustrated in the following way:

> We chose this compiler because it:
> a. is fast
> b. has good diagnostics
> c. implements advanced language features.

Here it should be obvious that *a, b,* and *c* are parallel elements. Structurally they all begin with a verb and semantically they all are characteristics or features of the compiler that we are discussing.

While everyone tends to use parallel sentence elements, not everyone uses them grammatically. You often run into this incorrect construction:

> We chose this compiler because:
> a. it is fast
> b. good diagnostics
> c. implements advanced language features.

The best that can be said about this example is that each of the three elements has something to do with the characteristics of the compiler. Structurally though, the sentence is terrible. Part *a* is a complete sentence in itself, part *b* is simply an adjective phrase, and part *c* is a sentence fragment beginning with a verb.

Another bad example is the following:

> We are using ILLIAC-IV because of its matrix processors and to solve our differential equations faster.

The two ideas after the word *because* should be parallel in structure, but they are not. Either of the two following examples is preferable:

> We are using ILLIAC-IV because of its array processor and its ability to solve differential equations faster.

> We are using ILLIAC-IV because of its array processor and its faster solution of differential equations.

3.2.5 Pronouns

When you use a pronoun such as *he, she, it, they, his,* or *her,* make sure that your reader knows what the pronoun refers to. For example, in the following sentence the reader is not sure whether the second *his* refers to the manager or to the subordinate:

> A DP manager should teach his subordinate to write good documentation as part of his job.

If *his* refers to the subordinate, a better sentence would be:

A DP manager should teach his subordinates to write good documentation as part of their jobs.

If *his* refers to the manager, you could write:

As part of his job, a DP manager should teach his subordinate to write good documentation.

3.3 SPELLING

Many of the people who attend my class have ten to twenty years of data processing experience and admit with embarrassment that they have spelling problems. I could indict the school systems and claim that spelling was not properly taught in the sixties and seventies, but that would be looking backward rather than forward. What is the best way to deal with poor spelling?

First of all, you might ally yourself with a dependable secretary/typist who is alert to spelling errors and who will do a conscientious job of cleaning up manuscript in letters and other data processing documents. Second, recognize spelling for what it is—a social mark. It is the difference between writing with class and getting by. It has, however, almost no real impact on communication. For example, if you read in a document that "Use of this function will *affect* the throughput of the system," it matters not whether you spell *affect* with one *f* or two. As far as the communication value is concerned, everybody understands that you mean *affect*.

Third, remember that it is possible to learn to spell just as it is possible to learn to remember the names of people to whom you have been introduced. The trick is the same, namely to make the situation important to you. If it is important to you to remember your senator's name or your mother-in-law's name, you will remember it. Likewise, if it is important to you to distinguish between *affect* and *afect* then you will do so.

Obviously you will not learn to spell all words at the same time. You should make lists (spelled correctly) of the words which cause you trouble. You should continuously add new words to your spelling vocabulary, perhaps one a day or one a week. If you really care about your spelling, then you will put in the time. If you make it important, you will succeed.

Quick spelling. References are essential to a good spelling repertoire.

For that reason, I have included in the bibliography a list of spelling dictionaries which should be kept close at hand.

3.4 NAMING AND DEFINING COMPUTER TERMS

It is often easier to name something than it is to define it. Sometimes naming it is all you can do, because defining adds very little clarity. For example, calling something a *disk driver* gives it a name.

But is it a

- function
- capability
- feature
- module
- program
- subprogram
- routine
- subroutine
- task

or an

- architectural component?

You can think of justifications for all of these terms. In technical writing, it is best to *make the distinctions between these terms anew with each document and be consistent within that document.*

For example, my firm had a contract to develop a set of several programs which collectively made up a system. However, the contract called for a *single* entity—a model. A model should be a single program—that is a software entity. The firm's solution to the naming problem was to link the programs up by a master control program which links to the others—thus creating a single entity. The programs were then referred to as "modules" of the model, that is as program modules.

3.5 HIGHLIGHTS

- Overcome the "blank page syndrome" by simply putting down ideas as they occur. Then organize these ideas later on.
- Good grammar and usage will result in succinct, easily understood writing.
- Learn to spell correctly by making lists of problem words and by using reference books.
- If necessary, define vague terms anew with each document as the same term may mean different things in different contexts.

4

Writing Clearly

Before getting into the matters of the content and organization of the computer professional's written documents, consider this question: What qualities make any business document an effective document of communication?

4.1 PLAIN WRITING

For the four basic qualities of good communication I am indebted to Mona Shepherd and her government training course "Plain Letters for Managers" (see bibliography). These four qualities are called the Four S's. They are *shortness, simplicity, strength,* and *sincerity.*

An effective business or technical document is a *plain* document. That is, it is one that is short, simple, strong, and sincere. A plain document is *effective* for several reasons. It takes less time for the author to dictate or handwrite the document because it is short. It takes less time for the typist to type it out, and less time for the author and his supervisor to review it. The whole revision cycle takes less time. The audience expends less energy in trying to read and understand the document because it is easier to read. A *plain* document saves time for everyone concerned.

4.2 SHORTNESS

A document is more impressive if it is totally without padding. Paraphrasing Shepherd's ideas, every word that is in the document should either *tell* or *sell*, unless the word is needed to provide tone, flow, connection, interest, or rhythm.

4.2.1 Unnecessary Words

Examples of unnecessary words include the phrase *as you know*, which often shows up in correspondence. If the reader does know, then you are citing the obvious to him. If he does not know, then you are being sarcastic. In either case, the tone has a negative effect on the reader. In addition, such phrases are trite and they waste the reader's time.

You probably have acquaintances whose speaking and writing habits fall into the needless words category. A business associate of mine has a rather exasperating habit of prefacing every spoken sentence with the words *like I say*. In a typical business meeting I find myself counting the repetitions of *like I say*. Fifty to sixty per hour are not at all uncommon with him. Such habits carried over into written documents are a severe test of the reader's patience.

4.2.2 Needless Information

Information is needless if it is information that the reader either already knows or has readily available to him. For example, a sentence which begins, "Our System 370, which is IBM's upgrade of the System 360 . . ." contains needless information. Computer professionals know that IBM's System 370 is a generation or so beyond the System 360.

If you want to make the point that the System 370 is the newest machine acquired by the writer's computer center, then you should say something like this, "Our newer machine, the System 370 . . . ."

Over-referencing is another example of needless information. In correspondence one often sees this sort of thing:

> Reference is made to your invoice SAI-3456, of April 7, 1981, for programming services performed at our facility during the month of March, 1981 . . . .

The problem is that the writer has written the same thing three times (see figure 4-1). Presumably the invoice numbers are unique. Presum-

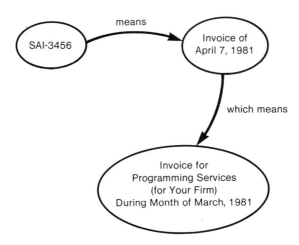

Figure 4-1. Over-Referencing

ably the firm normally issues only one invoice to a particular customer on a given day, and presumably it only invoices one time for a given piece of work. The invoice number alone would be sufficient as in the following:

> Your invoice number SAI-3456 is currently being processed.

Under-referencing is even worse than over-referencing. You must always provide the minimum amount of information which the reader needs in order to find the file, letter, or report to which you refer.

4.2.3 Long Sentences

Sometimes writers violate the shortness principle, not by adding extra words or unnecessary information, but by making sentences too long. Sometimes so many words are put into a sentence that it becomes unreadable. Every word may be important, but it is better to use several small sentences instead of one long one. For example, it is more effective to say:

> Calculate the economic reorder point. Next, compute the shipping quantity. Finally, establish the optimum freight volume.

Those three sentences are easier to digest than the following:

> The optimum freight volume should be established, but
> this requires computation of the shipping quantity, which
> cannot be done until the economic order point is calculated
> and that should be done first.

4.2.4 Qualifiers

The most frequent cause of overly long sentences is the addition of too many qualifiers. Do you find yourself writing sentences like the following?

> Because time-sharing costs were getting so high, while the
> computer mix was shifting more and more to scientific and
> to research and development type applications, we elected
> to go to an in-house batch processing computer.

The patient reader struggles mightily to find where this sentence is going. A much more effective way to say the same thing is the following:

> The cost of time-sharing was getting out of hand. The mix
> of jobs was shifting to scientific. We were becoming an
> R&D shop. These considerations forced us to shift to an
> in-house batch processing system.

Often, it is better to state the condition in one sentence and the conclusion in the next sentence rather than to bind the two together in the same sentence (see figure 4-2). That way the reader can absorb one simple idea at a time and then connect them together. This is easier than trying to find his way through a series of intricately interconnected thoughts as he looks for the main point of the sentence.

One example of the qualifying thought trap should suffice. Suppose you want to write:

> Your computer program was redesigned in September.

Your hand begins to move over the page putting pen and ink to paper. As you write you decide to add your judgment that the computer program is long overdue and prone to error. Perhaps you want to say so in order to put your reader on the defensive. Then it occurs to you that the reader may not know what program you are talking about, so while your hand is still moving you add the phrase

> to compute missile trajectories

Harder to Follow

> We needed real-time access to warehouse inventory records in order to maintain our competitive position, but we could not justify a large timesharing mainframe, so in order to get the work out we procured and installed an interactive inventory control system, consisting of a single minicomputer with several inquiry stations.

Easier to Follow

> We needed real-time access to warehouse inventory records in order to maintain our competitive position, but we could not justify a large timesharing mainframe.

> In order to get the work out we procured and installed an interactive inventory control system, consisting of a single minicomputer with several inquiry stations.

Figure 4-2. Placing Condition and Conclusion in Adjacent Sentences

to tell the reader what program it is. Next, wanting some credit to accrue to your team, you point out that the redesign work was done with sophisticated and modern techniques, such as HIPO. When you mention the fact that it was redesigned in September, you decide to get some additional credit by pointing out that it will be ready in December. So the sentence becomes:

> Your long overdue and error prone computer program to compute missile trajectories was redesigned using HIPO methods of structured programming in September and should be coded by the end of December.

This is quite a heavy sentence for the reader to digest.

One problem with adding such qualifiers as you go along is that these extra thoughts are not always important to the reader. Frequently, they are important only to you. If they are important to the reader, then they are probably important enough to deserve separate sentences. A better version of the preceding sentence might be:

> Your missile trajectory program has suffered from developmental problems. It took too long to develop and was very difficult to debug. It has been redesigned and should now be ready by the end of December.

4.2.5 Verbs Versus Noun Phrases

Another effective way to tighten your writing is to use dynamic sentences based on action verbs. A typical action verb is the word *run*, as in "I will *run* the program." Sometimes to give the appearance of greater erudition writers mistakenly weaken the action verb by stretching it into a dull noun phrase. For example:

> I will *make a run.*

The action verb *run* has been converted into a noun phrase. Nouns are static words. Also, the new verb *make* is cloudy. Thus, the writer takes something that was vigorous and changes it into something that is dull. Other examples from data processing writing are the following:

Verb	*Noun phrase*
to copy	to make a copy
to test	to conduct a test
to fix	to apply a fix
to meet	to hold a meeting
to compile	to get a compilation

A typical example of overkill with noun phrases is the following:

> We reached a decision to place an order for a second CPU so that we could make a better distribution of the workload.

The offending phrases are *reached a decision, place an order,* and *make a better distribution.* A much more straightforward and dynamic form of the same sentence is the following:

> We decided to order a second CPU to improve workload distribution.

Note also that using a noun phrase like *make a distribution* in place of the verb *distribute* results in using three times as many words.

4.2.6 Redundancies

Using redundant expressions like *absolutely finished* instead of *finished* will also add undesirable length to your writing. If something is finished, it is, by definition, finished absolutely. Of course the programming manager may claim that in the realm of management there is no such thing as a project that is *really* finished, or absolutely finished. It is a truism that computer projects always require maintenance. Nonetheless, in writing, the phrase *absolutely finished* is a redundant phrase.

Are you in the habit of writing redundant phrases like *ask the question* instead of *ask, cooperate together* instead of *cooperate,* and *consensus of opinion* instead of *consensus* because you use such phrases in spoken English? In spoken English you may use many different methods of communicating including vocal inflection and facial expression.

You may also use very flowery turns of speech and very elaborate forms. In writing, on the other hand, particularly technical writing, you should always communicate directly and economically.

4.2.7   Roundabout Phrases

In technical writing authors tend to clutter up the page with other vocal communication holdovers as well. For example, there is the phrase *at the present time,* which is a very wordy way of saying *now.* Likewise, *in a satisfactory manner* can be replaced by *satisfactorily.* Roundabout phrases have no place in technical writing.

4.2.8   Rhetorical Considerations

To use too many redundant phrases makes the writing look loose, imprecise, and childish. It distracts the reader and is counter-productive. However, an occasional roundabout phrase or redundant phrase might add a bit of interest to the writing, a brief change of pace that will be welcome to the reader. When editing so as to make your writing more effective, you should be careful not to be too rigid.

4.3   SIMPLICITY

The second of our Four S's stands for simplicity. The simpler the statement, the more likely to be understood. However, in order to simplify something, you must know your subject. Conversely, it is an old and self-deluding trick in technical writing to *attempt* to conceal ignorance of subject matter by writing in a complicated style.

4.3.1 Getting Right to the Point

Suppose you have to turn someone down and you're writing a letter to do so. The right way to do it would be something like the following:

> We are sorry that we cannot provide time on our PDP-11/45 at present; however, your excellent project . . . .

Now the most important point about this letter is telling the applicant "no." Your very first words give him that negative response—"We are sorry." In the example, there is also a subordinate thought. He may be able to take his project elsewhere. You have added that to the letter as a word of friendly advice.

The wrong way to do it is like this:

> In response to your inquiry regarding the possibility of getting machine time on our PDP-11/45, we feel that the project you have outlined is meritorious and that it would make a valuable contribution to the life sciences. However . . . .

Here you have committed several sins. First, it takes you a long time to get to the point. Second, you redefine the problem before you respond to it. Third, you give the subordinate response—that you like the project and feel that it ought to get a chance somewhere—before you give the primary response. The most important thing and presumably the thing you were initially asked, namely whether you would or would not give machine time, is answered near the end of the letter. This circuitous wording does the reader a cruel injustice. It builds up his hopes and then it tears them down. *Getting right to the point gets the job done right.*

4.3.2 Simple Words

In technical writing the objective is to communicate. Thus, anything that interferes with communication is bad. For example, using lots of long words with lots of syllables tends to intimidate the reader rather than to communicate with him. When writers try to use long, multisyllabic words in order to impress the reader the result is usually communication failure and audience alienation.

Conversely, the easier a piece of writing is to read, the better the impression it will make on the reader. He will want to read more of what you write, because he gets the concepts more quickly, he learns faster, and he gets the help he needs for his work.

4.3.3 Fog Index

It is popular these days, particularly in government circles, to speak of the fog index of a person's writing. The intention behind the fog index is to have an objective measure of the readability of a piece of writing. Indeed the fog index is a surprisingly reliable indicator of readability.

There are several fog indexes. One that can be described quite simply is the fog index developed by Robert Gunning in *Technique of Clear Writing* (see bibliography).

A simplified version of Gunning's fog index is computed as follows:

- Pick any 100-word segment of the text.
- Count the number of sentences in the 100-word segment; a fragment of a sentence at the beginning or ending of a text portion may be counted as a whole sentence.
- Divide 100 by the number of sentences, giving average sentence length.
- Count the number of words with three or more syllables in the 100-word sample.
- Add the two numbers—the average sentence length and the number of words with three or more syllables; multiply by 0.4.
- Round off to the nearest whole number (see example, figure 4-3).

This gives the grade level required to understand the material. It is important to stress that a fog index is a very rough tool for estimating the difficulty of written material, and cannot be used as if it were a precise instrument.

I have found that the Gunning fog index is fairly effective when used to estimate the reading difficulty of a document for an audience of readers who are not familiar with the technical material. For example, a document dealing with automated economic analysis might have a Gunning fog index of twenty, indicating that a Ph.D. level of education is necessary to understand the document. This might be accurate for a reader whose primary computer experience had been in a completely different field such as programming of missile trajectories. But to a person familiar with automated economic analysis, the material would not seem nearly as complex. In other words, the fog index is a relative, not an absolute measure.

In *Writing with Precision*, Jefferson Bates (see bibliography) suggests a way of reducing the fog count while you are in the act of writing, but without trying to do a lot of mental arithmetic which would distract you from the actual writing task. He suggests that you keep your sentences

The Gunning fog count is to be computed for this document.

EXECUTIVE SUMMARY

Our company is participating in the specification and development of operating systems software for automation of the XYZ program. [We have completed a general review of the software development environment.

In our review we found that the software development environment lacked two things—a standard methodology for software development and a standard configuration of systems software.

The first section of this report addresses the problem of standard methodology. It describes the fundamental constraints which will affect all applications software in the XYZ system. It also identifies the hardware configuration on which the applications software must run. It shows the importance of software uniqueness, flexibility, transportability, reliability and maintainability. It also shows the importance of establishing extensive rights to applications] data.

a)	Number of words between square brackets =	100
b)	Number of sentences between square brackets =	6
c)	Average number of words per sentence (100 ÷ 6) =	16.7
d)	Number of words with 3 or more syllables =	27
e)	Sum of (c) and (d) =	43.7
f)	Product of (e) and .4 =	17.48
g)	Gunning fog index (rounded)	17

Figure 4-3. Example of Gunning Fog Index Calculation

short, aiming for twenty words or less per sentence. He suggests also that you simply steer away from using long words.

Figure 4-4 shows some target fog counts for the kinds of technical material that data processing professionals write. The rationale for this table is roughly as follows. Documents which are intended for a management audience will reflect that audience's higher experience and formal education, but should not penalize any individual if he skipped college. So, documents like the Problem Statement, the Study, the Ven-

Problem Statement	13
Study	13
System Specification	15
User Manual	11
Run Book	11
Program Specification	15
Operator's Guide	11
Program Maintenance Manual	13
Data Base Management Manual	11
Data Base Loading Plan	13
Test Plan	13
Procurement Specification	13
Installation Plan	13
Parallel Operations Plan	11
Cutover Plan	11

Figure 4-4. Target Fog Counts

dor Survey, the Data Base Loading Plan, and the Installation Plan, which are selling-and-planning documents, are at a level appropriate to those who have a high school education plus a year or so of college.

Those documents which are by nature more intricate and more technical, such as the System Specification and Program Specification, have the highest fog count, about fifteen or so. A fog count of fifteen means the document is intended for readers with a college education or equivalent experience.

Some readers are in a position on the job where they must look something up in a hurry and take some action, usually a straightforward, simple action. Their documents ought to be designed for straightforward, ready reference. Documents of this type, such as the User Manual, the Run Book, and the Operator's Guide, should have a lower fog count, approximately eleven. This lower fog count does not imply that users and operators are less well-educated than managers, programmers, or systems analysts. Rather the lower fog count simply reflects the fact that users and operators have very little time to read a manual.

The Air Force publication listed in the bibliography gives a further explanation of the fog index.

4.3.4 Unfamiliar Terms

In documents intended for managers, users, and operators, unfamiliar terms will inevitably be introduced and used. Such technical manuals as Systems Specifications and the Programming Specifications, contain terms familiar to the writer but unfamiliar to the reader. This is particularly the case when new concepts are being developed and when applications are being programmed for the first time. Such terms should be defined in the text.

For a lay audience, such as managers, you must define such terms as *floppy disk, hexadecimal, re-entrant,* and *transfer vector.* For the user, you may need to be explicit in defining such terms as *text editor, prompt, protocol,* or *driver.*

Even for a technical audience, you may need to define such terms as *cyclic redundancy check, Hamming code, paging,* and *logical port.* Since these terms arise in the internal logic of systems, they may not even appear in the more general documents that users, managers, and operators see.

Audiences are rapidly becoming more sophisticated in every computer shop, but words that are sufficiently esoteric will always need proper definitions.

4.3.5 Tying Thoughts Together

Look at the following example:

> Charlie designed the system. We developed the programs
> from his designs.

Here the verb *designed* links up very neatly with the noun *design.* Even if there had been an intervening thought or two, the reader would probably still have no difficulty in making the connection.

Good sentence-to-sentence and paragraph-to-paragraph flow also links ideas logically. Always write so that the connection between sentences within paragraphs is stronger than the connection between paragraphs. For example:

> paragraph 1   sentence 1. The hardware won't work.
> sentence 2. We're fixing it.
>
> paragraph 2   sentence 1. The software won't work.
> sentence 2. We're fixing that, too.

Figure 4-5 illustrates this relationship.

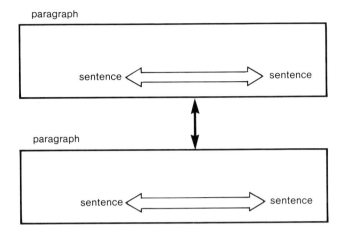

Figure 4-5. Comparison Between the Interconnective Strengths of Paragraphs and Sentences

4.3.6 Rules for Writing Simply

When trying to write a technical document that is simple and direct, follow these rules:

- First, consider how the document would sound if it were read to a third party, someone who is not familiar with the material and who has an objective view. This will indicate to you how much additional explaining is required and whether the document is capable of standing alone.
- Try for one sentence to one thought. This will lead to short sentences. Indeed shortness and simplicity are very closely interrelated.
- Reconsider when tempted to add a qualifying thought.

4.4 STRENGTH

When you put strength into your writing, you are writing for clarity, for conciseness, and for cogency. In other words, you are writing with precision. Jefferson Bates (1978) calls precise writing writing that cannot possibly be misunderstood.

4.4.1 Avoiding Bureaucratese

Writing has strength as well as sincerity when it goes right to the point and says what it has to say.

Have you ever written a bureaucrat a letter of inquiry and received an answer with so much boilerplate at the beginning of the letter that the answer was almost irretrievable? Some writers have a habit of listing all the restrictions placed upon their computer center by budget, manpower, law, and other regulations before they get around to telling you what they can or cannot do in their letter. Figure 4-6 is a good example of this kind of bad writing. The point of the letter finally appears in the fifth paragraph.

4.4.2 Using Specific Terms

Strong writing means using specific terms rather than general ones. For example, it is stronger to say *keypunch services* than to say *data services* because *keypunch* is specific while *data services* is ambiguous. Likewise, the phrase *payroll program,* conveys a more definite image to an individual than does the word *software* which is a somewhat amorphous term. Figure 4-7 shows a list of terms in three columns. Those terms in the left column tend to be more general, more amorphous in meaning than the terms in the third column. The ones in the middle are sort of in-between. Note that it is easier to make a mental picture of the items in column three, than it is to make a mental image of those in column one.

4.4.3 Creating Vague Terms

Another way that writers rob their writing of strength is to take words that have a clear meaning such as *initial, parameter,* and *final,* and turn those words into very vague, imprecise terms by adding *ize.* Computer people have the unfortunate habit of using words like *initialize, parameterize,* and *finalize.* The following quotation from Bates (1978), quoting the Kidner report, says it very well:

> Bureaucracy never utilizes use when utilize can be utilized. It also totalizes, rarely does it total. It systematizes; it seldom arranges. Programs are prioritized.

UNITED STATES POSTAL SERVICE

Dear Boxholder:

Getting your mail delivered—on time and where you want it—is as important to us as it is to you. That's why proper addressing is necessary to assure that we can do just that, deliver your mail quickly and where you want it.

Consequently, effective October 1, 1980, all post office boxholders became subject to the one year forwarding provisions applicable to all other postal customers. What this means to you is that, if you filed a forwarding order to your post office box on or before October 1, 1980, the forwarding order you filed will expire on September 30, 1981. If you initiated a forwarding order to your post office box after October 1, 1980, your forwarding order will expire one year after the date of filing. After that date, your mail will be delivered exactly as addressed, i.e., to the location listed immediately above the city and state. Thus, items addressed to your physical location will be delivered there and items addressed to your post office box will continue to be delivered through your post office box.

In the past, you, as a post office boxholder, have been able to specify where you wanted your mail delivered, either to your physical address or to your post office box address. In some cases, you have even been able to specify that different types of mail be delivered to specific locations. For instance you may have directed us to deliver your letters to one address and your parcels to another. This can cause delays and costly rehandlings such as when a letter has to be redirected from the delivery unit at your physical location to the delivery unit where your post office box is located.

In spite of the additional cost involved, we at the U.S. Postal Service have endeavored to provide this service, but ever increasing volumes of mail, spiraling costs driven by inflation, and an ever increasing number of delivery stops make this impractical.

We suggest, you simply notify your correspondents as to how you would like your mail delivered—either to your post office box or your physical location—and ask them to address it accordingly. You can even use a dual address provided you put the desired delivery location on the line immediately preceding the city, state and ZIP Code as shown in these examples.

MR JOHN JONES		MR JOHN JONES	
801 N ERIE STREET	Mail will be	PO BOX 1502	Mail will be
PO BOX 1502	← delivered here	801 N ERIE STREET	← delivered here
TOLEDO OH 43603	ZIP Code corresponds	TOLEDO OH 43604	ZIP Code corresponds
	to PO Box		to street address

We ask your cooperation in helping us hold down postal costs and assuring proper delivery of your mail

Sincerely,

Your Postmaster

Figure 4-6. Bureaucratese Circa 1981

Weak	Stronger	Strongest
draft animal	horse	Clydesdale
tape	magnetic tape	tape cassette
tape	paper tape	8-level paper tape
data services	data entry	key-to-disk services
system development	programming	coding
study	data collection	forms completion
computer	microcomputer	microprocessor
mass storage	disk storage	5¼″ flexible disk
dp professional	system analyst	senior system analyst
programmer	scientific programmer	simulations programmer
building	computer center	machine room
hardware	central processor	register

Note: the terms labelled "stronger" or "strongest" are more specific, i.e. less abstract, than those labelled "weak."

Figure 4-7. Example of a Ladder of Abstraction

4.5   SINCERITY

4.5.1   Personalizing

Of all the four facets of plain and clear writing—shortness, simplicity, sincerity, and strength—the most difficult one for most organizations to accept is sincerity. Some organizations actually have a policy which prevents the use of personal pronouns or direct references to people or organizational entities. Too bad.

Your writing is much more real, it is much more factual, it is much more meaningful if you, the writer, are willing to admit who you are and what you have done. For example, in a study reporting on a survey of branch offices, it is all right to say "We interviewed one hundred people." In fact, it is preferable to saying "One hundred people were interviewed." The latter has the liability of being in the passive voice which means that it takes more words to express a given thought. It is also less informative because it does not tell who actually did the interviewing.

There are ways to identify yourself personally and thus be sincere without violating some of the corporate rules against the personal pronoun. For example, instead of saying "We interviewed one hundred people," you might say "The study team interviewed one hundred people." Instead of saying "We recommend that a new computer be installed," you might say "The computer steering committee recommends that a new computer be installed."

4.5.2 Direct Questions

Sincerity means asking the reader direct questions, as in the following: "Could you attend a meeting on March 15th?" Question marks are actually quite acceptable in a letter. A question is much more effective than the flat statement: "If you would attend a meeting on March 15th, we would appreciate it."

The former, carrying its question mark, indicates that an explicit answer is required. The latter simply reflects a frame of mind, namely that you would appreciate it if the individual came, but that you are not attempting at this time to find out whether he intends to come. I suspect that when you write the sentence, "If you would attend a meeting on March 15th, we would appreciate it," you do want to know whether the individual is going to attend and, in fact, you urgently want him to appear.

4.5.3 Tone

A sincere letter or report strikes just the right tone. It avoids appearing gushy. It avoids appearing childish. For example, the phrase *extremely important,* while all right in spoken conversation, carries no more impact in a letter or document than the single word *important.* Likewise, *very anxious* is just a nonprofessional way of saying *anxious* and *critically urgent* is simply gushier in a written document than the equivalent word *urgent.*

In fact, overuse of superlatives in writing has all the appearance of a cover-up. If a colleague sends me someone whom he writes is "extremely competent," I am immediately suspicious. I think a competent person is good enough.

If someone recommends an organization to me as being a "most responsive service organization," I wonder why it is not simply "a responsive service organization" or just a "service organization." Presumably an organization that is in business to provide service would not stay in business if it were not responsive to its customers' needs.

Likewise, I am worried about people who are "highly qualified" in a particular subject area. If they are qualified, they are qualified. How much more qualified can a person be? What does it mean to be highly qualified?

When you try to seem too sincere, you tend to make the reader suspect that you are being insincere. When you write a thank you letter, thank the person only once in the letter. Do not thank him again and again.

There is often a misunderstanding about when, in the business world, you should even send a thank you letter. A good rule is this. If a person performs a service for you and that service is part of his job, then do not send a thank you letter.

For example, if you have written for a computer tape from a librarian whose job it is to copy tapes and return them, then it is not necessary to thank him for this service. On the other hand, if it is a private organization such as a wholesale distributor which is not in the software business, but which has generously provided you a copy of its inventory control system, then you should definitely send a thank you letter.

The word *please* should not be used more than once in a letter. When you request something, it is appropriate to say *please*, but, when dealing with subsequent matters in the same letter do not repeat your *pleases*.

4.5.4   Angry Letters and Memo Wars

In the "Plain Letters" course taught by the National Archives and Record Service at the General Services Administration, teachers point out that the author of a letter should be neither arrogant nor groveling, and that he should be prepared to admit mistakes. He should read over his letters to make certain that his tone does not alienate the reader. They give as examples of alienating phrases the following:

- "As we told you in our last letter . . . ."
- "We are at loss to understand why you . . ."
- "It should have been clear to you . . . ."
- "You claim you did not receive . . . ."
- "Your attention is again called to . . . ."

Some letters that you receive may have tones that offend you. In fact, you may occasionally get letters that make you very angry, particularly those that attack you or the way that you are handling your job. Do not reply to an angry or offensive letter with an angry or offensive letter. Bates (1978) says, "Don't write when you are angry; or if you do, tear up your letter, don't mail it."

To that, I would add this point. If you do well in an organization, you will invariably make enemies on the way up. Hopefully, most of them will be unintentionally made. If you previously wrote angry letters to people, they will keep those angry letters and they will continually refer to them. The more visible you become in the organization, the more frequently those letters will be taken out and gossiped about, to your detriment.

There's a corollary to this angry letter business, which has received recent attention. "Be nice to the people you meet on your way up, because you will meet those same people on the way back down again."

4.6   APPLYING THE FUNDAMENTALS

How do you apply the fundamentals to an actual piece of writing? Figure 4-8 shows pages extracted from a government report. Since you will be critiquing the writing, not the writer, I have deleted explicit references to the government organization and its project.

The writing is obscure. It is jumbled. It is replete with passive voice constructions resulting in sentences with widely separated subjects and predicates. Note, for example, the second sentence of the second paragraph. The report employs redundant or meaningless phrases, such as *system wide conventions* and *integrated top-down strategy*. This conveys little useful information to the reader.

Figure 4-9 shows what happens when you apply the principles of plain writing. The passive voice has disappeared. The offending phrases have been replaced by the more meaningful *standard methodology* and *top-down strategy*. Note the use of parallel construction in figure 4-9.

Figure 4-10 gives a quick review of the fundamentals.

4.7   HIGHLIGHTS

The following principles and axioms appear in the text *Writing with Precision* (Bates, 1978), a good reference on creative writing skills.

4.7.1   Principles

- Prefer the active voice.
- Don't make nouns out of good, strong "working verbs."

EXECUTIVE SUMMARY

This report represents the conclusion of the System Overview phase of an overall effort to specify and develop the next generation of systems software for the Automation of the XYZ program. The report is divided into two major portions. The first defines the system wide conventions to be followed throughout the software development process. The second identifies the major software components which together comprise the XYZ system software suite.

Fundamental considerations for all software are first discussed, including the identification of the target hardware configuration. Several necessary software characteristics, among them uniqueness, flexibility, transportability, reliability, and maintainability, and their importance to the success of the program are presented. In addition, the need for extensive data rights to the developed software is shown.

An integrated top-down strategy for the design, coding, and testing of all developed software is proposed. This proposal defines the techniques to be employed and discusses the advantages of these techniques from both a technical performance and program management perspective. Comprehensive documentation produced during the development cycle is defined in detail, as is the schedule for its production.

Four major classes of required software are defined in the latter portions of the report. Foremost among these is the Operating System, a real-time multi-tasking system capable of supporting both system-level and background applications programs. The need for a high level Systems Development Language and its compiler is also discussed in some detail, and candidates for this role are identified. Other language processors, including a Fortran compiler and a Basic interpreter, are described briefly. Finally, several fundamental utility programs are identified as necessary, and the processing performed by them is briefly presented.

—End of the Executive Summary—

Figure 4-8. Extract from a Government Report

EXECUTIVE SUMMARY

Our company is participating in the specification and development of operating systems software for automation of the XYZ program. We have completed a general review of the software development environment.

In our review we found that the software development environment lacked two things—a standard methodology for software development and a standard configuration of systems software.

The first section of this report addresses the problem of standard methodology. It describes the fundamental constraints which will affect all applications software in the XYZ system. It also identifies the hardware configuration on which the applications software must run. It shows the importance of software uniqueness, flexibility, transportability, reliability, and maintainability. It also shows the importance of establishing extensive rights to applications data.

The first section also explains the top down strategy for designing, coding, and testing applications software. It proposes that this methodology be used to develop XYZ software. It shows the improvements to be achieved from applying this methodology. Improvements should be possible in both technical performance and program management.

The section also describes the documentation which should be produced. It proposes a schedule for software development.

The second section defines the four classes of systems software required for XYZ:

- *the operating system,* a real time multitasking system which can support both systems code and applications programs
- *a systems development language,* a language for developing systems code
- *other language processors,* compilers for writing applications programs
- *utility programs,* special routines for routine tasks.

Figure 4-9. A Rewrite of the Government Report

Shortness

- Avoid Needless Words
- Use Active Voice

Simplicity

- Get to the Point
- Compactify
- Use Short Forms

Sincerity

- Identify Sources
- Set Professional Tone

Strength

- Write Exactly What You Mean
- Don't Hedge

Figure 4-10. Main Points of Good Writing

- Be concise.
- Be specific.
- Keep related sentence elements together (e.g., noun-subject with verb and noun-object).
- Prefer the simple word.
- Don't repeat a word or words unnecessarily.
- Make sentence elements parallel.
- Arrange your material logically.

4.7.2 Axioms

- Do not write without good reason.
- Slant your presentation to your audience.
- Get straight to the point.

- Show the reader.
- Be consistent.
- Rewrite-rewrite-rewrite.[1]
- Allow in your planning for production delays.

[1] The reader will observe that this is one point where I disagree with Bates, who is concerned with creative writing in general and not with DP writing in particular. In DP writing we want to strive for a clear statement. Once we have achieved that, we go on to something else, cutting and pasting if necessary from what we have already produced.

5

More Effective Writing through Better Time Management

5.1 USING TIME EFFICIENTLY

In writing for computer people, you will often be able to save time by reorganizing your material rather than rewriting it. In order to produce a given document, chances are you can draw upon a previously written clear statement of the technical information that you want to convey if it is written at an appropriate level for the audience you are addressing. Probably you will only have to cut and paste.

Frequently, the reader is looking for a specific technical fact. Place at the front of your document the information which is the most critical to the reader so that he can find that first. A good table of contents is invaluable. A document which is intended to be archival, that is, to be used as a reference for a long time to come, should also have a complete index.

5.1.1 Rewriting

Rewrite only when the document is unclear. As indicated above, many of the computer professional's documents can frequently be improved by simply moving paragraphs and sections around.

5.1.2   Time Limits

When you are writing letters, establish a time limit for the recipient's reply. The following is an example: "If we do not hear from you within thirty days, we will assume that this approach is acceptable to your staff."

5.1.3   Reviews and Clearances

Within your own organization, limit the number of reviews and clearances that are required. In one particular study of Pentagon paper-pushing, it was reported that a typical letter required forty-five days and twenty-two signatures before it got out of the building—a prime example of review and clearance overkill. A letter should be sent directly to the individual in an organization who can take action on it. If you send it to his boss or his boss's boss, that will only add to the delay. Reserve the use of the higher authority signature for those cases where there may be legal considerations.

5.1.4   Retyping

The author should not insist on letter-perfect letters. If there are very minor errors, say one or two, have the typist make them neatly in pen and ink and send the letter out. The sensible businessperson will consider this a way to save executive time, not an example of office sloppiness. Probably the only time a letter needs to be perfect is when the letter deals with a legal matter, and even legal documents contain typos.

5.1.5   Preassembled Tissues and Carbons

A simple step, which is of no direct benefit to the writer but which does save the secretary time, is using preassembled tissues and carbons. It saves the secretary the time of finding carbons and paper, and getting them all straight in the typewriter.

5.1.6   Automated Signatures

For mass mailings use automated signature pens. These save the author boring hours of writing his name over and over again.

5.1.7   Selected Paragraphs

Computers and word processors can generate letter perfect letters from a file of selected paragraphs. Such a letter may give an impression of neatness, but it frequently amounts to overkill. Remember, your emphasis should be on effective communication, not on letter perfect letters.

When exact wording is important in order to avoid legal problems, using selected paragraphs has a definite advantage. Individual paragraphs can be given proper thought well ahead of time and can be approved by the legal department before being made available for use.

5.1.8   Form Letters

If your business gets certain kinds of inquiries over and over again as does the Internal Revenue Service, for example, then it would be appropriate to use form letters. These are letters which are already printed. You simply check the appropriate paragraphs and fill in the blanks.

5.1.9   Endorsement Letters

An endorsement letter is a two-way memo which consists of an original and two carbons. The inquiry and its reply are typed on the same letter. An endorsement letter keeps the file of correspondence integral to one letter and saves time because you do not need to make copies of people's comments. It also saves typing time because the appearance of the letter is not as important as it would be on letterhead paper.

5.1.10   Routing Slips

Use a routing slip when transmitting material around the organization. This saves you the time required to write letters of transmittal and the cost of duplicating copies of the material. If several people in your organization need to see a document, send the original with a routing slip. If you want to send a personal note to one of the readers, just write that out in longhand on the routing slip.

5.1.11   Window Envelopes

Window envelopes not only save the typist the time required to type a separate address on the envelope, but they also save you the time required to check and make sure that the typist got the right letter into the right envelope.

I recently learned about a study in which a government agency required six months to process and return license applications. It turned out that the majority of the wasted time was caused by having to match up envelopes with insertions. When the system was changed to a self-mailing form, the backlog was eliminated.

5.1.12   Distribution Lists

Limit the distribution of your letters and documents to *only those people who are directly involved.* This practice avoids wasting the time of people who are not involved since they would otherwise have to read the document, classify it, and decide where to file it.

5.1.13   Word Processing

Used properly, word processing equipment can be very effective. However, such equipment alone will not make for better communication.

Without indicting the industry by saying that word processing equipment has been oversold, I will indict the modern office by saying that word processing equipment has been overbought. Audit groups within the federal government have shown that the typical word processing machine is merely a status symbol. One executive secretary has one, so another executive secretary has to have one as well.

A typical example is the executive who feels his secretary's work is below par, so he spends tens of thousands of dollars to get a word processing machine which will turn out letter perfect letters. A better use of the organization's money would be to send the typist back to typing school for a refresher course. A week or so of refresher training would only cost a few hundred dollars compared with tens of thousands for the word processing equipment.

Word processing equipment often sits idle. Government audits have found that the typical typist may spend less than two hours each day actually engaged in typing. The rest of the typist's time is spent in filing, answering telephones, composing letters, running errands, making xerox copies, and so on.

5.1.14   Electronic Correspondence

Electronic correspondence means the use of computer message switching through telephone lines. Electronic correspondence's primary advantage is speed, but it has other advantages as well. First, a permanent record is kept of all communication. This means you can go back and review the history of a particular communication especially if there has been a dispute. Second, a communication can be directed to any number of recipients in different organizations and locations.

I am a great believer in discipline as this book will show. Electronic correspondence has the advantage of imposing the discipline of writing on the person who is doing the communicating. In a telephone conversation you can be fairly loose and imprecise in your conversation, but when you write down the query or write down the answer to the query, you must take more pains to be correct. Paraphrasing Francis Bacon, "Writing makes a man exact."

Another advantage is that electronic correspondence is less expensive than the typical office letter. A letter is normally written by one person, typed and proofread by another person, then reviewed again by the author, possibly proofed and retyped, reread, signed and then sent out by the typist. With electronic correspondence systems, the author often does his own typing. Correct spelling is not as important in electronic correspondence as the preciseness of the writing and the speed with which it can be transmitted and received.

5.1.15   Telephone

A typical telephone call might cost five dollars for three minutes across the country during prime time, but a letter or two going each way, which would accomplish the same objective, might cost almost a hundred dollars considering the secretary's time at each location, the author's time at both locations, as well as material and postage.

5.1.16   Telegrams

Telegrams have the same advantages as electronic correspondence systems except that a third party (the carrier) is involved. This adds to the cost and may take longer than an inhouse electronic correspondence system.

5.1.17 Facsimile Transmission

Facsimile transmission is the use of specialized telephone equipment to send graphic material. Through the use of facsimile transmission, individuals at offices separated by hundreds of miles can work on a design or on a draft document and save thousands of dollars in travel costs.

5.2 MEETINGS

5.2.1 The Usefulness of Meetings

Meetings can either save time or waste time depending on how they are conducted.

General meetings where several people are in attendance are less productive than discussions between two individuals. Two people can usually thrash things out but a general meeting with several people participating frequently gets bogged down with nuances and personal views so that the technical issues are not resolved.

When there is a technical matter at issue, try to have it resolved between two people. If there is need for precise documentation, use correspondence rather than meetings. Most meetings need some kind of precise record-keeping in order to be truly effective. Otherwise each attendee goes away with a different version of any conclusions that were reached. Use larger meetings only for the exchange of general information and for essential, but wider-ranging, topics.

If the objective of the meeting is one-way communication, that is, communication between a boss and his subordinates, for example, then he should call a meeting, describe the issue to all of his subordinates, and pass out documentation at the same time. This preserves the person-to-person approach and answers the questions that will occur in people's minds later. A meeting to discuss a reorganization of the project team is a typical example of such a meeting.

5.2.2 Structured Meetings

A meeting should be structured just as correspondence is structured. It should be limited to only those people who can make a direct contribution. Meetings are generally more effective when everybody around the table is at roughly the same level in the organization. Every meeting should have a fixed time limit so that people will concentrate on the agenda in order to get the work done in time.

The topics on the agenda should be communicated to all attendees prior to the meeting. A meeting should be announced at least a day ahead of time. If there is need to review a document for discussion at the meeting, then that document should accompany the announcement. Make a follow-up phone call to be sure that everybody has received the material.

When people show up at the meeting obviously unprepared, use diplomacy and tact. I try to use euphemisms like the following: "Joe, I know that you were tied up when the document was distributed for review and have not had time to read it. I think it would be unfair to take your time while the rest of us discuss the document, so why don't we excuse you for this one?"

The meeting chairman should discourage any discussions which ramble off the subject and should be hard-nosed about keeping the meeting focused on exactly the things that were supposed to be discussed. I find that there are many people who are not anxious to go home at night. Such people will tend to carry on afternoon meetings until midnight or later. I suspect they enjoy the social interchange that takes place at meetings, and I suspect that they enjoy sending out for pizza to keep the meeting going past eight o'clock.

A subtle technique that works for me with such individuals is to schedule meetings around ten o'clock in the morning. The same individuals who will not go home at night do like to get out at lunchtime. A meeting which is scheduled to go until lunchtime tends to adjourn at lunchtime.

5.3 DOCUMENTATION MORALE

One of the big problems facing a study team, or any other team of professionals who are writing a long and complicated document, is the long dry spell between positive reinforcements. The writers go for such a long time working toward an apparently nebulous end that they lose their early enthusiasm. Productivity falls. To remedy this situation, I strongly recommend this Principle of Frequent Successes—what encourages people to do well is success.

5.3.1 Positive Reinforcement

The execution of the Principle of Frequent Successes is this. Break the assigned task into smaller tasks which are so small as to be almost ridiculously easy. Force each of these subtasks to culminate in an end product. Produce each end product in turn, look at it, admire it, say to yourself, "I have accomplished this." Get someone to compliment it.

Through a succession of such subtasks, you build up your ego and reinforce your will to achieve the final result. Each new success adds to your self-confidence. Soon you are "walking tall."

I have seen people who were victims of the trials and tribulations of a difficult computer office become brand new people after experiencing only a handful of these almost trivial successes. For someone who has been continually beset by near failures, even insignificant successes lead to happiness on the job and personal satisfaction.

5.3.2 Easy Steps First

There are many corollaries of the Principle of Frequent Successes. One of them is "Concentrate on the Do-able." Often when I have discussed their schedule with my subordinates, I find them committed to achieving some formidable objective which looks nearly impossible. I counsel them to keep that objective in mind, but only as a down-the-road sort of thing. I urge them to identify as their first deliverable something which they are completely confident they can accomplish, and, in fact, can produce almost overnight.

If the long-range, difficult commitment prevails, I end up with frustrated and defensive subordinates. If instead they commit themselves to something simpler as a preliminary step, I find myself developing subordinates who are willing workers and who are getting a lot of satisfaction out of putting an "easy one" over on the boss. Even the big jobs get done with this technique—one step at a time.

5.4   **HIGHLIGHTS**

- By using time-saving techniques—automated signatures, selected paragraphs, form letters, endorsement letters—you can save writing time.
- Productive meetings have a definite agenda. Those attending should have previously read any documents that are being discussed.
- To avoid getting bogged down in a long project, keep up your morale by breaking up the task into small, easily accomplished steps.

6

An Overview of Data Processing Documents

The documents that DP professionals produce can be combined into groups according to the nature or purpose of each document—investigative, analytic, developmental, archival, instructive, directive, and promotional.

6.1 INVESTIGATIVE WRITING

A large percentage of an analyst's or programmer's time is spent in writing for the purpose of finding out about something. Analysts and programmers write letters to their peers in other organizations, to vendors of hardware and software, and to government organizations to get information about equipment, applications, and systems software.

Within their own organizations, in the initial phases of a project, they initially write tentative problem statements, seeking to obtain general agreement about the objectives of an application that is being automated. Subsequently, they will have to write a study and a report. *The study is an attempt to get hold of all the relevant and available information about a problem and to organize that information into a format for decision making.*

In the early stages of system development, surveys must be conducted: Vendors must be surveyed about their products to provide input into the decision-making process for buying equipment. Users are surveyed to find out how they would use a new system, and potential clients must be surveyed to find out what they are inclined to buy.

6.2 ANALYTIC WRITING

The analytic phase of the system development lifecycle follows the investigative phase. In analytic writing it is assumed that all the facts have been gathered and that the investigation is complete. Ahead lies the task of making sense out of the information and putting together a logical system which will do the job.

Occasionally additional studies are performed in the analytic phase. These studies are not usually fact-finding studies. Instead they are analytic studies where the collected data are examined very minutely and the special interrelationships among them are very carefully worked out.

The logical structure that emerges during the analytic phase is refined and focused, developing the shape of the emerging new system. The end product of this activity is called the *system specification*. It is known by other names as well, including *functional specification* and *external specification*. The naming of these documents and the roles they perform will be discussed later on.

6.3 DEVELOPMENTAL WRITING

After the fact-finding and the analysis are completed, it is time to build the system. The building activity consists of converting system specifications into programming specifications, converting programming specs into programs, and converting programs into reliable working systems. The entire system development cycle is illustrated in figure 6-1.

In *Structured Analysis and System Specification* (see bibliography), Tom DeMarco calls the output of structured analysis a system specification. In *Composite/Structured Design* and in *Reliable Software through Composite Design* (see bibliography) Glen Myers calls the result of structured design a program specification. The result of applying structured programming techniques to a structured programming specification is

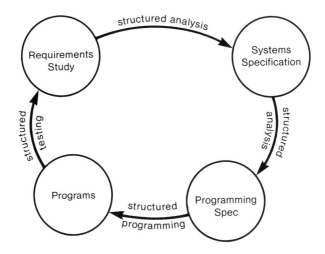

Figure 6-1. Documents and Activities of the System Development Cycle

the program itself. Both Glen Myers and Robert Glass talk of structured testing. However, this writing manual is the first single book that I know of that shows the very elegant, almost mathematical, yet very practical and effective linkage between these structured approaches.

6.4 INSTRUCTIVE WRITING

Many people in business, government, education, and industry consider the computer professional and his instrument, the computer, to be esoteric and intimidating. What the computers do and what they require others to do must be carefully explained. There are several documents that supply this education to the user.

First there is correspondence by which the analyst, programmer, or manager explains to his user community and to his bosses what he is trying to accomplish and what the system requires of its user community.

Next there is the maintenance specification which is used by support personnel to keep the system running after the analysts and programmers have gone on to other projects. Usually the maintenance specification is just a program specification with some extra goodies such as indexes, glossaries, tables of error messages, and sample printouts.

User manuals are written to instruct neophytes about using the system, and also to provide ready reference to experienced users under emergency or high-pressure conditions.

Operator's manuals are written as detailed subsections of the run book. These manuals show operators very explicitly how to handle individual components or subsystems of a system application.

Executive summaries are written for the nontechnical executive who does not have the time to go through the mass of information in a large specification or study but who needs to be acquainted with the contents.

6.5 DIRECTIVE WRITING

Certain kinds of data processing writing are intended to tell people what action to take, for example, explicit written directions given by a manager to his subordinates about how to do something. The generic term for such a document is "directive." A directive implements a policy by being both a description of the policy and a blueprint for carrying it out. Such a document, therefore, consists of a statement of policy and a procedure. Frequently directives are called other names such as *notices* and *bulletins.*

6.6 ARCHIVAL WRITING

Certain of the documents already mentioned have not only developmental significance but historical significance as well. These documents include the system specification document and the programming specification document. Normally these documents need to be polished up before they are suitable for filing away as historical documents.

It is also useful to have a record for the file of how the system is to be operated. For this reason the run book, which is used for instructive purposes, is edited and placed in the permanent record.

6.7 PROMOTIONAL WRITING

Every data processing professional eventually finds himself in a position where he must sell something, promote an idea, motivate users to adopt

Document	Audience	Author	Sponsor	Source
Correspondence	Specific	Specific	—	—
Study	User, Sponsor	Systems Analyst	User, Top Management	Technical Libraries, User Personnel, Personal Observation, Commercial Surveys
Flyer, Notice, User Bulletin	User	Systems Analyst, Manager	Manager	Existing Documentation and Policy
System Spec.	Systems Analyst, Programmer	Systems Analyst, Programmer	Manager	Design Analysis Experience, Technical Refs. (e.g. mfr's)
Program Spec.	Programmer	Programmer	Manager	System Specs., Technical Refs.
Run Book	Systems Analyst, Programmer, Operators	Programmer	Manager	Design Specs., Program Specs.
Maintenance Spec.	Programmer	Programmer	Manager	Design Specs., Programming Specs.
General Information Manual	General	Systems Analyst	Top Management	Design Specs.
Operator's Manual	Operator	Programmer	Manager	Design Specs., Programming Specs.
Proposal	Customer	Manager, Systems Analyst	Top Management	All of the above

Figure 6-2. DP Documents: Audiences, Authors, Sponsors, and Sources of Information

his system concept, convince top management to upgrade a computer facility, solicit support for increasing the size of his budget, obtain approval to attend a training course, or convince someone to hire or promote him. These activities call for effective written communication.

Computer professionals keep users, programmers, and analysts aware of developments in the computer center by writing computer center newsletters, announcements, and bulletins. These documents announce the acquisition of new hardware and software systems, changes in job submittal procedures, and revisions to old programs and systems. Computer people write proposals to sell products and services to clients. They also make presentations to executives to interest top management in new directions or to acquaint top management with the status of various projects.

6.8   AUDIENCE, AUTHOR, SPONSOR, AND SOURCE

Figure 6-2 tabulates the various documents which data processing people produce, indicating the audience, author, sponsor, and source of each document.

As the figure shows, the audience of a document is not necessarily the same person as the sponsor. The audience is the reader of the document. The sponsor is the person who is paying the bill or who has the idea in the first place. He is the motivating force behind the project or the activity.

Material appearing in a document comes from a variety of sources. Sometimes it comes from policy, sometimes from other documents, and sometimes out of the mind of the individual or group writing that document.

6.9   DOCUMENT CHAINS

Sometimes it is easier to describe a DP professional's work in terms of the products of that work, than to try and describe the tasks themselves. Let's look at the documents that are in only one chain of the system development cycle, namely the software cycle:

Task	*Document*
• problem identification task	problem identification
• problem definition task	problem definition

• study task	study report (definitive requirements statement)
• system analysis task	system specification
• system design task	programming specification
• programming task	programs
• test task	system test report
• maintenance task	system maintenance manual

For any system development there are many related chains. For example:

- the software development chain
- the user chain
- the operations chain
- the data base management chain
- the hardware procurement chain
- the quality assurance chain

Many of these chains contain subchains. For example, in software development, within the programming chain there are the following chains:

- coding chain
- programmer test chain
- program library maintenance chain
- test data development chain

Depending on the application there are other chains as well. For example, in inventory control systems there may be another chain devoted to the mathematics of the simulation model.

The major chains and their related documents are depicted graphically in figure 6-3.

6.10   HIGHLIGHTS

- The documents that DP professionals produce fall into basic groups—investigative, analytic, developmental, archival, instructive, directive, and promotional.

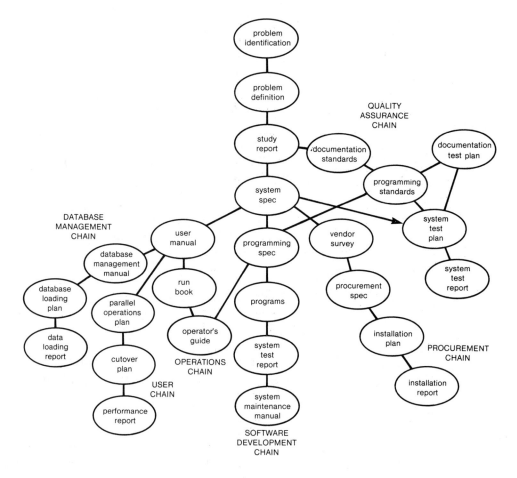

Figure 6-3. Major Document Chains in the System Development Cycle

- Each of the document types has its own audience, author, sponsor, and source.
- There are many separate chains in the system development cycle, and each chain produces its own series of documents.

PART B

Technical Writing

This kind of writing is done primarily by system analysts and programmers and consists of investigative, analytic, instructive, and directive documents.

7

Investigative Documents: Studies

7.1 THE STUDY

7.1.1 Why Studies are Done

Why do a study? The study is the earliest systematic treatment of a problem and solution in the system development cycle. The *objective of a study is to write a report.*

Data processing people are never asked to do a systems study to find a simple answer. For example, you will not be asked to do a study to find out the balance of a checkbook or how many tons of coal were loaded at a particular dock on a particular day. These answers are too easy to get. Instead you will be asked to do studies which do not have definitive answers.

You may be asked, for example, to find out whether it is feasible to automate a warehouse. There is no one definitive answer to such a question. To one group of people it may seem quite feasible, but to another group it may not seem feasible at all. The whole thing is a matter of perspective and daring, seasoned, of course, with good professional judgment.

Another study task with an "impossible" solution is the following: Determine the state of the art in electronic photocomposition. Such a request is meaningless because all over the world people are continuing to develop new concepts, new techniques, and new capabilities in electronic photocomposition. There is no way you can absolutely define the state of the art in electronic photocomposition at any particular instant.

Another typical study assignment is to find out whether there is a market for product X. Here again, you cannot say with accuracy whether there is a market until the product has been produced and the customer has stepped forward and paid the price for the product. Therefore, you would only be crystal ball gazing.

A typical study assignment is to determine the requirements of a future data communications network. This entails analyzing your company's present needs and projecting from that analysis into the future. No answer you come up with will be 100 percent accurate. *When doing a study, you don't just wake up one day, discover that you have the answer, and start writing.*

7.1.2 What Doing a Study Really Means

Well then, what *can* you do in data processing studies? Again the answer lies in your point of view. You must acknowledge that it is not possible to answer study questions in a literal sense. You can only supply information and organize that information so that it makes some kind of sense to the reader.

A particular study is defined by its objective:

- to determine how to accomplish a given thing
- to determine whether a given thing is feasible
- to determine the state of the art
- to determine whether there is a market for a particular thing

The definition of the study tells you what you should work towards. The rest is a matter of being resourceful:

- *To determine how to accomplish x* means to develop system design alternatives.
- *To determine whether something is feasible* means to identify the conditions under which it is practicable to automate that application, to identify the conditions under which it is not practicable, and to assign costs.
- *To determine the state of the art* means to find out as much about the subject and recent developments as possible within reasonable limits of time and money.
- *To determine whether a market exists* means to identify some likely customers and to extrapolate from their estimated share of the market, the size of the buying population.

Reason	Per Cent
Poor Study	60
Poor Analysis	*
Poor Design	*
Poor Programming	10
Poor Maintenance	*
Poor User Relations	20

* Less than 10 percent

Figure 7-1. Why Systems Fail

Do not think in terms of giving *the* answer but in terms of *how much* answer to give, that is, how much information to develop and how far to go in obtaining data.

7.1.3 Why Systems Fail

Figure 7-1 is a chart, based on my own observations, showing the reasons why systems fail. Well over half of all systems fail because of a poorly performed study. It is much less frequent that systems fail because of poor systems analysis, poor systems design, poor programming, or poor maintenance. A failed system is one that was initially built at substantial expense and subsequently abandoned, that is, taken off the computer altogether.

A study may turn out badly for any of several reasons: The system requirements were poorly defined; the user's needs were inadequately understood; the difficulties of the developmental effort were underestimated; or the system concept was inadequate or inappropriate to the task.

7.2 THE STUDY REPORT

7.2.1 Importance of the Study Report

The most important single document in data processing is the one that is often the most poorly researched and the most amateurishly produced. That is the study report. This is ironic because it is the study document which gives rise to all the other documents and which is the foundation for the system development work that follows. The study report contains the initial concept for the entire system.

The study report also contains the economic justification for a system. It tells what the requirements are, and what the user's needs are perceived to be. In addition, it examines the feasibility of any project effort. The report identifies the policy behind the user system, that is, it puts the company's position into writing. Without a good, thorough study report, no system development project should be launched.

The study, itself, is the starting point for every development project. The study is the first formal application of systems technology, primarily systems analysis, to a problem to be solved. The study report contains the results of that scientific analysis. It describes the action to be taken as a result of the findings of the study team.

7.2.2 Ingredients of the Study Report

The essential ingredients of the systems study report are the problem definition, the summary of the data that were collected subsequent to identification of the problem, the findings that are derived from the data, the conclusions drawn from the findings, and the recommendations advanced to solve the problem.

7.2.3 Problem Specification and Problem Definition

The two documents which precede the study report, namely the problem identification and the problem definition documents, are much less formal than the study. What they do initially is to put in writing the first statement of the problem as perceived by the sponsor and subsequently to elaborate on the problem so that everyone can understand what the sponsor is talking about. Normally these two documents will be incorporated later into the body of the study report.

7.3 GETTING STARTED

7.3.1 Defining the Problem

Assume that your study deals with the feasibility of developing a certain system. First of all try to get an accurate statement of just what it is that is being considered. For example, what does it actually mean to automate the warehouse? Are you talking strictly about control of inventory or are you also talking about writing and filling orders? Are you talking about automated decision making, or are you talking about automation carrying out the decisions made by human beings? Are you talking about automating one warehouse or all warehouses in the company? Are you talking about automating one product line or one type of product or all products and all product lines? Are you constrained to develop the system on your firm's existing computer?

In other words, try to get a *definition of the problem*. Write a one paragraph statement of the problem if this has not already been done. If the problem cannot be stated in a paragraph, chances are no one really understands the problem or it has been defined too vaguely. Do not proceed with the study until you can write a concise statement of the problem. Poor problem definition leads to poorly developed or failed systems.

Next get yourself organized to write a report—set up a plan for carrying out the study—as organization is of prime importance. Then go out and acquire the information that you have identified as necessary. In the process of acquiring that information you will be writing things down and continually refining what you have written. On the day that the money and time run out you will deliver your study report.

One of the most effective managers of technical studies I have ever known gave me the following advice: "The study is over when the money runs out." To what he has said, I have my own corollary: "The study is over when the time runs out." Neither of these statements is meant in the Machiavellian sense that it might seem. Neither that consultant nor I meant "Grab the money and run," or "Fool around until the money is all gone and then turn in your work." What we *are* saying is this. It is not possible to give a simple answer to any of the things that a study team is assigned to do. What a study does do is to give as much of the answer as can be given within its operating constraints.

It is never a question of giving *the* answer, but of how much of the answer to give. In the business world the constraints are time and money. Studies can be accomplished within these fundamental constraints if the team uses structured, particularly top-down, techniques. A top-down approach solves the whole problem at a general level, then divides the problem into subproblems which are solved at a more detailed level and continues in this way until the work is finished (see figures 7-5 through 7-9).

I have sometimes been embarrassed for my colleagues who were assigned to do a study, went all the way down to the deadline, and then reported to their managers that they did not have the study completed.

Sometimes they gave the excuse that the problem was more complicated than they had anticipated or, putting it another way, that they had fewer resources than they had anticipated. Invariably they asked for more time and for more money. Such conduct is absolutely unprofessional and shows a complete lack of understanding of what it means to do a study.

There are no studies to study the whole world; there are no open-ended studies. Therefore, the knowledgeable professional makes a reasonable estimate of the cost and the time of doing the study and establishes these as controlling limits. He then proceeds to organize his time and his team so that a professional study report comes together when the time and the money are used up.

In other words, he has answered the question, "How much information can I give?" by saying, "I will give all the information that I can obtain within the time allotted, and see to it that I am able to make sense of the data. I will prepare a sensible, reasonable, and professional report so that someone can understand what I have learned and follow the logic of my conclusions and my recommendations."

7.3.2   The Wrong Way and the Right Way

The naive and unprofessional way to do a study is shown in figure 7-2. Here the study team allot themselves a certain amount of time to go out and find facts. After that time, they plan to sit down and write the report. Such an approach is guaranteed to be an abysmal, unprofessional effort and to produce a late report, for the following reasons:

- It will turn out that not all the necessary data has been collected.
- It will turn out that certain data will be found to be indispensible to the study, but they will be identified too late.
- There will not be enough time to write up the study because the fact finding will continue right on through the time allotted for writing.
- The different parts of the study will not fit together, the writing will be disjointed, and there will be glaring differences in quality among the chapters.
- Everyone on the project team will feel that there is not time enough, and they will drag out whatever writing they do.

The first task of your study team should be to write the charter (see figure 7-3). The charter shows not only the team but those people who are going to be involved with the study team, what the team has been

FACT FINDING	WRITING

GUARANTEED TO BE LATE

NO END TO THE FACT FINDING

NEVER TIME ENOUGH TO WRITE

TOO MANY LOOSE ENDS

Figure 7-2. The Wrong Way to Do a Study

assigned to do. The charter should be short and simple so that it can be readily understood. It should also be complete, giving the study team the scope needed to do the job. Frequently a sponsor may ask a study team to do a particular study, but, after the initial interview, the sponsor discovers that the five-man study team has five different versions of what the study is all about. Writing down the study charter forces unanimity among the study team.

After writing the charter, your team can begin the study itself. Figure 7-4 shows the right way to do a study—the top-down approach. The next task is to produce the outline. Yes, it is indeed possible to write an outline for a report of a study before you begin to gather data. A typical general fact outline is shown in figure 7-5. Once the outline is written, the study team can proceed to identify the general facts that have to be found.

An ad hoc committee, under the leadership of John A. Jones, has been appointed to study and report on Company A's communication network requirements. The study team is to investigate means of reducing current communication costs and of improving the level of service and the effectiveness of our current operations through modern computer-based communications methods. The team is authorized to collect cost data and to examine representative computer communications systems. They are to limit their projections to a five-year time frame. The study is to be completed within six months.

Figure 7-3. A Sample Charter for a Study Team

OUTLINE

    GENERAL FACTS

        DETAILED OUTLINE
        _____

            SPECIFIC FACTS

                REWRITE
                _____

ALWAYS ON TIME—BECAUSE IT IS ALWAYS "FINISHED"

ALWAYS KNOWS WHAT FACT THE TEAM IS FINDING, AND WHICH
  ONE IS NEXT

ALWAYS TIME TO WRITE, BECAUSE THE TEAM IS ALWAYS WRITING

NO LOOSE ENDS FROM THE VERY BEGINNING

READY AT ANY MOMENT TO "MAKE A PRESENTATION"

Figure 7-4. The Right Way to Do a Study

The next step is to find those general facts. In the case of figure 7-5, general facts "I" and "II" might come from an interview with the study's sponsor; fact "III" from an interview with the company's communications officer; fact "IV" from calls to company X's competitors and to communications vendors and from some perusal of communications periodicals.

The study team assigns the logical skeletons to facts "V" through "VII." Naming fact "VIII" at this stage is merely assigning a number to something before it is written.

The next step is to write an outline of the more specific level of facts that have to be discovered (see figure 7-6). Then the team must get those facts.

Next the team writes the third level of facts down in outline form (see figure 7-7). It goes out and obtains those facts, and comes back and polishes the report in its final form.

When is the actual writing done? The writing is done as the facts are found. Every member of the study team must learn to write up his facts as he acquires them. An example of a fact to be found, the fact itself, and the draft writing of it is shown in figure 7-8.

COMMUNICATIONS NETWORK REQUIREMENTS FOR COMPANY X

A STUDY

I. General Antecedents for the Study

II. Charter of the Study Team

III. Current Communications in Use in the Company

IV. Current Communications Comparing Three Different Network Systems

V. Five-Year Projection of Communication Needs

VI. Projected Comparison of the Three Networks

VII. Analysis of the Projections

VIII. Recommendations

Appendix A—General Systems Concept

Appendix B—Systems Implementation Plan

Figure 7-5. General Fact Outline for a Typical Study

COMMUNICATIONS NETWORK REQUIREMENTS FOR COMPANY X

A STUDY

I. General Antecedents for the Study

    A. Annual Cost of Company X Communications

    B. Delay in Order Processing

    C. Need to Interface with Company Y Network

    D. New Capabilities Company X Can Use

II. Charter of the Study Team

    A. Company X Records to Examine

    B. Competition to Critique

    C. Vendors to Contact

    D. Systems to Review

    E. People to Interview

Figure 7-6. More Specific Fact Outline

III. Current Communications in Use in the Company
   A. Corporate Level
   B. Manufacturing
   C. Sales
   D. Warehousing/Shipping
   E. Finance/Personnel

IV. Current Communications Comparing Three Different Network Systems
   A. Corporate Level
   B. Manufacturing
   C. Sales
   D. Warehousing/Shipping
   E. Finance/Personnel

V. Five-Year Projection of Communication Needs
   A. Corporate Level
   B. Manufacturing
   C. Sales
   D. Warehousing/Shipping
   E. Finance/Personnel

VI. Projected Comparison of the Three Networks
   A. Corporate Level
   B. Manufacturing
   C. Sales
   D. Warehousing/Shipping
   E. Finance/Personnel

VII. Analysis of the Projections
   A. System 1 Costs and Benefits
   B. System 2 Costs and Benefits
   C. System 3 Costs and Benefits

VIII. Recommendations
   A. Appropriate Parts of System 3
   B. Modifications to System 3 With Justification
   Appendix A—General Systems Concept
   Appendix B—Systems Implementation Plan

Figure 7-6. (cont.)

COMMUNICATIONS NETWORK REQUIREMENTS FOR COMPANY X

A STUDY

I. General Antecedents for the Study

    A. Annual Cost of Company X Communications
        1. Telephone
        2. Telegram
        3. Messenger
        4. Facsimile
        5. Mail

    B. Delay in Order Processing
        1. Monthly Sales Order Backlogs
        2. Estimates of Sales Lost to Competition
        3. Samples from Audit of Order Processing
        4. Analysis of Present Order Processing Cycle
        etc.

Figure 7-7. Third Level Fact Outline

Identified Fact
I.A.1 Annual Cost of Company X Telephone Communications

Substantive Fact
Item a. Company X Telephone Bill for January 1980 and its contents

Item b. Company X Telephone Bill for February 1980 and its contents

Item c. Company X Telephone Bill for March 1980 and its contents
etc.

Draft
The cost of telephone services for the year 1980 totalled $1,380,991.55. This included both use of the telephone facilities and rental of telephone equipment, which are $1,122,444.03 and $258,547.52 respectively.

Figure 7-8. Identified Fact, Substantive Fact, and Draft

7.3.3 Top-Down Fact Finding

How does a study team organize its fact finding into a top-down form? There is a ready-made instrument that can frequently be used. That instrument is the organization of the user group. Consider the organization chart in figure 7-9. The three levels of that organization chart correspond to the three levels of specificity with which you might be working when you do your fact finding for the company's network needs. This facilitates organizing the fact finding into a top-down mode. Note that this approach is guaranteed to be on time. Since the approach is top-down, it means that all the bases are covered all the time. For example, each level of the chart represents the complete user organization.

At any given time, the study exists in draft form. It was in draft form from the first day because, on the first day, the general outline was written. Therefore, the study report can be put in its final form at any time. In fact, if for some reason the study report is called early only minor polishing is required to produce the full study report. Of course your study will still look like an outline, but it is complete. If, however, the sponsor gives your team two or three days notice, a few words of

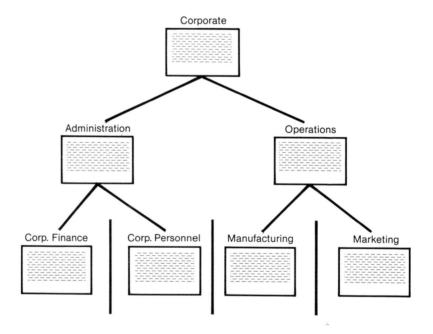

Figure 7-9. Top-Down Corporate Organization (Note Partitioning)

padding here and there will produce a draft that looks respectable. Such a study report is always ready to go.

Because the study team has been trained to write things down, there will always be material with which to give presentations. More will be said about DP presentations in section 10.5.

For now, remember that your team must begin writing the report on the very first day. That way, no matter what happens, there is a product—a tangible return on all the labor invested. Next, remember to work top-down just as in programming.

7.3.4   Quick Studies

When it comes to studies, there is no such thing as a "quickie" for the company. Neither is there such a thing as a skimpy but good study. Poor studies never seem to die; they just get reinterpreted again and again, often leading management to make poor decisions which would never have been considered if the work had been carefully done in the first place.

7.4   MANAGEMENT OF THE STUDY

7.4.1   Data, Sources, Methods

After the charter and general outline have been written (see section 7.3.2), your study team should make a list of the kinds of data that they will be collecting. It is a natural tendency to want to work at a very detailed level right away. If you are the study manager, you will find that your team members will want to go off and pick out the areas in which they are interested and study them at great depth. It is important in the early stages to keep the team working at a general level. At this stage the list of data should be a list of generic entries. The kinds of data that would go into this list are the following:

- management information needs
- operational data (data about internal operations)
- organizational data
- equipment capabilities
- performance data

- productivity data
- document descriptions
- similar systems data
- precedents in the company
- software development capabilities of the company
- vendor services
- software packages

The next thing to write down is the sources for these information items. Corresponding to the above list, the study team should identify sources such as the following:

- top management—for organizational information
- supervisors and foremen—for operational information
- clerks and users for documents—for inputs and outputs
- manufacturers' surveys—for equipment capabilities
- the head of the computing center—for computing capabilities
- software development manager—for software development capabilities
- vendors (primary sources)
- vendor survey articles and services (secondary services)
- technical periodicals—for precedents and similar systems

Next the team must write down the methodologies that will be applied in gathering the data:

- questionnaires
- literature review
- interviews (in person and by phone calls)
- phone calls (for specific questions)
- time and motion studies
- letters of inquiry
- compilation of journal articles
- announcements of invitations to submit information
- mathematics or statistical techniques
- graphic analysis techniques
- graphic presentation techniques

(After working with the same study people for a period of time, you may not need to specify in advance the latter two methodologies.)

Many of the data collection methods can be used for several different sources (see figure 7-10). After establishing the methods, identify

Sources	Questionnaires	Literature Reviews	Interviews	Phone Calls	Time & Motion Studies
Top Management	X		X	X	
Supervisors & Foremen	X		X	X	X
Clerks	X		X	X	X
Manufacturers	X	X	X	X	
Head of Computer Center			X	X	
Technical Periodicals		X			
Software Development Manager			X	X	

Figure 7-10. Relationship Between Information Sources and Information Gathering Methods

the timeframe, allowing time for processing the information, and you're ready to start collecting data.

7.4.2   The Fact-Finding Activities

The most important thing about managing the fact finding team is to keep the members on track, that is, following the top-down approach, and to get them to write things down.

To keep team members on track, give them short-term assignments, restricting an individual piece of research to not more than two or three days' duration. In a research environment people tend to wander off on tangents, following the path that looks most interesting at the moment.

It is often said that research cannot be managed, the implication being that creativity is spontaneous and, since research is a creative task, its results cannot be controlled. Without arguing the point too much, I can only stress what has been my experience. The top-down approach permits the project to be managed through focus of attention. It is true that you cannot tell people how to think or what to imagine, but you can tell them on what to focus their attention.

Figure 7-11 shows a succession of tasks in a top-down order for a fact-finding study. The bringing together of the general facts at the

Task 1. Review of Communications Requirements as Envisioned by Top Management

Task 2. Review of Administration Division's Communications Requirements

Task 3. Review of Operation Division's Communications Requirements

Task 4. Review of Finance Department's Communications Requirements

Task 5. Review of Personnel Department's Communications Requirements

Task 6. Review of Manufacturing Department's Communications Requirements

Task 7. Review of Marketing Department's Communications Requirements

Figure 7-11. Top-Down Task Plan

highest level will identify what the next set of facts are to be examined. It also insures that there are no gaps in the data.

Making the assignments of short duration will not guarantee that the individuals doing the work do not wander off the track, but it makes it possible for you to monitor more closely what is being done. Left to themselves, the members of a team tend to let the work be delayed or pile up so that it will be done at the end of the project. Avoid this problem by making short-term assignments. The short-term approach guarantees that the work will be done when it is supposed to be.

The next most important thing is to make sure that people write things down. The source and the date for every fact should be recorded with that fact. A good manager will run a strong quality assurance program to make sure this is done.

Obviously you cannot spend the time to check every fact that your team encounters. To do that would mean that you were duplicating everyone's work. If you were a member of a five-man team, you would end up doing five times as much work as anyone else on the team. While you may indeed end up doing more work than anyone else, you obviously cannot duplicate, nor would you want to duplicate, the time that the others have put in on their individual assignments.

The technique which I have used is to take a random set of facts that have been discovered and check them to make sure that the sources were accurately identified and that there were no errors of transcription.

This verifies that what was given by way of instruction to a subor-

A Checklist for the Study Author Who Wants to Write Effectively:

- Keep the schedule uppermost in your mind.
- Make outlines good enough that rough drafts can be prepared from them. (Outlines can be continuously refined during the study using top-down techniques.)
- Be prepared to commandeer rough drafts as finals.
- Be prepared to cut and paste.
- Use copiers to avoid getting into retyping queues when editing or revising text, especially if several writers are working on the same section.
- Treat every document as a potential cut and paste inclusion in the final draft.
- Have reports from team members reorganized and edited to serve as inserts.
- Treat every document as a working document.

Figure 7-12. Checklist for Managing Study Documents

dinate was understood by the subordinate. It verifies that the subordinate had the tools and the access that he needed to get his work done. The manager who leads a team by assuming its work is done properly without ever looking at the work is not a manager at all; he is a dreamer.

You may feel that I overemphasize the management and control aspects of doing a system study. However, the study is the part of the system development process which most often goes wrong. The fix for these errors is the simplest imaginable, just hard-nosed management. Figure 7-12 shows a checklist for writing effective studies.

7.5 CONTENTS OF THE STUDY REPORT

Every study has certain ingredients which are so important they might as well be the chapter or section headings of the final report.

7.5.1 Executive Summary

An executive summary is needed only if the study report exceeds twenty pages. It is a concise statement of the problem, the conduct of the study, the findings, the conclusion, and the recommendations. The executive summary should be not longer than three pages—preferably less.

7.5.2 Introduction

This chapter will identify the original problem, give a precise statement of the problem, tell how the team was organized and how it conducted its study, and explain the contents of the remaining parts of the report. The statement of the problem may contain two versions: the problem as originally identified and the problem as the team finally came to understand it.

7.5.3 Methodology

If the techniques used to obtain the data for the study were standard (such as tabulations with computations of averages and comparisons of large and small numbers), you do not need to have a special chapter on methodology. However, if the methods used were original (such as the design and utilization of a questionnaire), or if the methodology is esoteric to the sponsor or the report's readers (such as analysis of covariance, regression analysis), then the method should be explained in layman's terms in this chapter.

Your team should include references for further investigation of the methodology, particularly if it is part of a body of specialized knowledge such as sampling statistics.

7.5.4 Findings

This is a detailed description of the different findings that the study team uncovered. Any trends, costs, and other special considerations would be described in this chapter. Data presented should be generalized, not detailed.

7.5.5 Conclusions

Here the authors should describe and separate into categories the conclusions that the study team has drawn about things that can be done.

This section should include the results that can be expected from applying each of the possible measures.

7.5.6   Recommendations

In this section your study team would present the different actions that could be taken, each based on a unique concept that would achieve the results identified in the conclusions section. Costs and benefits would be presented separately for each alternative (see figures 7-13a and 7-13b).

	Cost	*Benefit*
Alternative A	$2,000,000	• faster response • interface to System X • more complex inquiries
Alternative B	$1,000,000	• shorter development time • interface to system Y

A good comparison. Here, by implication, B is slower, since A is faster. Alternative B obviously does not interface to X, but it does interface to system Y. Since B has shorter development time, then A must have longer development time. Since A handles more complex inquiries, then B must handle simpler inquiries.

The Right Way—Costs and Benefits of Each Alternative Stand on Their Own

	Cost	*Benefit*
Alternative A	$2,000,000	1,000 transactions per day
Alternative B	500 transactions per day	$1,000,000

This says that the advantage of Alternative B is that it costs only half as much as Alternative A. The cost (or disadvantage) is that it only handles half as many transactions. Yet Alternative A and B are really the same. Each costs $2,000.00 per daily transaction.

The Wrong Way—Costs of One are Benefits of the Other

Figure 7-13a. The Right Way and the Wrong Way to Present Costs and Benefits

Attribute	Alternative A	Alternative B
Cost	$2,000,000	$1,000,000
Response	faster	slower
Interface	System X	System Y
Development Time	longer	shorter
Inquiries	simple and complex	simple only

Figure 7-13b. Another Version of the Right Way to Show Costs and Benefits

7.5.7 Appendix

Any data needed in the report for illustration or back-up purposes belong in this section. The sources of data should be indicated as well, including organizations, individuals (at least by position, if not by name), and published references. Raw data do not actually belong in the body of the report. I have seen very unprofessional looking study reports that were nothing more than page after page after page of raw data stapled together.

7.5.8 Bibliography

This is an optional list of related readings for those who are new to the technology. You must judge the level of interest and receptivity of your audience before preparing this section.

7.6 DATA, FINDINGS, CONCLUSIONS, AND RECOMMENDATIONS

The most frequently misunderstood terms in systems studies are the following: data, findings, conclusions, and recommendations. You must have a precise understanding of what each of these terms means.

7.6.1 Data—Isolated Facts That Have Been Observed and Written Down

Assume that a study team has been asked to find out how to reduce costs in a nationwide telecommunications network. The following are typical facts that it may have uncovered:

- The office in Des Moines, Iowa, uses a teletype terminal but could just as easily use a video display terminal.
- One particular manufacturer, Company X, markets a particular video display terminal (VDT) that costs less than a teletype terminal.

The preceding two items are facts that have been obtained from documented sources. For example, the fact about the Des Moines office may have been obtained in an interview with the branch office supervisor in Des Moines. Likewise, the fact about the cost of the terminal could have been obtained from a terminal survey publication such as Auerbach's or DataPro's.

7.6.2   Findings—The Results of Analysis Performed Upon Data

By tabulating the responses to its questions, the study team may have found that the majority of the company's offices were using teletypes or hard-copy terminals and would be willing to switch to VDT terminals. Perhaps also by simple tabulation, the team discovered that there were dozens of firms marketing video display terminals which cost less than the hard-copy terminals the company is now using. These discoveries are findings.

7.6.3   Conclusions—Implications Drawn from Examination of the Findings

Drawing conclusions is a logical process for which I cannot give a formula. Basically, it consists of looking at the findings and answering sensible questions about those findings. For example, in the telecommunications study a logical conclusion would be that video display terminals could be substituted for teletype terminals and that costs would thereby be reduced. The report could state this in the following way: "We can save money by substituting VDTs for teletype or hard-copy terminals in most of our branch offices."

7.6.4   Recommendations—A Formula for Action

Recommendations are a blueprint for management to follow in order to get results. For example, a recommendation proceeding from the above conclusions might be as follows: "The company should set up a conversion schedule to convert offices X, Y, . . . , Z from hard-copy to VDT devices. The schedule should be developed so as to begin within the next six weeks and be completed within one year. Commitments should be made to take advantage of VDT prices now in effect. The schedule should include a preliminary solicitation of the following vendors."

By identifying and describing recommendations, studies can make creative results come from resourceful people. Different alternatives can be different in a generic way, for example, manual versus automated, or different in a specific way, for example, a particular big system versus a particular little system.

There is no rule about *how different* the alternatives must be. Don't always assume there can only be the three classical choices:

- batch
- on-line
- left as is.

This kind of thinking is an example of what psychologists call "self-imposed limitations."

A perfectly viable set of alternatives might be:

- the whole thing
- a part of it
- development by stages.

Another set is:

- the whole thing
- a prototype, followed by the go-ahead decision.

7.7 FORMATS

As author of the study, you are bound by the rules of effective writing discussed in chapter 2. First of all, you must remember to write to the particular audience who will be reading your study. Usually this audience will consist of managers. Many managers prefer a study report to be organized in a problem-solution format which corresponds to the outline I have been discussing. Other managers prefer a solution-problem format. In that case, the recommendations would be given first, then the findings and conclusions. Another variation is to have recommendations, conclusions, then findings.

During the Nixon administration, I was in charge of a system-development project for the Executive Office of the President. In that

The current hardware configuration is not adequate to handle the daily workload. An additional one million bytes of main memory and two more printers should be installed immediately.

Figure 7-14a. Example of Problem-Solution Format

particular era, the upper management of the Office of Management and Budget (OMB), who reviewed our reports, were inclined to the solution-problem approach. They preferred a report to begin with a statement of action, for example, "Step X should be taken immediately." The report would then continue on to say why the action should be taken. In fact, they preferred that each paragraph be organized the same way. In other words, the paragraph began with a statement of urgency, grabbing the reader's attention. Then the words following would amplify that point. Examples of the two contrasting approaches are shown in figures 7-14a and 7-14b.

7.8 WORDING

By skipping over or improperly researching their facts, data processing people frequently do studies that look as if the team is trying to get away with something. A typical example is the transparent attempt to justify a position by appealing to an invisible majority. "It is generally considered . . . " or "It is understood . . . " or "It is assumed . . . "

If in fact the things that you are putting into your study are really facts, that is, if they are really true, then you produce a stronger document by identifying the body that has been referenced. For example, the phrase "It is generally considered" could be replaced by "The official position of the DPMA is that . . . " Likewise, in place of "It is assumed

An additional one million bytes of main memory and two more printers should be installed immediately. The current hardware configuration is not adequate to handle the daily workload.

Figure 7-14b. Example of Solution-Problem Format

. . ." you could say "The 1980 Professional Salary Survey indicates that . . ."

If you have done a study well, then you should be able to make positive statements about your data. For example, you should say something like, "Over half of the branch offices have eliminated punched cards." That is much stronger than starting out with one of the following: "apparently," "it seems," "usually," or "in general."

When doing a study, your professional approach should be to let the facts speak for themselves. Using a phrase like "in our opinion" merely challenges the reader to see if he can find a contrary opinion.

7.9 PERSONNEL RELATIONS

7.9.1 Employee Cooperation

Getting the right people to do a study and keeping them effective is one of the hardest parts of any study effort. Most organizations, even those with the largest DP shops, do not have a full-time staff to do system studies. Why this should be I do not know unless the industry assumes that the real DP work does not begin until system analysis and design are underway. Whatever the reason, the study team is typically brought together on an ad hoc basis, with its members drawn from different organizations, its charter of short-term duration, and its internal organization a purely temporary arrangement.

No one really wants to be drafted for any but the most glamorous studies. This causes certain problems. Even those individuals who are particularly good at doing system studies are reluctant to leave the familiar environment of their own office to go to work, even briefly, in a strange office with an unfamiliar group of people.

Where possible I recommend that the actual study work be done in close proximity to the team members' offices and that members have a certain amount of time every week to spend back in their home office.

The actual study work, however, should be done out of its own base office so that the individuals come to look upon themselves as a team. The proper environment helps to make a team spirit possible.

Studies do take time and during an average study, say of three month's duration, a team member may feel anxious about what is happening back in his home office. He may wonder about other people getting reviews, merit increases, and promotions, and worry about losing out.

To alleviate this anxiety, I recommend the following: The manager of the study team should meet with the supervisor of each individual assigned to the study just as soon as the charter has been set up and a schedule has been laid out. The manager should then make the supervisor aware of the overall schedule and the responsibilities of his particular subordinate as a member of the study team. In particular the manager should make the supervisor aware of the deliverables which are the responsibility of that team member and the dates on which those deliverables are due.

Armed with this information, the supervisor can then meet with his subordinate on a regular basis and talk confidently of the work that the individual is doing and the results that are expected of him. Since they are meeting frequently, the team member will know that his work is visible and important to his supervisor.

If this arrangement is maintained, then the individual who has successfully completed his study assignment can move naturally and comfortably back into his old niche in his organization and continue to be in line for personal advancement as the opportunities come along.

7.9.2 Effective Personnel Management

I advocate the following management actions for getting the work done:

- *Assign members of the study team in their area of specialty.* The more experienced the individual team members are, the less guidance they will need. A study should not be considered an opportunity to learn a new skill. Certainly people on the study will learn about the application if it's unfamiliar to them and DP professionals should not be reluctant to tackle areas new to them. But if one person, for example, is a hardware specialist and another is a software specialist, then the hardware specialist should work in a study area that involves hardware, and the software specialist should work in the part that involves software. They should not be trained on the job in a study. The study is too important.

- *Use senior people.* The study is not the place to assign junior people. If the company feels it necessary to put inexperienced people on the study team, then they should be assigned simple data collection or data reduction tasks under senior supervision. They should not be assigned data collection responsibilities which require more mature discretion, because they will be too easily led astray.

- *Make a top-down approach the rule.* All team members should know how to make an outline and be aware of its usefulness.
- *Agree on the statement of the problem.* This gives every team member a sense of direction. The problem statement is a point of reference for the entire study effort.
- *Keep the turnaround time short.* Too long a turnaround schedule encourages waste.
- *Insist on citations for specific sources.* These references should include page numbers, if applicable. The study manager bears the responsibility for errors in the final report.

7.10 PACKAGING

Avoid the "consultants' syndrome"—that is, putting an inferior report inside a classy cover. Everyone likes a pretty package, but the report's appearance should be compatible with the position and tastes of the audience. Its general attributes are these:

- understated cover
- neat appearance
- readability and intelligibility
- an executive summary that tells the whole story
- two volume packages for very large reports
  —Volume I to include summaries of findings and methodology.
  —Volume II to include details of longer sections and raw data, even to the extent of reproducing actual survey notes, if necessary.

To be professional, the style of the report should be absolutely atonal. Avoid a folksy or too familiar narrative form, remembering the guidelines set down in chapter 4. Watch the wording of gripes and pet peeves. Substantiate every point. Avoid overselling your recommendations as they should speak for themselves.

7.11   HIGHLIGHTS

- The study report is the most important document in data processing, yet it is often given little attention.
- When doing a study, give the best answer you can, given the amount of time and money at your disposal.
- Your team must write a charter, then, using top-down techniques, produce an outline.
- Write as the study progresses, not at the end.
- Your report will probably contain an executive summary, an introduction, a section on methodology (optional), findings, conclusions, recommendations, an appendix, and a bibliography (optional).
- Studies may be written in a problem-solution format or a solution-problem format.
- In your study report, assign responsibility for facts wherever you can.
- If you are managing a study, meet frequently with your team members' supervisors so members will not feel they are being forgotten at their home offices.

8

Analytic and Developmental Documents: The System Specification

8.1 SYSTEM DEVELOPMENT TASKS AND DELIVERABLES

Before discussing the principal systems development documents, let us recapitulate the major tasks and deliverables of the software development cycle. These are shown in figure 8-1. Figure 8-2 shows the cross-reference between the terms used in this book and those of the government standard FIPS-38.

The actual tasks of programming, testing, and maintenance are outside the scope of this book. The study was discussed in the previous chapter. Systems analysis and its written deliverables are covered in this chapter. System design, its deliverables, and program listing documentation are discussed in chapter 9.

System development begins where the study leaves off. You will recall that the study is a top-down deliverable and a milestone for the design and implementation work to follow. The study provides background, identification of users and user communities, and the general systems concept. The readers of the study were the users who would be directly involved with the new system, sponsors who would pay the bill, and the systems analysts who would be doing the system design. All these readers figure in the systems development to come.

Task	*Deliverables*	
Feasibility Study	Problem Statement	⎫ Requirements
	Problem Definition	⎬ Statement
	Feasibility Study Report	⎭
Systems Analysis	System Specification (sometimes called the structured spec)	
System Design	Programming Specification (sometimes called the structured design spec)	
Programming	Programs	
Testing	Operational Programs	
Maintenance	Maintenance Notebook	

Figure 8-1. Major Tasks and Deliverables of the Software Development Cycle

8.2 THE SYSTEM DEVELOPMENT CYCLE AND QUALITY CONTROL

The key to turning out a good, professional document is quality control. Figure 8-3 shows my company's quality control cycle. This cycle is based on the premise that *a successful system satisfies the user's needs.*

8.2.1 The Requirements Statement and the System Specification

The requirements statement is just that—a statement of the user's requirements. The system specification is a rigorous restatement of these refinements in terms that are more nearly the terminology of data processing. The essential question is "Does the system specification satisfy the user requirements?" In other words, "Are the two documents equivalent except for a difference in terminology?"

A professional quality control program will ensure that there is a task in the project which verifies that the two are equivalent. The task could be any one of several testing methods. For further information about testing, consult the catalogue of testing procedures in the *Software Reliability Guidebook* by Robert L. Glass and the statement of testing philosophy found in *The Art of Software Testing* by Glen Myers (see bibliography).

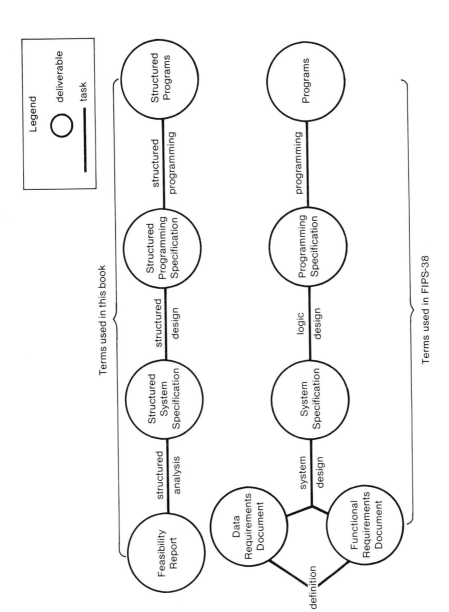

Figure 8-2. Cross-Reference Between Deliverables and Tasks in Life Cycle Schematics

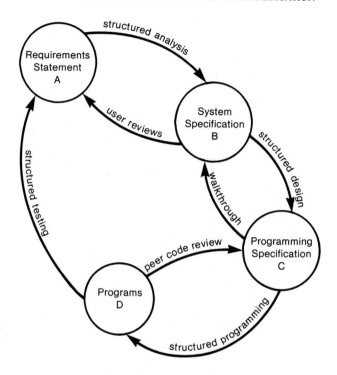

Figure 8-3. The Quality Assurance Life Cycle

8.2.2   Testing the System Specification

My firm uses the particular quality control test called the user review. In this method, a concerned user or group of users reviews the system specification with the systems analyst who developed it. The user need not be experienced in data processing in order to read and deal with the structures and terminology in the systems specification document.

The successful system review by the user will follow a structured format. A small piece of the document to be reviewed should be identified as the topic for a particular meeting. The material should be given out a day in advance so that everyone has a chance to review it before the meeting. Then the user and the people who wrote the document can come to the meeting and go through each item in that particular section.

No manager should be present so that the workers will not be intimidated and will feel free to speak critically. This should be a frank, but constructive, discussion of what the questionable items mean and whether they satisfy the corresponding requirement in the problem statement document. Meetings should continue until the system specification has been accepted by the user as being equivalent to the user requirements statement. At this point, the specification satisfies the user requirements, i.e., that document A equals document B. The mathematics of A = B turns out to be very important further along.

8.2.3   The System Specification and the Programming Specification

Next the same sort of thing is done for the programming specification. The system design task is the task of converting the system specification into a programming specification. The review task is the task of ascertaining that the programming specification document is equivalent to the logic of the system specification document. This review is attended by the systems analysts who developed the specification and by their peers among systems analysts and senior programmers. More than likely, some interested users will attend these quality control test sessions as well.

8.2.4   Testing the Programming Specification

Next the programming specification is tested. In one effective testing method, the *structured walk-through,* a particular line of logic is followed to make sure that it is handled correctly in the specification document.

At the end of this testing process, you will again have document equivalence—the programming specification satisfying the system specification—that is, a new document C (the programming specification) equivalent to document B (the system specification).

Notice that the objective is only incidentally to have document B equal to document C. The real objective is to have document C equivalent to document A (the requirements statement), because that is what good, reliable system development is all about, to have the system as developed satisfy the user's requirements. The rules of logic tell us that if A is equivalent to B and B is equivalent to C, then A is equivalent to C also.

8.2.5   The Programming Specification and the Program

The next process is to undertake a programming task which will produce the document called a program or programs. The quality control task that verifies the code is not, as is frequently assumed, testing the programs all at once on the computer. This is sometimes called the "Big Bang" theory of testing. Instead the program code that is written is checked against the specifications in the program specification document.

8.2.6 Testing the Program Code

For illustration purposes, I will use the testing technique called peer code review. The steps of peer code review will verify that the code as written matches the code that was specified in the programming specification.

The result is a situation where the new document, document D (the program code), is equal to document C, but you already know that document C is equal to document A. So we have $A = C$ and $C = D$; hence $A = D$. Thus, the program code is equivalent to the statement of user requirements.

8.2.7 The Requirements Statement and the Program

Perhaps I should say that you *feel* you have achieved equivalence between the two documents. Since you are dealing with human beings and with language, obviously you will not have a rigorous mathematical relationship. There are going to be oversights and errors in the quality control process as with most other human activities. But, generally speaking, the structured approach to quality control described in the preceding paragraphs is very effective and better than anything else available to date. So you can safely assume that the documents are in good shape when you go into final testing.

8.3 THE SYSTEM ANALYSIS TASK AND THE SYSTEM SPECIFICATION DOCUMENT

8.3.1 System Analysis

The first task of system development is the task of system analysis. The job of the system analyst is to do the work that was done in the systems study but to do it more rigorously. In fact, the rigor should be sufficient to commence what traditionally is called programming.

System analysis is the work of defining data elements and of defining the interrelationship between elements of the system. These elements include not only data but also processes. This analysis is necessary, first, so that the system to be programmed can be understood and, second, so that the existing system can be improved by combining some things, eliminating some things, and refining others.

The subtasks of system analysis are the following:

- collection of data
- analysis of the current physical system
- analysis of the underlying logical system

Name of document: Bulk Shipment Order
Number of copies: 3
Originated by: Marketing
Used by: Warehouse clerk, picker, loading dock
Ultimate disposition: Account Department
Description of uses: Clerk receives form, verifies validity, gives 2 copies to picker who locates stock and places 1 copy on loading dock
Volumes per day/week/month: 200/day

Field name	Description, use, and comments
date	MMDDYY, dates form
billing address	4 lines used for billing
ship-to-address	4 lines used for shipping
item number	stock number of item to be picked; repeated as needed
description	one line description of item; repeated as needed
each	amount of each item to be shipped; repeated as needed
per	number of basic units packaged together; repeated as needed
clerk number picker number loader number	id number or initial of individual handling form

Figure 8-4. Document Description Form Used for Data Collection

DATAFLOW NAME: Bulk Shipment Order Form

ALIASES: Bulk Order Form

COMPOSITION:

date + billing address + ship-to-address
+ {item no. + each + per + description} $_1^n$
+ clerk # + picker # + loader #

NOTES: in 3 copies, clerk receives form, verifies validity, gives
2 copies to picker who locates stock and places with one
copy on loading dock

Figure 8-5. Dataflow Entry in Data Dictionary

- refinement with alternative man/machine interfaces
- selection of the target man/machine interface
- final polishing of the system specification

The above list follows the approach described in *Structured Analysis and System Specification* by Tom DeMarco (see bibliography).

Data collection First, you must collect data about the system which is to be investigated. To do this in a systematic way, you should use forms (see section 8.4). In the computer industry today there must be thousands of good, useful forms available to you. The bibliography lists several of the many sources of data collection forms.

Analysis of the current system After the data are collected, the next step is to analyze the current system by diagramming the current physical system setup. My company uses a method described very effectively

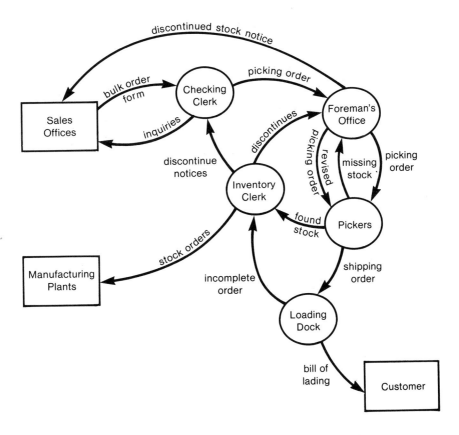

Figure 8-6. Dataflow Diagram of Physical System for Warehouse Inventory

in DeMarco's book and in *Structured System Analysis: Tools and Techniques* by Chris Gane and Trish Sarson (see bibliography).

Example of data collection and analysis of the current system As an example of these forms and diagrams in action, the following figures show an inventory control problem. Figure 8-4 is an illustration of data collected from a warehouse. Some of the data collected on the form came from direct analysis of documents, others from interviews. Figure 8-5 shows these data converted into a data dictionary entry (see section 8.5). Figure 8-6 shows the physical system which gives rise to those documents, treated in the systems analysis technique called *structured systems analysis*. Figure 8-7 depicts the underlying logic of the current physical system.

Example of man machine interface In figure 8-8 a man/machine refinement of the system is shown. Various man/machine alternatives are presented to management with a suitable executive summary. Man-

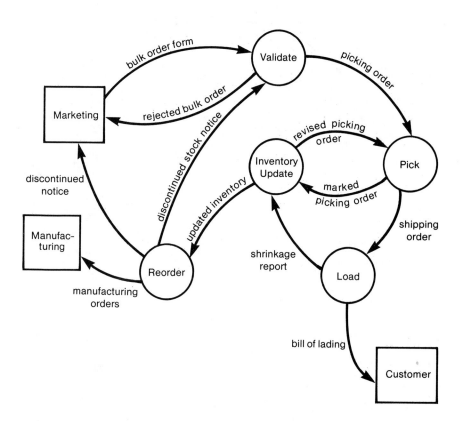

Figure 8-7. Dataflow Diagram of Logical System for Warehouse Inventory

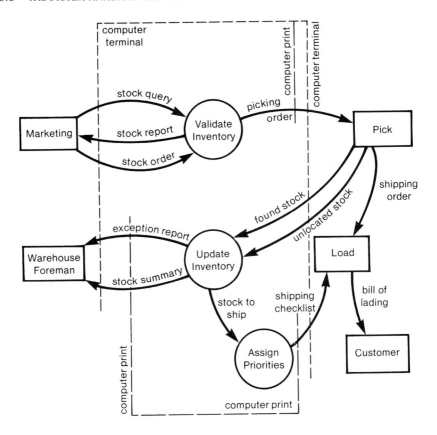

Figure 8-8. Man/Machine Refinement of the Logical System

agement reviews the alternatives and selects one alternative. Other variations are usually developed to help management make a cost/benefit decision.

Final polishing of the system specification The next step is to polish the specification by fleshing out the selected alternative into a final system specification. To "flesh out" means to close all logical gaps, checking to make sure that every requirement has been satisfied and that all the details are worked out.

8.3.2 The System Specification Document

Figures 8-9 through 8-13 show excerpts from a finished structured system specification. This system specification is taken from a different

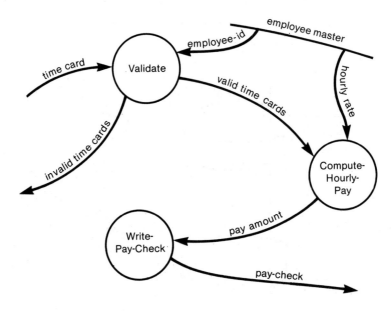

Figure 8-9. Dataflow Diagram from Structured System Specification for a Payroll System

example, one concerned with the ubiquitous "payroll system" problem.

Anyone who reads the analysis documents should be able to go back and look at the system requirements study and compare that with the system specification. The reader should be able to trace a very logical developmental growth from the study which is the kick-off document to the system specification which is the first document once system development gets underway. Subsequently the reader should be able to see the same evolution from the system specification to the programming specification.

8.4   FORMS AND FORMATS IN DATA COLLECTION, ANALYSIS, AND DESIGN

The data used in systems analysis are systematically collected on forms. Other forms, as you will see, are used to *perform the analysis and design tasks* of systems development. Each form has its own format which imposes an organization upon data in system development. In other words, forms and formats help to structure the data which are collected.

FILE OR DATABASE NAME: Employee master

ALIASES:

COMPOSITION:

Header $+ \, _0^n$ {employee record}

ORGANIZATION:

NOTES:

Figure 8-10. Datafile Definition from Structured System Specification for a Payroll System

---

PROCESS NAME: Compute hourly pay

PROCESS NUMBER:

PROCESS DESCRIPTION:

1. For each employee time card
   1.1 get employee record
   1.2 extract hourly rate and deductions
   1.3 multiply rate × hours worked giving base pay
   1.4 calculate withholding using base pay and deductions
   1.5 subtract withholding from base giving actual pay

2. -----
   2.1 -----
   2.2 -----

NOTES:

Figure 8-11. Process Definition from Structured System Specification for a Payroll System

DATAFLOW NAME: Time card

ALIASES: greencard

COMPOSITION:

    employee name + employee id + no. hours worked

NOTES:

Figure 8-12. Dataflow Definition from Structured System Specification for a Payroll System

DATA ELEMENT NAME: Employee id

ALIASES: Executive id

VALUES AND MEANINGS:

$${}_{1}^{5}\{\text{digit}\}$$

-or-

digit + digit + digit + digit + digit

NOTES:

Figure 8-13. Data Element Definition from Structured System Specification for a Payroll System

8.4.1 Structuring Data Collection

Structure in the development process *leads to correct designs* which in turn lead *to correct systems.*

There are many different forms and many different formats. Some are better for some applications than others. Forms are also used to perform analysis upon the collected data and, as in the case of HIPO (see section 9.1.2), to perform actual systems design.

8.4.2 Forms Selection

Analysis and design should be structured but not blindly structured. Choice of forms and formats is up to the analyst—but he must make the decision *before* collecting the data or doing the analysis or design. Sometimes choosing a form breaks the inertia that holds the analysis back.

8.4.3 Sample Forms

A systems analyst should be free to select or design his forms to suit the application, but he can get some very good ideas from other people. For this reason, I have included a few of my favorites from *Systems and Programming Standards* by Susan Wooldridge (see bibliography). They are the following:

- document description form (figure 8-4)
- data/document cross-reference chart (figure 8-14)
- document analysis form (figure 8-15). Developed on machine readable basis for keypunching and incorporating into computer analysis of application. Listings can be produced; file can be updated; cross references can be examined.
- input description form (figure 8-16). Part of a data dictionary.
- file abstract form (figure 8-17). Gives file description, disposition volumes (sizes). Permits estimation of capacity and access rates in configuring hardware and software.

Some other forms illustrating useful ideas are included in figures 8-18, 8-19, and 8-20. These are reprinted, by permission of the publisher, from *Management Standards for Developing Information Systems*, by Norman L. Enger, © 1976 by AMACOM, a division of American Management Associations, pages 81 and 91. All rights reserved.

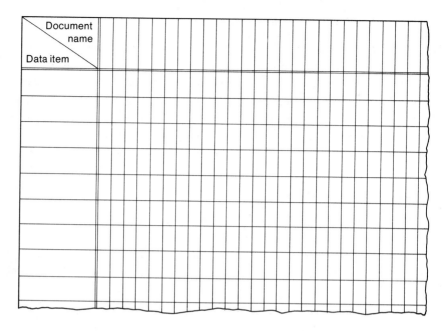

Figure 8-14. Data/Document Cross-Reference Chart

- input description (figure 8-18)
- output description (figure 8-19)
- file description form (figure 8-20)

8.5   DATA DICTIONARY

The notion of a data dictionary figures very prominently in systems analysis. The purpose of the data dictionary is to keep track of the inputs, outputs, and other data elements which will be used in the program. *A data dictionary is a document for the identification, definition, and description of data flows, data processes, data files, and data elements* (see figure 8-21).

A data dictionary is really a continuum of more and more detailed, properly filled out forms. Correctly designed and used, it feeds directly into the programming effort. From being an integral part of the system

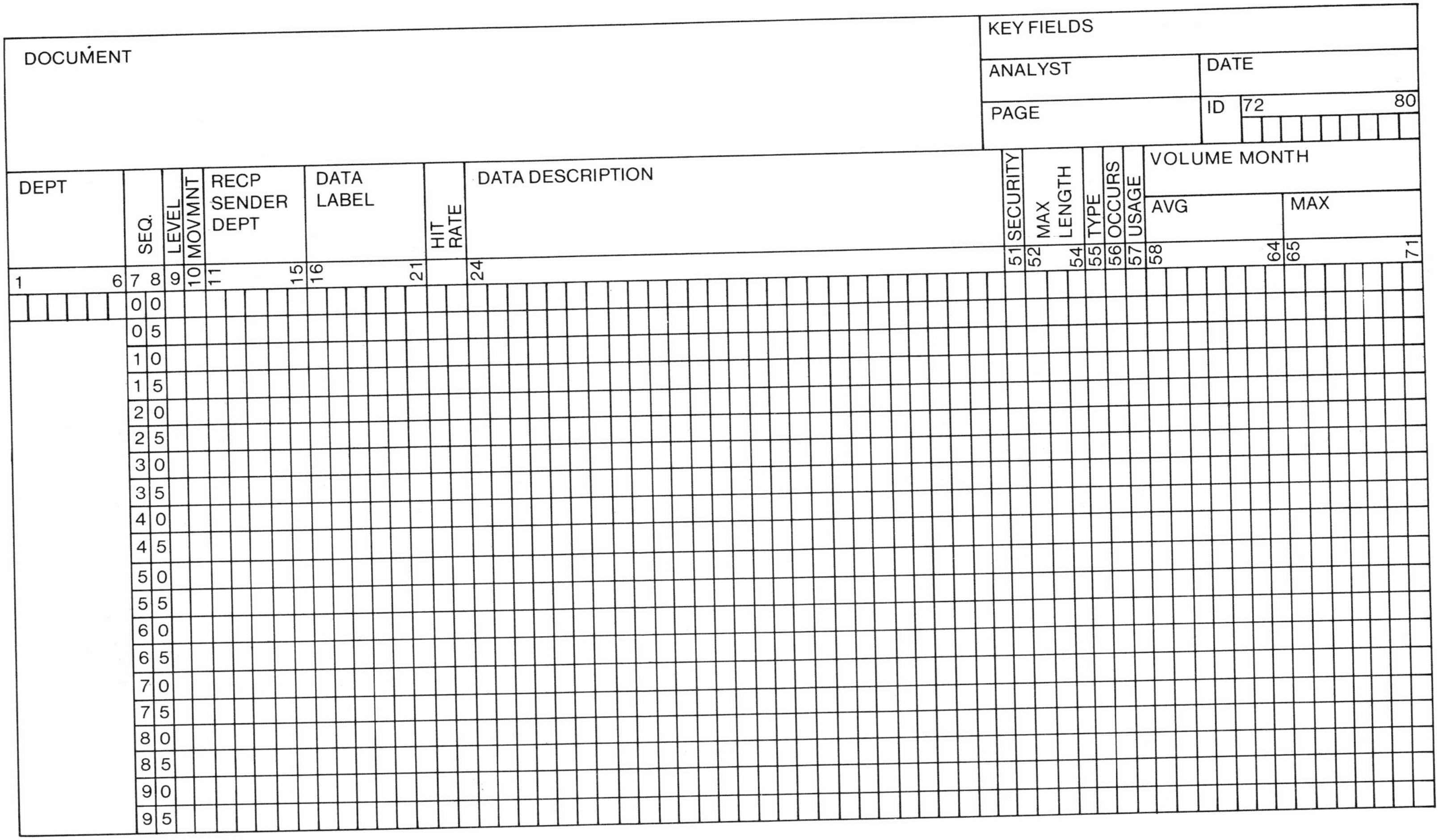

Figure 8-15. Document Analysis Form

INPUT DESCRIPTION FORM

	Identification
File no.	1
File title	2
Page no.	of
Brief Description	3
Date	4

	Input origin
Record name	5
From (title/dept)	6
Frequency	7
Take-on volumes(average/peak)	8
Normal volumes (average/peak)	9
Record size (average/max)	10
Input medium/device	11
Conversion method	12
Code	13

FIELD DESCRIPTION

Position	Correlation	Level	Field code names	Format & size	Occur	V	Ldg Zero	Sign	Further description (including details of validity checks to be applied on input).
19	18	20	21	22	24	25	26	27	28

File sequence

Key fields	Major	14
	Minor	

Cycling & security procedures

15

Programs using file

Program no.	Rw	Program no.	Rw
		16	

File description

Prepared by	17	Approved by

Figure 8-16. Input Description Form

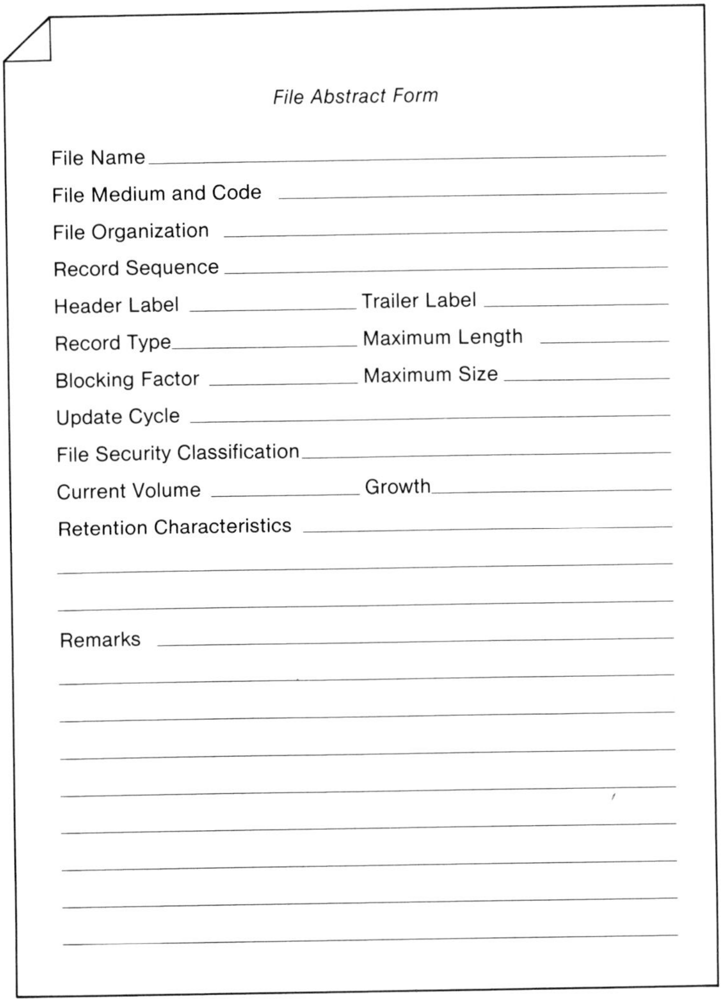

File Abstract Form

File Name _____

File Medium and Code _____

File Organization _____

Record Sequence _____

Header Label _____ Trailer Label _____

Record Type_____ Maximum Length _____

Blocking Factor _____ Maximum Size _____

Update Cycle _____

File Security Classification_____

Current Volume _____ Growth_____

Retention Characteristics _____

_____

_____

Remarks _____

_____

_____

_____

_____

_____

_____

_____

Figure 8-17. File Abstract Form

Name	Input				Frequency
	# Records	Record Size (Bytes)	Volume (Bytes/Mo)	Medium	

Figure 8-18. Input Description

Report Name	# Copies	# Parts	# Pages	Lines/Page	Frequency

Figure 8-19. Output Description

Data Element Name	Description	Origin	Size (Bytes)	Type Data	Volume	Frequency

Group Name

Remarks

Figure 8-20. File Description Form

Data Flow Diagram
Data Flow Definition
Data Element Definition ⎫
Data File Definition   ⎬ Data
Process Definition   ⎭ Dictionary

Figure 8-21. Documentation Elements of Structured Analysis

specification, the forms that make up the data dictionary go on to become part of the programming specification.

When they finally reach the programming specification, the data
elements sections of the data dictionary should include, as a minimum
for each element, the following:

- name of the data element (English and machine readable)

- description or definition of the data element

- source

- magnitude (in characters)—length

- range of acceptable values—different for numerical and alphabetic
  information

- type—alpha or numeric

- use—programs or applications

8.6 HIGHLIGHTS

- A successful system satisfies the user's needs.

- The system specification, the programming specification, and the
  program code must ultimately be equivalent to the user requirements statement.

- System analysis does the work that was done in the systems
  study, but does it more rigorously.

- Many forms and formats are available to help with data collection.

- After data is collected, the current system is analyzed by diagramming the current physical system setup. The final system specification is then "fleshed out."

- The data dictionary is a document for the identification, definition, and description of data flows, data processes, data files, and data elements.

9

Analytic and Developmental Documents: Program Specification and Program Listing

9.1 THE SYSTEM DESIGN TASK AND THE PROGRAM SPECIFICATION DOCUMENT

The program specification document is an intermediate document between the detailed system concept that resulted from structured analysis on the one hand and the actual program code on the other hand. My firm produces the program specification document using the ideas of Glen Myers in his various books on structured design (see bibliography). He calls his method modular decomposition.

The programming specification is concerned with the identification of programming modules, the organization of these modules and their relationship to one another, the interfaces between the modules, and the relationship between program modules and program data. The contents of a typical program specification are shown in figure 9-1.

The general logic of the various processes of the software system were developed in the system specification document described in chapter 8. An example appeared in figure 8-11. The corresponding programming specification section divides the general logic into segments of detailed logic. An example of the result is shown in figure 9-2. The algorithm of figure 8-11 is divided into detailed sections in figures 9-3 and 9-4.

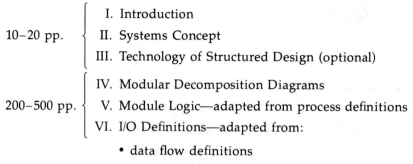

$$\left.\begin{array}{l} \text{I. Introduction} \\ \text{II. Systems Concept} \\ \text{III. Technology of Structured Design (optional)} \end{array}\right\} \text{10–20 pp.}$$

10–20 pp.
- I. Introduction
- II. Systems Concept
- III. Technology of Structured Design (optional)

200–500 pp.
- IV. Modular Decomposition Diagrams
- V. Module Logic—adapted from process definitions
- VI. I/O Definitions—adapted from:
  - data flow definitions
  - data file definitions
  - data element definitions

Figure 9-1. Contents of a Typical Program Specification

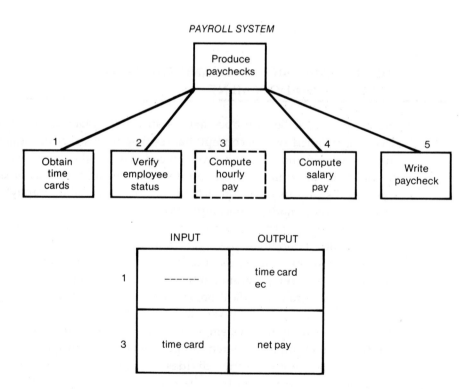

Figure 9-2. Modular Decomposition Diagram from Structured Design Specification

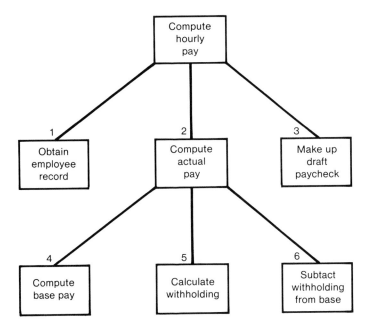

Figure 9-3. Second Stage of Modular Decomposition

9.1.1   Structured Design Through Modular Decomposition

The process of developing a programming specification using structured design principles is outlined in the following steps: First, using
the processes and data flow of the structured specification, lay out the
top level system design with one module of the top level design corre-

	Inputs	Outputs
1	employee-id	employee-record ec
2	employee-record time-card	actual pay
3		
4	hours worked hourly rate	base pay

Figure 9-4. Input/Output List for a Second Stage of Modular Decomposition

sponding to each process of the system specification. Be sure to give names with good working verbs to each of the modules thus defined. Next, list the interface between these modules. Then refine each of the modules one step further using any of the three standard methods of structural decomposition:

- functional decomposition
- transactional decomposition
- input process/output decomposition.

9.1.2   Structured Design Through HIPO

Another method of structured systems specification is the *hierarchy plus input-process-output (HIPO)* method. HIPO is described in *Systems Design and Documentation* by Harry Katzan, Jr. (see bibliography).

The HIPO process of program analysis and design specification consists of three elements:

- visual table of contents (VTOC) (figure 9-5)
- overview diagrams (figure 9-6)
- detailed diagrams with extended descriptions (figure 9-7)

The VTOC also serves as a system module diagram. In HIPO the system is constrained to be organized in the same hierarchial form as in the VTOC. The overview diagrams become a series of program specification general-level charts. The detailed diagrams (the third element) become a series of programming specification charts with data descriptions. Figure 9-8 is an example of the kind of double-duty document that comes naturally to HIPO. The worksheet of figure 9-8 will ultimately be redrawn as a detailed diagram such as in figure 9-7.

9.2   GRAPHIC TOOLS OF SYSTEM AND PROGRAMMING SPECIFICATIONS

My company has adopted the above-mentioned DeMarco graphics (see section 8.3.1) for structured analysis leading to the system specification document and Glen Myers' method of modular decomposition leading to the program specification document. This method is described in Myers' book *Reliable Software through Composite Design* (see bibliog-

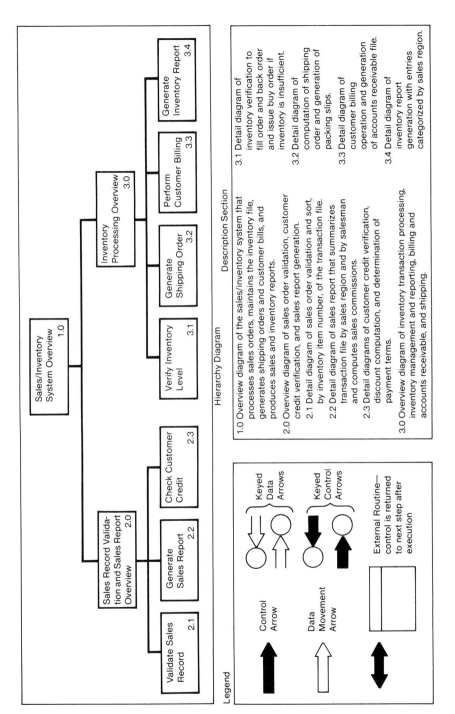

Figure 9-5. Visual Table of Contents of the HIPO Package Describing the Sales/Inventory System. From *Systems Design and Documentation* by Harry Katzan, Jr. Copyright © 1976 by Van Nostrand Reinhold Company. Reprinted by permission of the publisher.

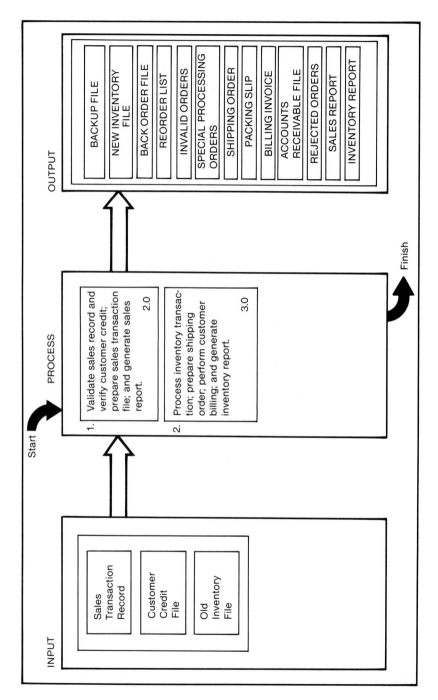

Figure 9-6. Overview Diagram Numbered 1.0 of the Sales/Inventory System (This is the Highest-Level Diagram in the HIPO Package.) From *Systems Design and Documentation* by Harry Katzan, Jr. Copyright © 1976 by Van Nostrand Reinhold Company. Reprinted by permission of the publisher.

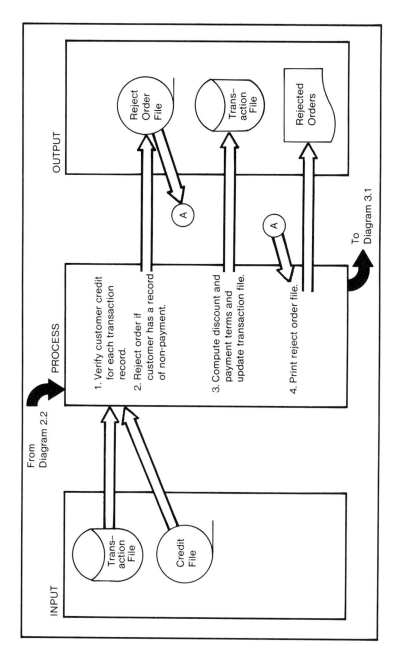

Figure 9-7. Detailed Diagram Numbered 2.3 of the Sales/Inventory System with Extended Description Omitted (This Diagram Corresponds to the "Verify Customer Credit" Subfunction.) From *Systems Design and Documentation* by Harry Katzan, Jr. Copyright © 1976 by Van Nostrand Reinhold Company. Reprinted by permission of the publisher.

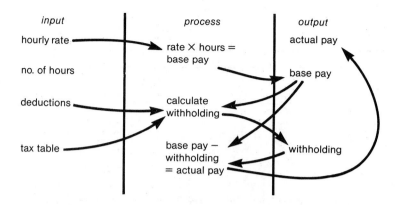

Figure 9-8. HIPO Worksheet for a Payroll Program

raphy). The firm has thus done away with almost all the graphics symbols except circles and squares. From time to time, the company is still called upon to produce systems flow charts of the type shown in figure 9-9. For such purposes, templates containing American National Standards Institute (ANSI) standard symbols are used (see figure 9-10). Also, to draw modular decomposition diagrams, such as those in figures 9-2 and 9-3, the firm occasionally uses a preprinted form with rectangles on it (see figure 9-11).

9.3 ORGANIZATION AND PRESENTATION OF DETAILED LOGIC

The secret of a reliable system lies in the readability and understandability of its development documents. High-level (general-level) graphics should always precede detailed logic. The detail can then be keyed to separate pieces of general charts as in HIPO. This avoids putting everything into one overly busy chart.

Thereafter, any changes in detail will involve only one small chart, not the chart of the entire system. Usually the more general charts will not need to be changed since corrections are made most often at lower levels. Something like the HIPO/VTOC scheme (see section 9.1.2) is very good for visual keying of information.

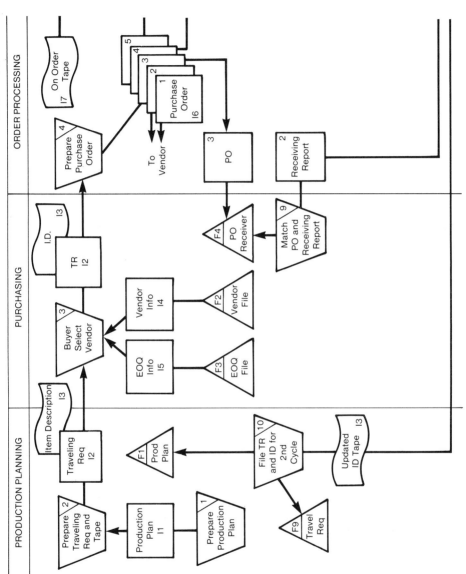

Figure 9-9. System Flowchart

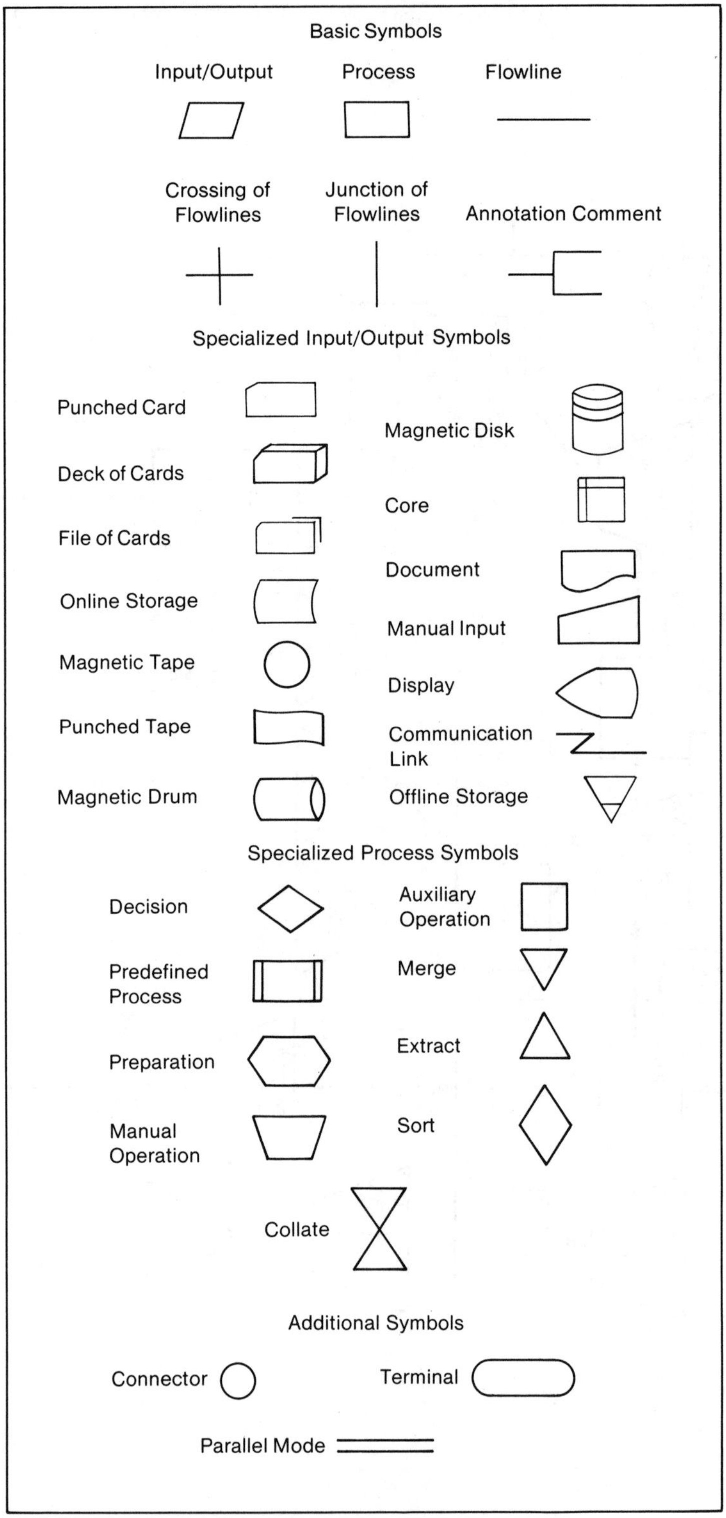

Figure 9-10. American National Standards Institute (ANSI) Flowchart Symbols

IBM Flowcharting Worksheet

| Programmer: _____ | Program No.: _____ | Date _____ |
| Chart ID: ___ Chart Name: _____ | Program Name: _____ | Page _____ |

Fold under at dotted line

┌ A1 ─ ─ ┐   ┌ A2 ─ ─ ─ ┐   ┌ A3 ─ ─ ┐   ┌ A4 ─ ─ ┐   ┌ A5 ─ ─ ┐

┌ B1 ─ ─ ┐   ┌ B2 ─ ─ ┐   ┌ B3 ─ ─ ┐   ┌ B4 ─ ─ ┐   ┌ B5 ─ ─ ┐

┌ C1 ─ ─ ┐   ┌ C2 ─ ─ ─ ┐   ┌ C3 ─ ─ ┐   ┌ C4 ─ ─ ┐   ┌ C5 ─ ─ ┐

┌ D1 ─ ─ ┐   ┌ D2 ─ ┐   ┌ D3 ─ ─ ┐   ┌ D4 ─ ─ ┐   ┌ D5 ─ ─ ┐

┌ E1 ─ ─ ┐   ┌ E2 ─ ─ ┐   ┌ E3 ─ ─ ┐   ┌ E4 ─ ─ ┐   ┌ E5 ─ ─ ┐

┌ F1 ─ ─ ┐   ┌ F2 ─ ─ ┐   ┌ F3 ─ ─ ┐   ┌ F4 ─ ─ ┐   ┌ F5 ─ ─ ┐

┌ G1 ─ ─ ┐   ┌ G2 ─ ─ ┐   ┌ G3 ─ ─ ┐   ┌ G4 ─ ─ ┐   ┌ G5 ─ ─ ┐

┌ H1 ─ ─ ┐   ┌ H2 ─ ─ ┐   ┌ H3 ─ ─ ┐   ┌ H4 ─ ─ ┐   ┌ H5 ─ ─ ┐

┌ J1 ─ ─ ┐   ┌ J2 ─ ─ ┐   ┌ J3 ─ ─ ┐   ┌ J4 ─ ─ ┐   ┌ J5 ─ ─ ┐

┌ K1 ─ ─ ┐   ┌ K2 ─ ─ ┐   ┌ K3 ─ ─ ┐   ┌ K4 ─ ─ ┐   ┌ K5 ─ ─ ┐

Fold under at dotted line

Figure 9-11. The IBM Flowcharting Worksheet

9.4   THE PROGRAM LISTING

In the early days—the late fifties through the early seventies—program listings were not only considered to be documentation, they were frequently the *only* documentation that existed for a program or even for some large-scale systems.

Even today with all that is known about structured programming techniques, peer code reviews, and other reliability measures among data processing professionals, you can still encounter DP shops where the program listing is the only documentation.

Even worse, many shops in their enthusiasm for on-line program development, their naive attitude toward record keeping, and their misguided efforts to save computer time or printing costs, neglect to maintain up-to-date printed listings of the computer programs. Such installations are headed for big trouble:

- They do not know with certainty which version is the current version of the system.
- They cannot say what changes or corrections have been implemented and which ones are still pending.
- They cannot recover from a system crash.
- They cannot assess the impact of adding a capability or deleting a function.
- They cannot make an effective use of desk check procedures.

9.4.1   Function of the Program Listing

The program listing has a very special function in the development cycle—the function of describing definitively what you have produced as of that moment. The program listing provides a point of reference so that you can go back and start off again in a different direction. It provides a static map of the execution sequence. In addition, it displays the logic in the mind of the program developers and shows how the interfaces were implemented. The program listing defines all the data that are used in the programs.

9.4.2   Who Maintains the Listing

In order for program listings to provide this function satisfactorily, they must be carefully prepared and carefully maintained. In one particular view of program development, the *chief programmer team* concept developed and exploited by the IBM Corporation, the program listing is considered to be so important that the maintenance of the listing is restricted to professionals who are especially qualified for just that function. Programmers must keep "hands off." Program listings are maintained by a listing specialist, usually the *librarian* or some other clerical specialist.

9.4.3   The Importance of Readability

Whoever maintains the program listing documentation should realize that the program listing has to be lucid. It must be readable by not only the person who wrote the program but by many others as well. There are many reasons for this. The programmer who wrote the code may take another job or be promoted. In either case, someone else will have to take over the further development and maintenance of the program code. In addition, other people may wish to review a programmer's code for close adherence to the programming specification. Finally, the programmer himself will need to read his own code to follow his thought processes through the listing.

9.4.5   Achieving Readability

Structured programming makes the task of understanding the code a little easier. In structured programming, the programmer uses three basic control structures (sequential, if-then-else, do-while) and develops his logic on a top-down basis so that the logic follows a visible pattern. He follows certain rules when defining variables and writing and arranging the program listing comments. Further, the programmer uses visual clues when guiding the reader through the listing. Indentation, blocking of sections, and pagination are examples of such visual clues. Examples of more readable and less readable program listings are shown in figures 9-12 and 9-13.

9.4.6   Visual Cues in the Programming Language

In figure 9-12, the programmer makes use of such visual cues as line spacing, comments, and indentation. These cues are virtually nonexistent in figure 9-13. Since it is less readable, this listing will be more

```
begin
  reset(journal, name);
  if eof (journal) then
      begin
        writeln('No data found in file.');
        close(journal,lock);
        exit(report);
      end;
  j:=0;
  while not eof(journal) do
      begin
        j:=j+1;
        jrec[j]:=journal^;
        get(journal);
      end;
  limit:=j;
  close(journal,lock);
  repeat
      no_change:=true;
      one_pass(no_change, sorttype);
      limit:=limit-1;
  until no_change;
  limit:=j;
  rewrite(journal, name);
  for j:=1 to limit do
      begin
        journal^:=jrec[j];
        put (journal);
      end;
  close (journal, lock);
end;
```

Figure 9-12. A Readable Program Listing

```
830  GOSUB 1200
840  GOTO 500
850  REM
860  YB = YF - (YF - YR) * (FO - CE) / (FO - RO)
870  IF YB < 0 THEN YB = 0
880  IF YB > VE THEN 1040
890  HCOLOR= 0
900  IF E1 THEN  HPLOT CE,N1
910  IF E2 THEN  HPLOT CE,N2
920  IF E3 THEN  HPLOT CE,N3
930  HPLOT X1,Y1 TO X2,Y2 TO X3,Y3 TO X4,Y4 TO X1,Y1: IF Y5 < VE THEN  HPLOT
     0,Y5 TO H0,Y5
940  HCOLOR= COL
950  IF F1 THEN  HPLOT CE,R1
```

Figure 9-13. A Less Readable Program Listing. Reprinted with permission. Creative Computing, 39 E. Hanover Ave., Morris Plains, NJ 07950.

```
960  IF F2 THEN  HPLOT CE,R2
970  IF F3 THEN  HPLOT CE,R3
980  HPLOT 0,YB TO RL,YR TO RR,YR TO HO,YB
990  IF YF < VE THEN  HPLOT 0,YF TO HO,YF
1000 X1 = 0:Y1 = YB:X2 = RL:Y2 = YR:X3 = RR:Y3 = YR:X4 = HO:Y4 = YB:Y5 =
     YF
1010 N1 = R1:N2 = R2:N3 = R3:E1 = F1:E2 = F2:E3 = F3
1020  GOSUB 1200
1030  GOTO 500
1040  REM
1050 XO = (VE - YR) * (FO - RO) / (YF - YR) + RO
1060  HCOLOR= 0
1070  IF E1 THEN  HPLOT CE,N1
1080  IF E2 THEN  HPLOT CE,N2
1090  IF E3 THEN  HPLOT CE,N3
1100  HPLOT X1,Y1 TO X2,Y2 TO X3,Y3 TO X4,Y4 TO X1,Y1: IF Y5 < VE THEN  HPLOT
     0,Y5 TO HO,Y5
1110  HCOLOR= COL
1120  IF F1 THEN  HPLOT CE,R1
1130  IF F2 THEN  HPLOT CE,R2
1140  IF F3 THEN  HPLOT CE,R3
1150  HPLOT CE - XO,VE TO RL,YR TO RR,YR TO CE + XO,VE
1160 X1 = CE - XO:Y1 = VE:X2 = RL:Y2 = YR:X3 = RR:Y3 = YR:X4 = CE + XO:Y4
     = VE
1170 N1 = R1:N2 = R2:N3 = R3:E1 = F1:E2 = F2:E3 = F3
1180  GOSUB 1200
1190  GOTO 500
1200  REM MAIN SUBROUTINE
1210 P1 =  PDL (1)
1220 PW =  INT (P1 * C5)
1230 PO =  PDL (0)
1240 V = D * V + DD * (PO * C3 + C8 + C4 * P1)
1250 CL = DC * DALT
1260 ALT = ALT + DALT
1270 VV = V * VC
1280  VTAB 22: HTAB 1
1290  PRINT  TAB( 2);"ALT"; TAB( 8);"CLIMB"; TAB( 16);"VEL"; TAB( 22);"DME";
     TAB( 28);"POWER"
1300  VTAB 23: HTAB 1
1310 AR$ = "-"
1320  IF ALT > P7 *  ABS (X - RW) THEN AR$ = "V"
1330  IF ALT < P5 *  ABS (X - RW) THEN AR$ = "^"
1340  PRINT  TAB( 1); INT (ALT); TAB( 8); INT (CL); TAB( 16); INT (VV); TAB(
     22); INT ( ABS ((X + ALT / Q3 - RW) / Q6)) / 10; TAB( 30);PW;"  "; TAB(
     38);AR$
1350 X = X - V
1360 DALT = E * DALT + EE * (C2 * P1 - V * C1 - C9 * PO + CZ)
1370  IF V < VM THEN DALT =  - ST
1380 HR = F * HR + FF * H1 * (Q1 - PO)
1390  RETURN
1400  REM LANDED!
1410  IF X > RW GOTO 1510
1420 X = X - 10 * V
1430  IF X < 0 GOTO 1630
1440  IF CL <  - RC GOTO 1780
1450  PRINT "YOU LANDED AT "; INT (VV);" MPH AND STOPPED "
1460  PRINT  INT (X);" FEET FROM THE END OF THE RUNWAY."
1470  PRINT "YOU WERE DESCENDING AT ";  - INT (CL);" FEET/MINUTE."
1480  GET Z$
1490  TEXT : HOME
1500  GOTO 20
1510  REM
1520  TEXT : HOME
1530  GOSUB 1850
1540  PRINT "YOU CRASHED "; INT (X - RW);" FEET SHORT"
1550  PRINT "OF THE RUNWAY AT "; INT (VV);" MPH. TRY AGAIN"
1560  GOTO 20
1570  REM
1580  TEXT : HOME
1590  PRINT "YOU OVERFLEW THE RUNWAY AT "; INT (VV)
1600  PRINT "MPH AT AN ALTITUDE OF "; INT (ALT)
1610  PRINT "FEET.  TRY AGAIN!!!"
1620  GOTO 20
1630  REM
1640  TEXT : HOME
1650  GOSUB 1850
```

Figure 9-13. (cont.)

difficult to debug. (Note, these program listing excerpts were chosen only on the basis of their readability. No criticism of the programming skill of either author is intended.)

The less readable listing is in the program language BASIC. Most of the small computers using BASIC will automatically nullify attempts at indentation in order to save internal storage space. Another problem with BASIC is that it has very limited facilities for assigning variable names and writing English language comments.

The more readable version is written in the programming language Pascal. This language was deliberately designed to emphasize readability as a means of achieving reliable software.

9.4.7 Comments in the Listing

Today many different standards are followed for program listing comments. One program listing standard may insist upon the program specification being carried over verbatim into the comments section of the program listings. Under this constraint the ratio of lines of comments to lines of code may be as high as five-to-one. At the other extreme, a different standard may merely identify the program modules by name and number. This standard considers the programming specification to be a one-to-one match to the listing and expects the reader to use both documents together.

Since there are so many standards, and all have merit, I will not recommend one procedure for maintaining programming documentation listings. However, I will offer several general guidelines. In addition, I will recommend to the reader the several volumes of programming proverbs which are mentioned in the bibliography.

9.4.8 Guidelines for Program Listing Maintenance

The following are recommended practices for making the program listings useful and readable.

- Each program module should be named, and its name or identification number should appear on every listing of that program. If the compiler or operating system does not title the listing, it should be titled by hand.

- The date of each listing should be printed out on the listing. If the operating system or compiler does not print the date, then it should be printed by hand. If more than one listing is taken in a given day, the listing should bear the time of day as well.

- The program name should be the same as that used in the programming specifications document.
- Each listing should bear the name and location or the phone number of the program author.
- Each listing should bear the name of the person who is currently modifying the program, that is, the person who made the modification for which the current listing has been obtained. His telephone number or other locating information should appear with his name.
- The opening comments should briefly describe what the program does. This should not take more than two or three lines of code.
- The opening comments should contain in a second paragraph the purpose of the most recent modification. This paragraph should also contain only two or three lines.
- Every line of code should be numbered or sequenced by either the compiler or the programmer. The sequence numbers should go up in steps of ten so that there is adequate room to insert corrections and modifications between lines.
- The program should be block-structured. Indentation and spacing will emphasize this block structure.
- Two separate central listings should be kept of all programs in the system. One listing is for the approved versions of each program and one listing is for the latest version of each program.

9.4.9   Approved Versus Latest Versions

The life of every program module consists of a series of plateaus as shown in figure 9-14. The first plateau is the first clean compile of the listing. This represents a benchmark. It is a milestone in the development of the system program.

Other plateaus follow. For example, there will be a time when certain functions in the program module may be considered "working," although others may not be. Sometimes, one person may need to use the program with its working functions as a submodule of the system he is working on, while someone else continues to debug the rest of the program. For this purpose, you will need an "approved" version of the program module. That is, you identify a particular version as being a milestone. Other people can use that milestone or approved version for

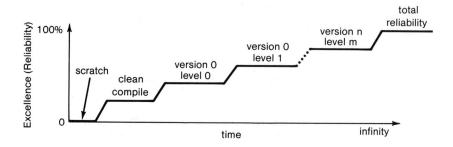

Figure 9-14. Plateaus in the Life of a Program

certain limited needs of their own. If someone testing the program to modify it snarls it up hopelessly, he can return to the approved version and start over again.

There should be a certain formality in transferring a program from the latest version stage of development into the approved version stage. This way the programmer and the librarian have to make a conscious decision to make the change. Even in a one-man project, there should be this conscious decision to take the program out of one category and place it in another.

9.5   PROGRAM MAINTENANCE DOCUMENTATION

9.5.1   Contents

Since program maintenance documentation is used *after* the program is written for the purpose of correcting and modifying existing systems, maintenance documentation is often not written until after the programs have been developed.

The program maintenance documentation contains up-to-date listings of the programs to be maintained, i.e., corrected or modified. It contains sufficiently detailed descriptions about those programs, the data upon which they operate, and the data files or data bases with which they are associated so that the corrections and modifications can be made rapidly, sensibly, and carefully.

But those two ingredients—the listings and the program and data descriptions—have already been developed. They are the program listing and the program specification document. Obviously these must be kept up-to-date in order for the maintenance documentation to be up-to-date. This is the purpose of program maintenance documentation, to reflect the current status of computer software.

Therefore, the program maintenance documentation is simply the up-to-date computer listings and programming specifications, reflecting all changes that have been directly applied to the system thus far.

9.5.2 Programming Change Requests and Programming Change Orders

In some DP shops the process of identifying errors and corrections to the errors is a highly formalized process. Identifying the error is the purpose of the programming change request (PCR) (see figure 9-15). Identifying

PROGRAMMING CHANGE REQUEST (PCR)				
SYSTEM NAME PROGRAM NAME	VERSION	LEVEL	☐ DEVEL. ☐ RELEASE STATUS ☐ PRODUCTION	DATE

Reason for PCR

    ☐ Performance does not satisfy structured system specs
    ☐ Specs inadequate or inaccurate
    ☐ Specs unclear
    ☐ New requirement; authorized by _____
                      (signature)

Description of Change Required (English Language)

[attach updated system specification pages]

For lead programmer's use only
           (dates)
Received _____
Verified _____
Assigned _____ to _____
                           (name)
Change Due _____ made _____ by _____
                                       (name)

Figure 9-15. Programming Change Request

the programming change is the function of the programming change order (PCO) (see figure 9-16). These two documents are generally used during the program testing activities.

Sometimes PCRs and PCOs arise from changes in requirements rather than from errors. In practically all shops, the requirements which

PROGRAMMING CHANGE ORDER (PCO)					
SYSTEM NAME	VERSION	LEVEL	☐ DEVEL. ☐ RELEASE		DATE
PROGRAM NAME			STATUS ☐ PRODUCTION		

Reason for PCO

    ☐ Performance does not satisfy programming specs
    ☐ Specs inadequate or inaccurate
    ☐ Specs unclear
    ☐ New requirement

Description of Change Required (English Language)

[attach updated programming specification pages and updated testing notebook pages]

For lead programmer's use only

Received_____
Verified_____
Assigned_____ to _____
                                            (name)
Test scheduled for _____ by _____
                                            (name)
Test made _____ by _____
                                            (name)

Figure 9-16. Programming Change Order

govern a system are modified after the system design and programming have proceeded. How soon and how much to change the requirement and the design is primarily an administrative decision.

The programming change request, the PCR, is an extension of the system analysis document. Likewise, the programming change order is an extension of the system specification document. Thus the complete cycle:

- Systems specifications are updated with programming change requests.
- Programming specifications are updated with programming change orders.
- Program listings are updated and inserted into the program maintenance documentation.

9.6 HIGHLIGHTS

- Always start off with a written statement of requirements; include a set of tests the system must meet.
- Always draw up a general (or systems) specification to show what computer approach you'll follow. Make sure it agrees with the requirements statement.
- Always draw up a programmed specification that converts the systems specification into computer modules and interfaces. Make sure it matches the systems specification.
- Always code in structured programming.
- Preferably use a higher level language as an intermediate between the specification and the language of the target computer.
  —It is easier to check a high level language against the programming specification.
  —Then recode for the target computer.
- Test your code (program listings) against the programming specifications.
- Test your executable code against the requirements tests that you developed at the beginning.
- Always write your specs in good clear English.
- Do the same with your program listings. Keep them clear and as much like English as possible.

10

The Complete Cycle: Analysis, Design, and Programming

10.1 DOCUMENTS OF DEVELOPMENT

10.1.1 The Documentation Continuum

It is a rare thing for a systems analyst or programmer to see the entire continuum of documentation in a system development life cycle. Typically the analyst sees only the early documents—the problem statement, requirements study, and systems specification. The programmer does not arrive on the scene till the systems specification is nearly finished. Consequently, he participates only in the programming specification and the programming and testing activities. Thus, the programmer may never see the early documents and the systems analyst may never see the later documents.

10.1.2 The Natural Fit of Structured Analysis into Structured Design

Although many managers and technical people have embraced structured techniques, comparatively few are aware of the precise and natural way in which structured analysis leads into structured design or structured design leads into structured programming and testing (described in section 8.2).

This chapter traces a sample project through the entire evolutionary cycle, looking at the results of the structured development activities— the deliverables.

10.1.3 Pyramid of Reports

The complete documentation of a system development project makes up a pyramid of reports (see figure 10-1). Documentation begins with the problem statement, represented by a report of a page or two in length at the apex of the pyramid. It grows to a volume or two of requirements study, then to several volumes of system specifications and program-

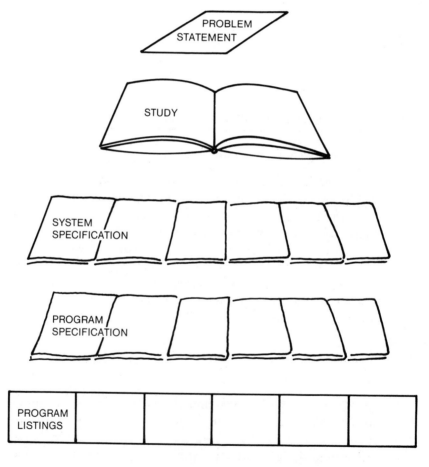

Figure 10-1. Pyramid of Documentation for a Complete System

ming specifications. Finally come the voluminous program listings which make up the base of the pyramid.

To place in this book the entire pyramid of documentation for even a relatively simple project would be totally impractical because of the number of pages involved.

10.2   A VERTICAL CUT

This chapter takes a vertical cut of constant cross section through the pyramid (see figure 10-2).

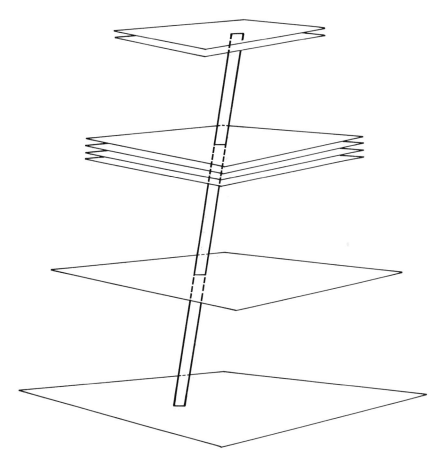

Figure 10-2. Vertical Section Through the Development Cycle's Documentation Pyramid

The dimensions of the constant cross section are about the size of a page. This size takes in almost the whole of the apex document, the problem statement. At each lower level, however, the extracted segment gets relatively smaller till at the pyramid's base the cross section includes only a very small percentage of the program code that appears at that level.

10.2.1 The Problem Statement

Figure 10-3 consists of a one-page cut from the problem statement. A quick reading of this page will show that it is actually the entire problem statement.

AUTOMATED GENEALOGIST'S CENSUS SEARCH

PROBLEM STATEMENT

An essential but routine and time-consuming task in genealogy is to check through the U.S. censuses for family names and members of households. The census for a particular year may be the critical source of linking a particular parent with a particular child.

Searching the census for a parent or child is a straightforward computer application, using either exhaustive search or keyed search strategies.

Some additional complications are:

- the condition of the data base—a handwritten record, available on microfiche
- spelling variations in both family names and given names
- the tendency of individuals to use initials or pet names and nicknames inconsistently from census to census
- the usual loss of the wife's maiden name, with its link back to her original family, when she marries
- the absence of certain census data resulting from fires at the archives in years past.

Determine one or more feasible ways of automating this census search and identify their costs and benefits.

Figure 10-3. The Initial Problem Statement

10.2.2   The Requirements Study

Figure 10-4 is one page from the requirements study which succeeded the problem statement. Assume that the requirements study was a thorough, professional study that examined many parameters of the genealogy problem. Assume further that this particular slice comes from the section of the study where findings and recommendations are explained and various system concept alternatives are presented. Since this is a relatively simple system, an entire system concept fits on one page.

AUTOMATED GENEALOGIST'S CENSUS SEARCH

ALTERNATIVE 2

SYSTEM CONCEPT

Data Base   The microfilmed data will be transcribed onto diskettes by a data preparation service. Provision will be made for data base corrections with appropriate housekeeping records. A separate file will be prepared for each county and each decade.

Hardware Configuration   A small business computer with high level language capability, a single console for operation and inquiry, a printer, and mass memory consisting of both hard disks and diskettes. Number of consoles and mass memory should be upgradable.

System Processes   The genealogist will be able to conduct searches of the following types:

- head of household names—with optional phonetic spelling
- members of household names.

Printouts   The system will display name, record number, head of household name and ages or date of birth for each match or near match; full record will be printed upon request. Initials will be treated as alternate spellings.

Nicknames   The user will put in nicknames or pet names as if formal names as variants of the primary inputs.

Decades   The data base will include all decades from 1850 to 1900 inclusive, with the exception of 1890—that census having been destroyed. The search will be conducted over any or all decades as directed from the console.

Figure 10-4. Part of the Requirements Study

Note that both the problem statement and the study are written in a clear, simple form of English which will be readily transferable into more rigorous and more formalized documents in the tasks ahead.

10.2.3   The System Specification

In figure 10-5 a schematic of the current logical system appears as the excerpt from the systems specification. This schematic, called a dataflow diagram, has been derived from careful analysis of similar schematics of the current physical system. In this particular case, the current system is totally manual.

Figure 10-5 is a top-level description of the logical system. Note that following the conventions of DeMarco's book (see bibliography), activities or agents external to the system are shown as rectangular boxes. Processes are shown as circles and data flows are shown as curved arrows. A file of information is shown as a straight line.

Lower-level (more detailed) versions of the system would be shown on subsequent drawings. For example, if the process "read exhaus-

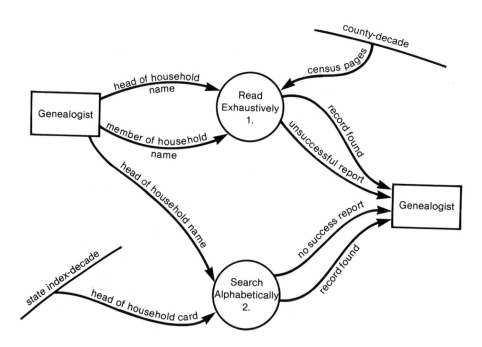

Figure 10-5. Part of the System Specification—Current Logical

tively," which is labelled number *1* on figure 10-5, were broken into
three subprocesses in the next level diagram, these latter processes
would bear the numbers *1.1, 1.2,* and *1.3.* If one of these, say *1.2,* were
further divided into say two subfunctions, this would represent a third
level of detail and the circles would be labelled *1.2.1* and *1.2.2,* respectively. Normally, it is not necessary to go beyond the third level in the
current logical system diagrams.

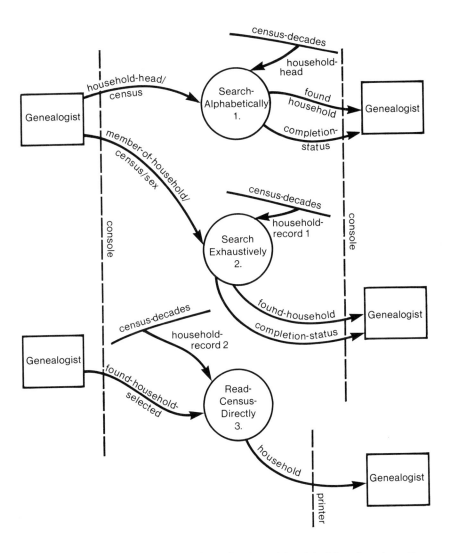

Figure 10-6. Part of the System Specification—Man-Machine Interface Overview

10.2.4   First Level Dataflow Diagrams

In figure 10-6 the new system concept has been worked up in dataflow diagrams. The figure shows an overview of the new system and indicates the man-machine interface with dotted lines. Notice that the system concept is still worded in near English terms, in symbology which would not intimidate a layman such as a user participating in reviews of the system specification with the systems analyst.

10.2.5   Second Level Dataflow Diagrams

Figure 10-7 is a second-level analysis of the proposed system. As indicated, it is a decomposition of the "search-exhaustively" process labelled number 2 in the earlier figure, figure 10-6. In figure 10-7 the "search-exhaustively" process has been broken into two subprocesses "complete-phonetic-spelling" and "read-serially-and-match." Note that the data which go into the process and the data which come out of the process are the same. There is, however, a new data flow introduced between the two processes.

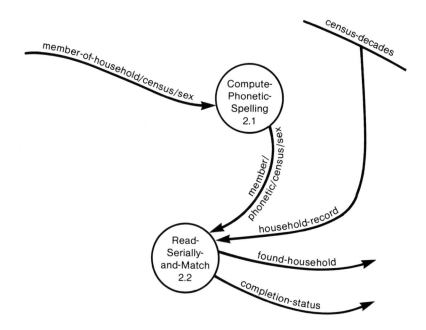

Figure 10-7. Part of the System Specification—Man-Machine Interface

PROCESS NAME: Read-Serially-And-Match

PROCESS NUMBER: 2.2

PROCESS DESCRIPTION:

1. Record member, phonetic, census, sex
2. Indicate zero count of households-found.
3. Open indicated census file.
4. For each household in file
    4.1 Read household-record.
    4.2 If sex matches head-of-household-sex then
        4.2.1 Compare member with head-of-household
        4.2.2 If match occurs (given names or initials) then
            4.2.2.1 Display head-of-household, age or date of birth
                and household number
            4.2.2.2 Add 1 to count of households-found
    4.3 If sex female then
        4.3.1 Repeat 4.2.1 through 4.2.2.2 for spouse
    4.4 For each member-of-household
        4.4.1 Repeat 4.2 through 4.2.2.2 for member-of-household
    4.5 If phonetic-spelling requested then
        4.5.1 Repeat 4.2 through 4.4.1 for phonetic spelling
5. Print completion-status using count of households found.
6. Close census file.

NOTES:

Figure 10-8. Part of the System Specification—Process Description

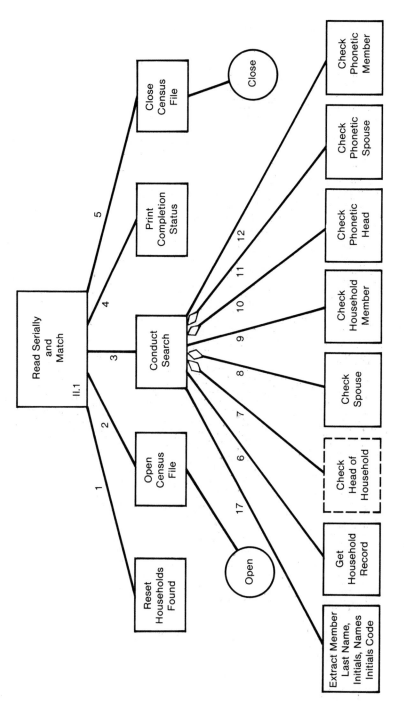

Figure 10-9. Part of Programming Specification—Modular Decomposition

	Input	Output
1	households-found	households-found,ec
2	filename	buffername, ec
3	buffername, households-found	households-found
4	households-found	ec
5	buffername	ec
6	buffername	household-record, ec
7	household #, member*, household-record, households-found	households-found
8	household #, member*, household-record, households-found	households-found
9	household #, member*, household-record, households-found	households-found
10	household #, member*, household-record, households-found	households-found
11	household #, member*, household-record, households-found	households-found
12	household #, member*, household-record, households-found	households-found

Figure 10-9. (cont.)

10.2.6 Process Description

The system specification is a thick document. Consequently a cut through it turns out to include also one of the other documents of the dataflow dictionary, namely the process description. Figure 10-8 is a description in English of the logic of the "read-serially-and-match" process. Although the description is obviously English, it is very formalized. In some shops, the verbs would even be preselected and the sentences confined to a particular structure.

10.2.7 Programming Specification

Figure 10-9 shows an excerpt from the programming specification. In this case, the excerpt is the decomposition of the process of the earlier figure into program modules. The upper module has been decomposed into five submodules by means of functional decomposition. One of these, the "conduct-search" module, has been decomposed into submodules that also differ functionally. The inputs and outputs are identified in the input/output table at the bottom of the chart.

The rules of modular decomposition say that decomposition concludes when the program code of the module is readily apparent to someone who reads the name of the module. In this example it is necessary to decompose one more level in order to achieve this level of obvious logic (see figure 10-10). The figure shows that the module called "check-head-of-household" has been decomposed into three submodules, using a source-transform-sink decomposition.

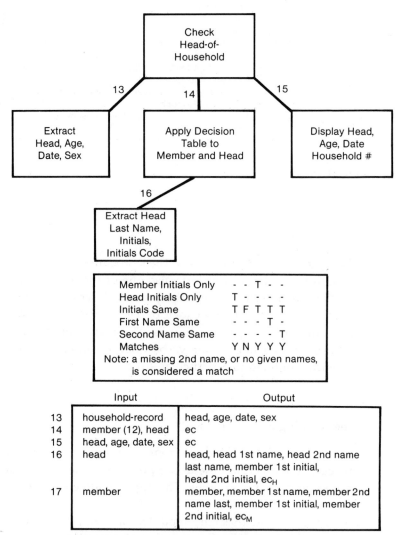

	Input	Output
13	household-record	head, age, date, sex
14	member (12), head	ec
15	head, age, date, sex	ec
16	head	head, head 1st name, head 2nd name last name, member 1st initial, head 2nd initial, ec_H
17	member	member, member 1st name, member 2nd name last, member 1st initial, member 2nd initial, ec_M

Note: 14 leads to a common subroutine for all checking modules.

Figure 10-10. Part of Programming Specification—Modular Decomposition—Levels 3, 4, and 5

10.2.8 Program Coding

Figure 10-11 shows the program code task of the system development project. As a first step, the logic of the program module has been written out in structured English.

Structured English Note that here the English is more formalized than it was in the system specification. The conventions used are very similar to the conventions of PASCAL, ALGOL, or PL/1 as far as identification of special words and the use of semicolons are concerned. As with the system specification, the logic is carefully written for readability. Notice the very effective use of indentation to show subthoughts and the

Apply Decision Table to Member and Head

0. Extract head-params.
   If head-last-name ≠ member-last-name
      then error-code = no-match
         exit;

1. *If* head-1st-initial *does not match* member-1st-initial
   or head-2nd-initial *does not match* member-2nd-initial
      then error-code = no-match,
         exit;

2. *If* head-initials-code = initials-only
      then error-code = match,
         exit;

3. *If* member-initials-code = initials-only
      then error-code = match,
         exit;

4. *If* head-first-name = member-first-name
      then error-code = match,
         exit;

5. *If* head-second-name = member-second-name
      then error-code = match,
         exit;

6. Error-code = no-match,

7. Exit;

Figure 10-11. Part of Program Code—Structured English

overall sequential flow of logic through the module. This structured English uses only the basic control forms of structured programming.

Computer language Figure 10-12 shows the results of rewriting the structured English into a computer language. In this case the language

```
SUBROUTINE DTMHED(HEAD$,MLNAM$,MFINT$,MSINT$,
MICOD, MFNAM$,MSNAM$,IERCOD)
DATA NOMATCH/0/INTOLY/0/MATCH/1/
CALL EXTRHN(HEAD, IHLNAM$,IHFINT$,IHSINT$,
IHICOD, IHFNAM$,IHSNAM$,IECH)
IF (.NOT.(IHLNAM$.NE.MLNAM$)) GO TO 10
    IERCOD = NOMATCH
    RETURN
10 IF (.NOT.((IHFINT$.NE.MFINT$).OR.(IHSINT$.N#.MSINT$)))
    GO TO 20
    IERCOD = NOMATCH
    RETURN
20 IF (.NOT.(IHICOD.EQ.INTOLY)) GO TO 30
    IERCOD = MATCH
    RETURN
30 IF (.NOT.(MICOD.EQ.INTOLY)) GO TO 40
    IERCOD = MATCH
    RETURN
40 IF (.NOT.(IHFNAM$.EQ.MFNAM$)) GO TO 50
    IERCOD = MATCH
    RETURN
```

Name Conversion Table

Structured Specification	Structured Code
head-last-name	IHLNAM$
member-last-name	MLNAM$
error-code	IERCOD
no-match	NOMATCH
head-1st-initial	IHFINT$
member-1st-initial	MFINT$
head-2nd-initial	IHSINT$
member-2nd-initial	MSINT$

Figure 10-12. Part of Program Code with Name Conversion Table

chosen was FORTRAN. In larger systems, it is frequently useful to take an intermediate step and go from the structured English into pseudocode and then into program code. In that intermediate step, final choice of data types and data names is made.

Data types and naming conventions   In the case illustrated by figures 10-11 and 10-12, the only necessary choices of data types were made by putting the alphanumeric data from the household record into strings permitted by this particular version of FORTRAN and identified by the use of the *$* sign at the end of the variable name. A second decision was to use FORTRAN integers for counters and codes. Thus the pseudocode step was not needed.

Choice of FORTRAN constructs   Note that the FORTRAN used here does not include the advanced block structures permitted in FORTRAN 77. Instead it uses the conversion conventions which place the IF statements and the statements which follow them in the *then*-followed-by-*else* form of structured English by using the negative of the condition in the IF statement.

Codewriting conventions   Figure 10-12 does not show the entire logic of the subroutine because part of the page is taken up by the conversion table for variable names. This is a housekeeping device which programmers can use so that the conversions are written down as they are made. This practice leads to fewer record-keeping problems. It would be just as convenient to use a separate page for the conversion table as long as it is kept handy while the programmer is doing his coding.

In coding, the programmer follows the steps indicated by the small circles on the left-hand side of the page (see figure 10-12). Circle *1* is an example of writing a statement which introduces variable names for the first time. As soon as the variable name has been invented, it is written down in the conversion table at the point shown by circle *2*. If the variable also requires some program definition, as with a DIMENSION statement or a DATA statement, that is done next in an area where space has been reserved, say circle *3*.

Note that the logic is very easy to follow and part of the testing process involves a comparative reading of figures 10-11 and 10-12. The two are directly comparable. Thus, errors are very easy to spot.

10.2.9   Data Development

The preceding figures deal primarily with system and program *logic*. Now let's take a look at similar cuts through the system's evolution of the *data*.

Figure 10-13 is the first of a series of cuts through the system specification where a data flow and its contents are defined. Figure 10-13 shows the household record as it is drawn out of the systems file.

Figure 10-14 shows a segment of the household records, dealing

DATAFLOW NAME: household-record
ALIASES: -none-
COMPOSITION: head + $_0^1${wife} + $_0^n${household-member}
NOTES: wife field not present if head is female

Figure 10-13. Part of the System Specification—Dataflow "household-record"

only with the head of the household. It shows, for example, that he may have a date of birth datum and/or an age datum.

Figure 10-15 shows the most basic entity in a data flow, the data element. It is designed to be 1 to n letters in length, representing the last name of the head of the household.

DATAFLOW NAME: head

ALIASES:

COMPOSITION:

head-last-name + head-1st-name + head-2nd-name + head-$_0^1${head-dob}

+ $_0^1${head-age} + head-sex

NOTES: Nonexistent second or nonexistent first and second names will be shown as blank.

Figure 10-14. Part of the System Specification—Dataflow "head"

<table>
<tr><td>DATA ELEMENT NAME: head-last-name</td></tr>
</table>

ALIASES:

VALUES AND MEANINGS:

$_1^n\{$letter$\}$

NOTES: 1. Assigned variable name IHLNAM$ in subroutine DTMHED, module "Apply Decision Table to Member and Head"
2. Value of n will be established in module "Get-Household Record"

Figure 10-15. Part of the System Specification/Maintenance Manual

10.3   CODING FOR MAINTENANCE

When the program logic is being constructed, programmers must concern themselves with facilitating future maintenance. The maintenance manual will be produced primarily from the programming specification manual. However, maintenance manuals also include the program listing and segments of the system specification. Converting the system specifications statements into useful program maintenance manuals includes such things as making the comment, indicated by Note 1 (see figure 10-35) in the data element definition. Note 2 makes the important point that, following good structured programming conventions, the actual format of the data file will not be established until the routine is designed that will manipulate this data file.

10.4 DESIGNING FOR TESTING

An important point should be made about test data. Notice that the system specification very clearly identifies the inputs to the system and the outputs to the system. Thus, it is possible at the time the system specification is written to make up a list of test inputs and outputs that can be applied to the system logic after the programs are constructed. This, of course, is the way to build reliable systems—to test from the user's point of view, not from the programmer's point of view.

10.5 PRESENTATIONAL EXTRACTS

While the systems analysts and programmers are working away at developing systems, management continues to fret in the background wondering what is going on with the systems tasks. It is in everyone's interest that the process of informing management should be as painless as possible. Remember the double-duty document described in chapter 2?

10.5.1 Graphics

Management needs graphic material as it is usually too busy to read textual material. One good visual presentation such as a flip-chart talk can cover many pages of text. Each graphic aid should have a specific objective.

10.5.2 Outlines

You may not have good drawings for everything. However, you can often fall back on the outlines you have made for your reports. Outlines make good bullet charts if they are not too crowded.

10.5.3 Questions and Answers

Always remember to consider the audience. The best presentation is one in which the questions raised on one chart are answered right on the chart behind it. This shows that you have put yourself into the mind of your audience, imagining, "What will be the first thing that occurs to them after they see this chart?"

10.5.4 Cutting and Pasting

Remember to "cut and paste," borrowing, if necessary, from what you have already written in the development documents. There is nothing wrong with using a good graphic right out of an analysis or design report. Figure 10-16 shows the kind of graphic analysis that might be used in a presentation in order to clarify an issue encountered in structured system analysis.

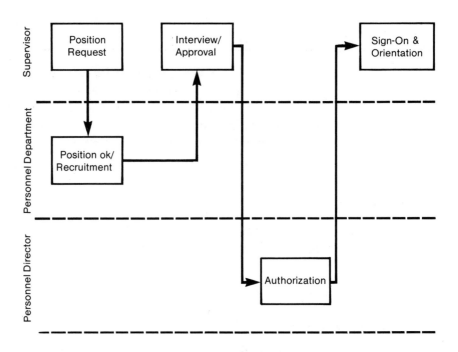

Figure 10-16. Graphic Analysis of a Personnel Recruitment Procedure

10.6   HIGHLIGHTS

- In this chapter you can trace a sample project through its entire cycle by looking at the results of the structured development activities—the deliverables.
- The documentation of a project can be shown as a pyramid with the brief problem statement at the apex and the voluminous program listings at the base.
- The flow from requirements statement to system specification to program specification to program listing can be shown to be very natural and logical.
- You can use graphics, outlines, and paragraphs from your developmental documents to make attractive presentations to management.

11

Instructive Documents: GIM's, User Manuals, and Operator's Guides

11.1 INTRODUCTION TO INSTRUCTIVE WRITING

As author of an instructive document in the computer industry you have the most difficult task imaginable—to explain the technologically complex to the technologically unsophisticated. The chief explaining documents in data processing are the general information manual and the user manual. These documents are intended for decision makers and lay users, respectively.

To the extent that educational manuals also help professionals to use a computer system, the operator's guide and the run book are also educational manuals. Although the operator's guide is a sort of guidebook, it is also treated in this chapter.

11.2 THE GENERAL INFORMATION MANUAL

The general information manual (GIM) represents a challenge in technical writing. As the writer, you must:

- understand the material well enough to explain it.
- explain the material without making it dull.

Program Product

Information Management System/360, Version 2 General Information Manual

Program Number 5734-XX6

The Information Management System/360 is a processing program designed to facilitate the implementation of medium to large common data bases in a multiapplication environment. This environment is created to accommodate both online message processing and conventional batch processing, either separately or concurrently. The system permits the evolutionary expansion of data processing applications from a batch-only to a teleprocessing environment.

    This manual includes a general description of the system and its various facilities and programs, listings of typical and minimum configurations, and sample applications.

Note: IMS/360 operates under several different operating systems (OS/MFT, OS/MVT, OS/VS1, and OS/VS2). For ease of reading, these are collectively referred to as "operating system" in this manual unless some function is peculiar to one of the operating systems.

Figure 11-1. Extract from IBM GIM—"Information Management System/360, Version 2"

- make it understandable to people whose technical background is different from your own, or is nonexistent.
- tell what the system or product does without going into the kind of detail that would be appropriate to a specification document.

The GIM is a dual purpose document. While it is a document for explaining the features of a specialized system to a manager, it is also a marketing tool. It should explain the features so well that it will tend to motivate the reader to acquire or to implement the system which it describes.

Whatever product you discuss in a technical document, especially an introductory one, should be given a name, preferably an original one. Otherwise, readers will have trouble following your discussion and will fail to get enthusiastic about the product.

The introductory section of a representative GIM is shown in figure 11-1. The general structure of a GIM is shown in figure 11-2.

11.3 THE USER MANUAL

11.3.1 The User Manual as a Substitute for You

Look upon the user manual as the document which substitutes for your own physical presence, providing everything in the way of guidance and assistance that you, yourself, would provide to the user of the system if you were there.

The user manual must tell what its own purpose is, as well as describing what the system is all about. The manual must delineate the user's role within the overall domain of the system and must give the

- Introduction
    Place subject in its historical context; show its significance
- General background; discuss its technological context
- General technical concepts
- What is new and important
- Other references according to reader interest

Figure 11-2. General Information Manual: Recommended Contents

user a procedure to follow so that he may use the system confidently in his day-to-day activities.

The user manual must be unambiguous. It must provide all the answers to the questions that may arise as the system is put to use. It must be self-contained so that it is all that the user will need under any conceivable circumstance.

11.3.2 The Self-Explanatory User Manual

User manuals vary in size with complexity of the system and the user's job in the system. The major features of the user manual are shown in figure 11-3. Notice that the introduction explains the purpose of the manual.

A good user manual must first *say* that it is a user manual. It must then proceed to tell the user exactly what the system is, how the system is to be used, how the user fits in, and how the book can help him.

11.3.3 Broader Context for the User

The user manual must give a larger picture of the system than an individual user is likely to experience. As a rule, users tend to have a very limited view of their roles in the system, and, consequently, when problems arise, they flounder helplessly. The user may be unable to comprehend any functions within the system other than those which he

- Introduction
    Objectives of the manual
    Purpose of the system
    Organization of the manual
- System Overview
- Role of the User (or this user if there are separate manuals for separate functions)
- Basic User Cycle—basic process
- Documents Needed When Using System
- Details of the Process—user dialogue or actions
- Table of Messages—appendix

Figure 11-3. User Manual: Recommended Contents

himself uses. When unexpected conditions occur, the user may not even know where to go for assistance.

A typical example of an uneducated user's dilemma is the situation that can arise when you call a computer-using clerk to ask him to research a delinquent bill from a telephone company or for a bank. When you ask why a particular item shows up, the only response he can give is, "That's what the screen says."

Such a person probably has almost no grasp of the total information capability of the system. If the system fails, he must sit back and wait for it to come back up. As far as he knows there are no resources that he can tap. He lacks the knowledge to exercise any independent judgment.

An example which shows the more desirable, broader context of the system is shown in figure 11-4.

The user manual is probably the most important single document that the system builders can leave behind them for the customer. It should be written with extreme care.

11.3.4   When to Write the User Manual

Write the user manual *before* the system is built. The user manual should be a driving document rather than a follow-on document to a system.

In the past, the user manual was written after the system was built, on the theory that there was no point in telling anybody how the system *should* work until the programmers found out how the system *did* work.

Today, however, programmers and users are no longer surprised by the way a system behaves because today programmers must *dictate* in advance how the system *will* behave. The way in which they dictate the system's behavior is by using structured analysis followed by structured design followed by structured programming with all the appropriate tests and checks along the way.

The user manual should be designed as soon as the system specifications are drawn up. That's when you know how the system *should* behave. If you design the user manual before the programs are written and the user confirms the contents of the manual, you have additional assurance that the system will satisfy the user's requirements because you will be developing a system to match the user manual.

11.3.5   Discrepancies Between the User Manual and the System

It may happen that in certain ways the system does not provide all the functions and capabilities in exactly the ways specified in the first draft

CHAPTER 2. ENVIRONMENT

Prior to discussing IMS/360, it is appropriate to describe the environment within which IMS/360 operates and to define terms and concepts that are used later in this manual.

Data Base

Traditionally, data files were designed to serve individual applications, such as inventory control, payroll, engineering drawing release, manufacturing planning, etc. Each data file was specifically designed with its own storage space within the computer, on tape or direct access devices. In many instances these data files included duplicate or redundant information. This information overlap would often result in one file being kept current while the other would remain static and fall out of date.

When the same data resided in different application files, it normally existed in different formats. This variance in the format of common data meant that application programs were tailored to specific data organizations and even specific physical devices. When new data management techniques and devices were introduced, the application programs normally had to be changed. Therefore, application programs could be in an almost perpetual state of change, adding appreciably to the overall cost of data processing.

These undesirable attributes of data files have been eliminated by the advent of the "data base." A data base is defined as a nonredundant collection of interrelated data items processable by one or more applications.

The data base provides for the integration or sharing of common data. As an example, a manufacturing company having an application for release of engineering part data may first integrate its data with an application dealing with a manufacturing part release (Figure 1). Subsequently, application data for assembly installation accounting may be integrated. Note that the data and the programs of the first two applications need not change when the data of the third application is integrated.

Figure 11-4. Example of a Broader Concept of a System from IBM's "Information Management System/360, Version 2, General Information Manual"

of the user manual. As a professional you should take this eventuality in your stride.

You will have to weigh the cost of changing the software to match the user manual against the benefit of having the user manual continue unchanged. Occasionally you may decide to change the user manual to match the software if this is all right with the user.

Such change should be minimal. That the system satisfy the user's needs should continue to be the main concern.

11.3.6 Updating

User manuals should be issued in draft form. Before the system is finished, this draft should be available for critique by users and sponsors. It is helpful to use a looseleaf binder so that the draft may be readily updated as errors are found or as system discrepancies and peculiarities are noted.

Figure 11-5 shows an updating practice that is used by IBM. Updating instructions are filed on a sheet at the end of the document. This sheet bears the latest revision number. The instructions tell which pages are being updated. It is not sufficient merely to replace pages with other pages bearing the same number, because you will frequently want to remove more or fewer pages than you insert.

If the revisions have become quite extensive, it may be necessary to bring out a whole new version of the manual.

IBM uses the solid bar on the side of the printed column to show which areas have been affected by the changes.

11.4 OPERATOR'S GUIDE

Another important education manual is the *operator's guide*, sometimes called an *operations manual*. Like the user manual, the operator's guide should be self-explanatory. After all no one wants to be awakened at 3:00 A.M. by an operator asking about the program. An operator's guide should be organized for quick reference since the operator is normally too busy to sit down and read an elaborate document.

The recommended contents of an operator's guide are as follows:

- name and purpose of the system
- overall systems flow

CONTENTS

Figure 11-5. Example of IBM Document Update Notation from "Information Management System/360, Version 2, General Information Manual"

Figure 11-5. (cont.)

- steps in each job
- data file management plan—what files to load, which ones to discard, how to label them
- responsible individuals and organizations. Be sure to use the individual's title, not his personal name; otherwise, the operator may call someone who was once, but is no longer, connected with the job.

11.5   INDEXES AND ERROR MESSAGES

When writing a user manual or an operator's guide, keep in mind that the person reading it may be all alone and separated entirely from the computer when he has problems. Therefore, you must provide sufficient information so that the user can proceed without any assistance from you or from any other person who was involved with the system design and programming.

It is a good idea to put as comprehensive an index as possible in the user manual.

11.5.1   The Error Message

Sometimes the user procedures are designed in such a way that the exits or decision points of the system display error message codes. All the error messages should be listed in an appendix of the manual such as shown in figure 11-6.

11.5.2   Abbreviated and Extended Forms

Users eventually become proficient with the system and come to recognize certain of the error messages, the ones that occur the most frequently. Thus, it may be desirable to have abbreviated error message explanations just to serve as a reminder to the experienced user.

An example of both the abbreviated and the extended forms are shown in figure 11-7. The abbreviated form merely identifies the problem and tells why it occurs. The more extensive form tells the inexperienced person exactly what the circumstances are and exactly what action may be taken.

ABBREVIATED ERROR MESSAGES

ERR 01 TEXT OVERFLOW
ERR 02 TABLE OVERFLOW
ERR 03 MATH ERROR
ERR 04 MISSING LEFT PARENTHESIS
ERR 05 MISSING RIGHT PARENTHESIS
ERR 06 MISSING EQUALS SIGN
ERR 07 MISSING QUOTATION MARKS
ERR 08 UNDEFINED FN FUNCTION
ERR 09 ILLEGAL FN USAGE
ERR 10 INCOMPLETE STATEMENT
ERR 11 MISSING LINE NUMBER OR
    CONTINUE ILLEGAL
ERR 12 MISSING STATEMENT TEXT
ERR 13 MISSING OR ILLEGAL INTEGER
ERR 14 MISSING RELATION OPERATOR
ERR 15 MISSING EXPRESSION
ERR 16 MISSING SCALAR
ERR 17 MISSING ARRAY
ERR 18 ILLEGAL VALUE
ERR 19 MISSING NUMBER
ERR 20 ILLEGAL NUMBER FORMAT
ERR 21 MISSING LETTER OR DIGIT
ERR 22 UNDEFINED ARRAY VARIABLE
ERR 23 NO PROGRAM STATEMENTS
ERR 24 ILLEGAL IMMEDIATE MODE
    STATEMENT
ERR 25 ILLEGAL GOSUB/RETURN USAGE
ERR 26 ILLEGAL FOR/NEXT USAGE
ERR 27 INSUFFICIENT DATA
ERR 28 DATA REFERENCE BEYOND LIMITS
ERR 29 ILLEGAL DATA FORMAT
ERR 30 ILLEGAL COMMON ASSIGNMENT
ERR 31 ILLEGAL LINE NUMBER
ERR 33 MISSING HEX DIGIT
ERR 34 TAPE READ ERROR
ERR 35 MISSING COMMA OR SEMICOLON
ERR 36 ILLEGAL IMAGE STATEMENT
ERR 37 STATEMENT NOT IMAGE
    STATEMENT
ERR 38 ILLEGAL FLOATING POINT
    FORMAT
ERR 39 MISSING LITERAL STRING
ERR 40 MISSING ALPHANUMERIC
    VARIABLE
ERR 41 ILLEGAL STR(ARGUMENTS
ERR 42 FILE NAME TOO LONG
ERR 43 WRONG VARIABLE TYPE
ERR 44 PROGRAM PROTECTED
ERR 45 PROGRAM LINE TOO LONG
ERR 46 NEW STARTING STATEMENT
    NUMBER TOO LOW
ERR 47 ILLEGAL OR UNDEFINED DEVICE
    SPECIFICATION
ERR 48 UNDEFINED SPECIAL FUNCTION
    KEY
ERR 49 END OF TAPE

ERR 50 PROTECTED TAPE
ERR 51 ILLEGAL STATEMENT
ERR 52 EXPECTED DATA (NONHEADER) RECORD
ERR 53 ILLEGAL USE OF HEX FUNCTION
ERR 54 ILLEGAL PLOT ARGUMENT
ERR 55 ILLEGAL BT ARGUMENT
ERR 56 NUMBER EXCEEDS IMAGE FORMAT
ERR 57 ILLEGAL VALUE
ERR 58 EXPECTED DATA RECORD
ERR 59 ILLEGAL ALPHA VARIABLE
ERR 60 ARRAY TOO SMALL
ERR 61 TRANSIENT DISK HARDWARE ERROR
ERR 62 FILE FULL
ERR 63 MISSING ALPHA ARRAY DESIGNATOR
ERR 64 SECTOR NOT ON DISK OR DISK NOT
    SCRATCHED
ERR 65 DISK HARDWARE MALFUNCTION
ERR 66 FORMAT KEY ENGAGED
ERR 67 DISK FORMAT ERROR
ERR 68 LRC ERROR
ERR 71 CANNOT FIND SECTOR
ERR 72 CYCLIC READ ERROR
ERR 73 ILLEGAL ALTERING OF A FILE
ERR 74 CATALOG END ERROR
ERR 75 COMMAND ONLY (NOT PROGRAMMABLE)
ERR 76 MISSING <OR> (PLOT STATEMENT)
ERR 77 STARTING SECTOR > ENDING SECTOR
ERR 78 FILE NOT SCRATCHED
ERR 79 FILE ALREADY CATALOGED
ERR 80 FILE NOT IN CATALOG
ERR 81 /XYY DEVICE SPECIFICATION ILLEGAL
ERR 82 NO END OF FILE
ERR 83 DISK HARDWARE ERROR
ERR 84 NOT ENOUGH MEMORY FOR MOVE OR
    COPY
ERR 85 READ AFTER WRITE ERROR
ERR 86 FILE NOT OPEN
ERR 87 COMMON VARIABLE REQUIRED
ERR 88 LIBRARY INDEX FULL
ERR 89 MATRIX NOT SQUARE
ERR 90 MATRIX OPERANDS NOT COMPATIBLE
ERR 91 ILLEGAL MATRIX OPERAND
ERR 92 ILLEGAL REDIMENSIONING OF ARRAY
ERR 93 SINGULAR MATRIX
ERR 94 MISSING ASTERISK
ERR 95 ILLEGAL MICROCOMMAND OR FIELD/
    DELIMITER SPECIFICATION
ERR 96 MISSING ARG 3 BUFFER
ERR 97 VARIABLE OR ARRAY TOO SMALL
ERR 98 ILLEGAL ARRAY DELIMITERS
ERR=1 MISSING NUMERIC ARRAY NAME
ERR=2 ARRAY TOO LARGE
ERR=3 ILLEGAL DIMENSIONS

Figure 11-6. Example of Error Messages Listed in Appendix & Example of Abbreviated Messages used in *Wang BASIC Language Reference Manual,* Wang Laboratories, 1976.

Section IX   Error Codes

CODE 80

Error: File Not In Catalog

Cause: The error may occur if one attempts to address a non-existing file name, to load a data file as a program or open a program file as a data file.

Action: Make sure the correct file name is being used; make sure the proper disk is mounted.

Example: LOAD DCR "PRES"

↑ERR 80

LOAD DCF "PRES"   (Possible Correction)

CODE 81

Error: /XYY Device Specification Illegal

Cause: The /XYY device specification may not be used in this statement.

Action: Correct the statement in error.

Example: 100 DATASAVE DC /310, X

↑ERR 81

100 DATASAVE DC #1, X   (Possible Correction)

CODE 82

Error: No End Of File

Cause: No end of file record was recorded on file and therefore could not be found in a SKIP END operation.

Action: Correct the file.

Example: 100D SKIP END

↑ERR 82

CODE 83

Error: Disk Hardware Error

Cause: A disk address was not properly transferred from the CPU to the disk when executing MOVE or COPY.

Action: Run program again. If error persists, call Wang Field Service Personnel.

Example: COPY FR(100,500)

↑ERR 83

Figure 11-7. Example of Detailed Error Messages used in *Wang BASIC Language Reference Manual,* Wang Laboratories, 1976

11.6 HIGHLIGHTS

- As the author of an instructive document you must be able to explain technologically complex material to those without a technical background.
- The general information manual explains the features of a system to a manager. It is also an advertisement for the system.
- The user manual gives procedures for using the system on a day-to-day basis. It takes the place of a teacher.
- Write the user manual *before* the system is developed to ensure that the system satisfies the user's needs.
- Like the user manual, the operator's guide should be self-explanatory. It should be organized for quick reference.
- A user manual should include an index and a list of error messages.

12

Directive Documents: Directives, Policies, and Procedures

12.1 POLICY + PROCEDURE = DIRECTIVE

A procedure is a set of rules for a person to follow in order to accomplish a particular objective. In the computing center this objective may be running a computer program or operating a large computer system. In the broader context of data processing, a procedure is a set of rules to be followed in order to carry out a *policy*. This policy may be articulated in a preamble to the procedure. The two components, the policy together with the procedure which carries it out, make up a document called a *directive*.

12.2 DIRECTIVES

A directive is the formal document that is needed to carry on the business of the organization when management is not physically present to give verbal guidance.

Figure 12-1 shows the characteristics of a good directive. For the particular list of observations shown in the figure, I am indebted to the General Services Administration's National Archives and Records Service's training program for records managers.

A directive is the documentation and issuance of policy or procedure. It:

- identifies the responsible party.
- defines relationships between parties.
- explains the work procedure.
- reduces training time through written instruction.
- prepares personnel for changes ahead of time.
- is part of a formal program of directives.
- is prepared in a standard format.
- states its status as temporary or permanent.
- is coded by subject classification or otherwise marked by subject for filing convenience.
- is coordinated with all entities involved.
- is clear.
- has been properly reviewed ahead of time for
  coverage
  duplication/conflict
  conformance to standards
  coordination.
- contains directive updating instructions (such as purging of obsolete directives).
- is distributed effectively.
- is stocked in adequate supply after distribution.

Figure 12-1. Characteristics of Directives

12.3 PROCEDURES

12.3.1 Attributes of a Good Procedure

To be useful, the procedures which accompany any statement of policy, and particularly those which are promulgated to assist users to run programs under various conditions, must meet several rigid criteria:

A good procedure is clear. It uses words which any reader can understand. It uses examples.

A good procedure is unambiguous. The procedural steps can be interpreted in one and only one way.

```
C:   ENTER 1 TO ADD TO
C:           2 TO SUBTRACT FROM
C:           3 TO INQUIRE ABOUT
C:   STOCK ON HAND
U:   ?_____
```

C—computer

U—user

Figure 12-2. Example of a Three-Way Decision Point in a Procedure

A good procedure is complete. Every eventuality is covered in the procedure. Sometimes a user procedure can go two or three different ways at a decision point as shown in figure 12-2. Each of these paths should be followed in the procedure so that the user can handle the eventualities which come up.

A good procedure is concise. It says what has to be said in the briefest possible way, so that the reader can absorb the material quickly and act quickly. It uses the active voice.

Sometimes a system condition will require a third party, such as a manager or supervisor, to take action. In this case, the procedure should clearly identify the separate roles that the user and the supervisor are expected to perform. The supervisor's responsibilities and the detail of the steps he takes need not be in the same procedures as the user's. See figure 12-3.

If the procedure includes making a phone call, the procedure should also include a form which makes certain that all the necessary information is at hand when the call is placed.

```
C:   NOTICE AUTHORIZED ORDER QUANTITY EXCEEDS
C:   QUANTITY ON HAND. CALL SUPERVISOR TO
C:   CONSOLE.
C:   ENTER SUPERVISOR ID.
S:   ?_____
```

Note: Supervisor's manual will advise how to take corrective action.

C—computer

S—supervisor (entry underlined)

Figure 12-3. Example of Procedure Requiring Supervisor Intervention

Every action item in a directive or procedure must have a time frame. There should be follow-up as well.

12.3.2 Testing the Procedure

A quick way to check that a procedure meets the above criteria is to try to follow the procedure yourself. Put away all the references which you had available to you when writing the procedure, but which would be unavailable to a person following it. Pretend you know nothing about the procedure other than what you see written down in front of you. Then try to follow the procedure as written.

If you can follow the procedure successfully with a minimum of difficulty, well and good. If you cannot, make note of the difficulties that you encounter and revise the procedure accordingly. When you have written the procedure to your satisfaction, attach the printouts or CRT dialogue to the procedure to illustrate it. If the procedure involves filling out a form, attach a filled-in example for the reader's reference. In the computer business a picture is worth a thousand words.

12.3.3 Illustrations for Batch Systems

In the 1950's and early 1960's, when computer programs were maintained entirely in trays of punched cards, it was customary to include a sketch of the program deck showing the various control cards and showing the order of the data input cards. This is still a good idea for batch systems.

12.3.4 Illustrations for Interacting Systems

For user applications on CRTs, you can illustrate user procedures by using typed or photographed representations of the computer dialogue. If you are reluctant to copy out the terminal dialogue because you may omit such important things as commas and other special characters, use a Polaroid or other instant camera. Then have the photographs of the terminal screen reproduced in the user procedure.

If other than alphanumeric graphics are involved in the CRT display, the same graphics can be drawn by an artist in order to illustrate the procedure. To show dialogue at the terminal in a procedure, use upper case for input and lower case for the computer response. This is shown in figure 12-4. Other techniques for differention are to use com-

HELLO
please enter id? ABLEBAKER
enter program name? PAYROLL
select payroll option:
   1-hourly
   2-monthly
   3-commission
   4-stop
?1
enter employee id? 12345
enter hours worked? 45
enter s to stop - p to proceed? S
print checks now? N
select payroll option:
       etc.

Figure 12-4. Example of Upper/Lower Case Dialogue

HELLO
please enter id? ABLEBAKER
enter program name? PAYROLL
select payroll option:
   1-hourly
   2-monthly
   3-commission
   4-stop
?1
enter employee id? 12345
enter hours worked? 45
enter s to stop - p to proceed? S
print checks now? N
select payroll option:
       etc.

Figure 12-5. Example of Italic/Gothic Dialogue

```
HELLO
PLEASE/ENTER/ID?   ABLEBAKER
ENTER/PROGRAM NAME?  PAYROLL
SELECT/PAYROLL/OPTION:
   1//HOURLY
   2/MONTHLY
   3/COMMISSION
   4/STOP
? 1
ENTER/EMPLOYEE/ID?  12345
ENTER/HOURS/WORKED?  45
ENTER/S/TO/STOP/+/P/TO/PROCEED?  S
PRINT/CHECKS/NOW?  N
SELECT/PAYROLL/OPTION:
                    etc.
```

Figure 12-6. Example of Shading Dialogue

binations of italic and Gothic typefaces or contrasting colors and shading (see figures 12-5 and 12-6).

A good procedure will make extensive use of these dialogue examples by cross-keying the explanations (see figure 12-7).

Examples of good procedures are shown in figures 12-8 and 12-9. Note that from step to step, the procedure addresses the user at the same level of experience. It assumes a certain base level of knowledge and does not deviate from that base level.

If both sophisticated and unsophisticated users will be following your procedures, you may have to write them out on two different levels. In such a case, two distinct user manuals may have to be written. If this is not practical, then the user manual can be divided into two sections, one for the experienced user and one for the inexperienced user.

12.4   EXAMPLE OF A DIRECTIVE

A directive includes both a statement of policy and a procedure for carrying out that policy. The directive shown in figure 12-10a—called by McDonnell Douglas Automation a Control Procedure—gives proce-

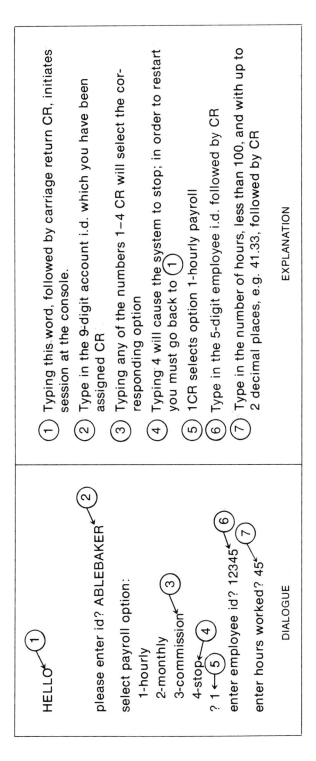

Figure 12-7. Example of Cross-Keyed Dialogue Explanation

PROC. AUTHOR W. D. Skees	COMPUTER PROCEDURE Diskette Copy	NUMBER CP13.01
PROGRAM(S) USED DKCOPY		DATE June 2, 19XX
VERSION-LEVEL(S) 0-0		REPLACES CP13.01 1-15-XX

PURPOSE:
> To make exact duplicate or backup copy of diskette containing programs, data or both

RESTRICTIONS:
> 8″ floppies, OSI format

STEPS:

1. Make certain that no other program is running
2. Disable both disk drives
3. Press console reset button
4. Place diskette UTILITY #3 in disk drive number 1
5. Enable disk drive number 1
6. Enter console commands

> LOAD—DKCOPY (RET)
> RUN (RET)

7. When console displays

> PLACE FROM DISKETTE ON D1

7.1 Disable disk drive number 1
7.2 Remove UTILITY #3 and insert diskette to be copied from
7.3 Enable disk drive number 1
7.4 Press (RET)

8. When console displays

> PLACE TO DISKETTE ON D2

8.1 Insert diskette to be copied to in disk drive number 2
8.2 Enable disk drive number 2
8.3 Press (RET)

9. When console displays

> COMPLETION
> TRACKS COPIED nnn
> NO. REREADS   nn
> NO. BAD TRACKS n

9.1 Disable both drives and remove diskettes

10. Record new contents and completion data in diskette notebook (page corresponding to "to diskette" number)—see example attached

Figure 12-8. Example of a Diskette Copy Procedure

PROC. AUTHOR W. D. Skees	COMPUTER PROCEDURE Abnormal Termination	NUMBER CP02.01
PROGRAM(S) USED any		DATE June 2, 19XX
VERSION-LEVEL(S) any		REPLACES CP02.01 12-1-XX

PURPOSE:
  To record sufficient information in the event of abnormal termination to facilitate program debugging *and* to permit routine recovery of processing.

RESTRICTIONS:
  None

STEPS:
1. Complete form CP02.01A (attached)
   1.1 Fill in date (A), time (B), operator name (C), and system, application, program, compiler or utility (D) being executed
   1.2 Fill in printer condition (E)
   1.3 Fill in diskette condition (F)
   1.4 Copy down terminating console message (G)
   1.5 Identify diskette from which executing code (H) was loaded
   1.6 Identify other diskettes in use (I)
2. Deliver completed form to computer supervisor
3. Re-run job or wait as instructed by supervisor

FORM DESIGN W. D. Skees	COMPUTER PROCEDURE FORM Abnormal Termination		NUMBER CP02.01A
DATE (A)			DATE December 1, 19XX
TIME (B)			REPLACES None
OPERATOR (C)	NAME OF EXECUTING CODE (D)	VERS./LEVEL	LOAD DISKETTE NO. (H)

PRINTER
  ☐ Loaded properly
(E) ☐ Loaded improperly
  ☐ Not loaded
	DISKETTE 1 DISKETTE 2
	LIGHT LIGHT
	  ☐ Error (F) ☐ Error
	  ☐ No Error ☐ No Error
			DISKETTE 1 DISKETTE 2
			No. ———— No. ————
			(I)

TERMINATING CONSOLE MESSAGE (G)			

Figure 12-9. Example of an Abnormal Termination Procedure with Form

MCDONNELL DOUGLAS AUTOMATION COMPANY

MCDONNELL DOUGLAS

CORPORATION

CONTROL
PROCEDURE

NO: CP 14.501-K
PAGE 1
DATE: 1 Aug XX (SMS)
SUPERSEDES: 14.501-K
dtd 22 Sep XX

SUBJECT: PREPARATION OF
COMMERCIAL LETTERS

A. SUMMARY
1. This procedure establishes the format to be used in the preparation of commercial letters. The consistent use of this format throughout MCAUTO will serve to promote a uniform image of MCAUTO to its commercial clients.
B. APPLICABLE TO:
All Departments and Subsidiaries.
C. DEFINITIONS:
None
D. REGULATIONS:
1. All letters will be prepared on MCAUTO stationery in accordance with the approved format.
2. Stationery:
a. Letter original—MCAUTO embossed or printed letterhead and matching continuation sheet.
NOTE: Embossed should be used (when available) for letters to clients and prospects, and letters concerning legal, contractual or obligatory matters. Printed rather than embossed should be considered in bulk mailing.
b. Copies—Letterhead (copy) or onionskin with MCAUTO logo printed at bottom edge.

c. Envelopes—Use appropriate size, imprinted with MCAUTO logo.
3. Abbreviations or acronyms shall be identified at first appearance in the body of the letter. Spell out in full the word or phrase to be shortened, immediately followed by the abbreviation or acronym in parentheses.
E. PROCEDURE I: FORMAT FOR PREPARATION OF COMMERCIAL LETTERS
1. Prepare letter in accordance with the following instructions; refer to Appendix "A."
a. Date—Show month, day, year.
b. Address—Insert name of addressee; if known; company; street; city; state; zip code.
c. Salutation—Use name of addressee; if no name, use Gentlemen.
d. Body of Letter—Use block style (text shown to demonstrate format only).
NOTE: For continuation pages, show page number beginning at left margin, skip one line and show name of addressee and company on next line as follows:

XX
Name of Addressee

NEW

NEW

NEW

REV

Figure 12-10a. McDonnell Automation Directive. Reprinted by permission.

NO: CP 14.501-K
PAGE 2
DATE: 1 Aug XX (SMS)

PROCEDURE I: FORMAT FOR
PREPARATION OF
COMMERCIAL LETTERS (Cont'd)

---

e. Complimentary closing—Use closing which conforms to general tone of the letter.
f. Signature—Refer to sample format shown in Appendix "A."
g. Dictator's and Stenographer's Initials—Place on left margin below signature.
h. Enclosures—Place below dictator's and stenographer's initials; denote number enclosures in parentheses.
i. Carbon Copy Distribution—Place below enclosures.

REFERENCES:
1. *Attachments*
   a. Appendix "A," Sample Letter.

J. Quackenbush

J. Quackenbush
Executive Vice President

Figure 12-10a. (cont.)

dures for writing commercial letters. An example of a piece of correspondence written according to the directive is shown in figure 12-10b.

This directive satisfies all the criteria. For example, it identifies the subject matter by classification. This makes it possible for those who need the revision to know where it goes in their manual. It makes it possible for people with other job descriptions which do not include that particular classification code to know they need not bother updating their directives manual.

Notice that the directive is dated and the initials of the individual responsible are indicated. The reader is told which document this directive replaces and how old the replaced document is. The revised procedure indicates with the word "new" and the word "revised," (written *new* and *rev*), where the important information of this particular issue is to be found.

Note also that the directive includes an example which the reader can follow. Anyone reading this directive will know unambiguously what the policy of the company is with respect to business letters, and be able to follow the procedure with minimum difficulty.

Page: 3 (last)
Date: 1 Aug XX (SMS)

APPENDIX "A"
MCDONNELL DOUGLAS AUTOMATION COMPANY

Bcx 616, Saint Louis, Missouri 63166

(a) July 2, 19XX

(b) Mr. Joe Reilly
Johannsen & Girand
6601 North Black Canyon Road
Phoenix, Arizona 85017

(c) Dear Mr. Reilly:

(d) Thank you for your interest in McDonnell Douglas Automation Company. As you requested, I am sending you a copy of Mr. John Baxter's mapping presentation.

I am confident that this program, along with the associated platting capabilities at our Company, can result in errorless right-of-way computations at reasonable cost.

I will have Mr. Gunther call you in a few days to answer any questions you may have.

(e) Very truly yours,

(f) MCDONNELL DOUGLAS
AUTOMATION COMPANY

Steven B. Wright
Marketing Representative

(g) SBW/bz
(h) Enclosures (2)
(i) cc: Mr. (name)

Figure 12-10b. McDonnell Automation Directive Implemented. Reprinted by permission.

12.5 HIGHLIGHTS

- A policy, together with the procedure which carries it out, is called a directive.
- A good procedure is clear, unambiguous, complete, and concise.
- One way to test if a procedure is well written is to try it out on yourself and see if you can follow it.
- Be sure to attach an example. It makes it easier for the reader to follow.

PART C

Management Writing

This kind of writing is done primarily by computer professionals with management responsibility. It includes budgeting, planning, project reporting, and performance monitoring.

13

Developmental Documents: Budgets, Project Plans, and Project Reports

13.1 BUDGETS

The budget is a bit of esoterica maintained in secrecy by management and viewed with awe and mystery by data processing subordinates. This may be because the training that data processing people receive is primarily technical whereas the budget process is primarily business and business management in nature. Actually there is nothing difficult about the budget process. It is partly based on data readily available from past history and partly based on professional judgment about what is likely to happen in the months ahead.

13.1.1 Budget Detail

Depending on the requirements of the company and of upper management, a budget may be very detailed, with lots of categories and individual projects, as in figure 13-1, or it may be quite simple with very few categories, as in figure 13-2.

Computer Center Budget for 19XX

	Administration	Operation	Project A	Project B	Project C	Maintenance	Total
Labor	124,000	180,000	90,000	150,000	150,000	300,000	994,000
Supplies	5,000	—	3,000	5,000	5,000	15,000	33,000
Computer							
Time	1,000	—	12,000	18,000	6,000	360,000	397,000
Equipment	—	—	35,000	5,000	180,000	—	220,000
Media	500	—	1,000	1,000	3,000	24,000	29,500
Travel	12,000	—	—	12,000	6,000	—	30,000
Education	200	—	3,000	5,000	5,000	10,000	23,200
Total	142,700	180,000	144,000	196,000	355,000	709,000	1,726,700

Figure 13-1. Detailed Departmental Budget

13.1.2 Budget Time Span

Normally a department's budget is prepared on a twelve-month basis as shown in figure 13-3. This need not always be the case. Some organizations, especially in state government, prepare biennial budgets, that is, budgets covering a two-year period. Conversely, a project budget may represent only part of a year.

Computer Center Budget for 19XX

	Administration	Operation & Maintenance	Development	Total
Labor	124,000	480,000	390,000	994,000
Equipment & Supplies	6,500	399,000	274,000	679,500
Travel	12,000	—	18,000	30,000
Education	200	10,000	13,000	23,200
Total	142,700	889,000	695,000	1,726,700

Figure 13-2. Simple Departmental Budget

Computer Center Budget for 19XX

	JAN	FEB	MAR	APR	MAY	JUN	JUL	AUG	SEP	OCT	NOV	DEC	TOTAL
Labor	75.0	75.0	75.0	75.0	75.0	75.0	80.0	85.0	85.0	95.0	95.0	104.0	994.0
Equipment & Supplies	56.6	56.6	56.6	56.6	56.6	56.6	56.6	56.6	56.6	56.7	56.7	56.7	679.5
Travel	2.5	2.5	2.5	2.5	2.5	2.5	2.5	2.5	2.5	2.5	2.5	2.5	30.0
Education	2.0	2.0	2.0	2.0	2.0	2.0	2.0	2.0	2.0	2.0	2.0	1.2	23.2
Total	136.1	136.1	136.1	136.1	136.1	136.1	141.1	146.1	146.1	156.2	156.2	164.4	1726.1

Figure 13-3. Twelve-Month Departmental Budget

13.1.3 Departmental Budgets

The budget for a department is normally made up of the budget from each of the projects for which the department is responsible plus the cost of maintenance, management, and support staff for the department (see figure 13-1).

13.1.4 Cost Centers

In this discussion the computer department is treated as a *cost center*. The assumption is that the center has no income with which to offset its costs and against which to figure profit. The opposite approach, called the *profit center* approach, to budgeting is deliberately left out of this text for two reasons. First, treating the computer center as a profit center is primarily a marketing consideration, having very little to do with data processing. Second, operating a computer center as a profit center is often more a matter of company politics than of logic.

13.1.5 Gantt Chart

Since a budget is built up from the costs of various projects, this discussion will concentrate on project costing first. Arriving at a project cost estimate is an iterative process.

Assume that the primary constraint on your project is a constraint

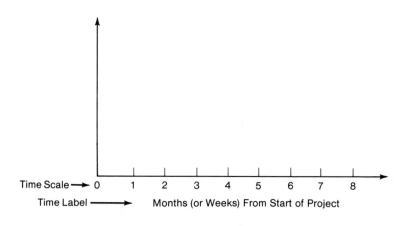

Figure 13-4a. Gantt Chart Showing Time Scale

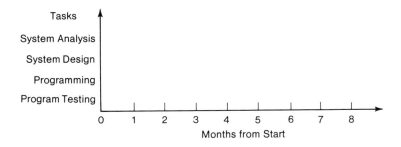

Figure 13-4b. Gantt Chart Showing Time Scale and Tasks

of time. Using pencil and paper, because you will have to make measures, lay out what is called a Gantt chart, or bar graph.

Time Scale The Gantt chart contains a time scale as shown in figure
13-4a with space above the time scale for depicting the tasks as individual bars.

Task Scale Next, list the tasks on the vertical axis as shown in figure
13-4b. Using your judgment of how long it takes to do these various
tasks, draw the bars as shown in figure 13-4c. If there is no overlap
between the tasks, previous experience should tell you that your plan is
in error.

It is very rare that one task ends on the exact day that the next task is

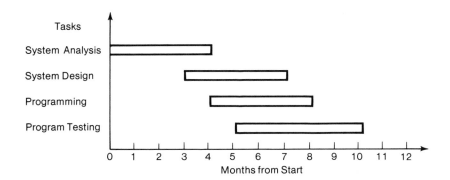

Features:
• elapsed time rather than actual dates (projects rarely start on date indicated)
• overlapped tasks—good project management

Figure 13-4c. Gantt Chart Showing Tasks within a Software Development
Project

supposed to begin. In fact tasks often seem to trail on and on until finally they fade into obscurity. The actual situation in the completed chart, figure 13-4c, is more in accordance with actual experience. In fact, the overlap between tasks is not only a matter of experience but a matter of technical necessity.

For example, a design task consists of several individually designed subtasks. It is not desirable to wait until all the various design subtasks have been finished to begin the programming because there is a programming subtask corresponding to each of the design subtasks. If all the design subtasks ended on the last day, the manager would never have any visible signs of progress in the interim. Practically speaking, on the last day he could be almost a hundred percent sure that the tasks were not completed.

The actual overlap is more like that shown in figure 13-5 where the

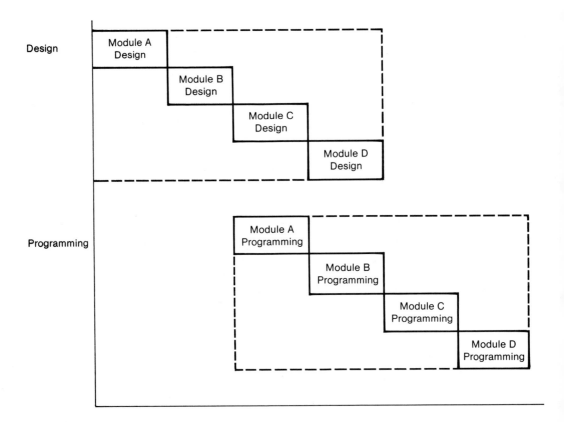

Figure 13-5. Subtasks of Design and Programming Tasks

individual subtasks that make up the design are shown with their relationship to the individual programming tasks. However, for the purposes of the budget, it is not necessary to go to that level of detail. Use your experience to estimate the overlap required.

Task Overlap for Staffing Purposes Another reason for the overlap is to facilitate carrying over people from each task to its successor task in order to preserve continuity of thought, knowledge, and purpose. In other words, you will want people on subsequent tasks who have experience with the preceding tasks. You do not want to bring in a completely new team to take over the work of the outgoing team and have no benefit of communication between the two teams. Arms-length relationships do not work in systems development.

13.1.6 Staffing

Next develop the staffing chart. The deployment of senior and junior talent and the number of people assigned to each task and subtask will depend on your own particular philosophy.

Assume that this is a medium-sized project and that the person in charge is capable of getting the project done in a manner that is consistent with the user's approval. Assume further that the project manager is *result-oriented.* He will see to it that the system is working to the satisfaction of the user in all of its major areas at the end of the time alotted.

13.1.7 Sample Staffing Formula

Assume a system development project staffing formula (SDPS) as follows:

- A simple programming task, that is, a simple system development task, requires a senior analyst and a senior programmer.
- A system of medium complexity requires three senior programmers and a supporting group of three junior programmers with corresponding numbers of senior systems analysts and junior systems analysts.

Cost and Labor Estimating This discussion of budgets does not attempt to be scientific about staffing, productivity estimating, or cost modeling. If you are interested in these topics, I recommend reading *The Mythical Man-Month* by Frederick Brooks, and Larry Putnam's article "Estimating Software Costs" (see bibliography). The literature is replete with hindsight or posteriori cost estimating, that is cost-tracking. Except for a few works such as Brooks's or Putnam's, there is very little in the literature that is worthwhile about a priori cost estimating.

Likely Staffing Pattern   For practice purposes, assume you are using three senior analysts and three junior systems analysts. It is unreasonable to expect that all six people will report on the first day and work at full speed from that day forward. Indeed, the classical picture of human productivity on a system project is not the uniform distribution curve shown in figure 13-6a, but the normal curve, or bell-shaped curve, explored by the mathematician Karl Gauss (figure 13-6b). Figure 13-7 shows the likely staffing relative to the Gantt chart. Note that for the majority of the tasks all the team members are present, but in the early stages there are fewer working, and in the latter stages people begin to drop out of the task as their part of the work is completed. Figure 13-8 shows the relationship of the normal curve to the Gantt chart that has been discussed.

Allocation of Talent   Here again is an opportunity to make use of the overlap. When I move from the analysis stage into the program design

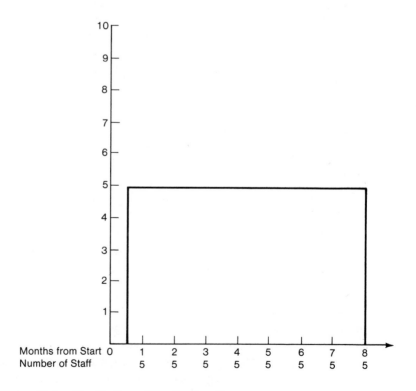

Months from Start	0	1	2	3	4	5	6	7	8
Number of Staff		5	5	5	5	5	5	5	5

Figure 13-6a. The Uniform Distribution Curve

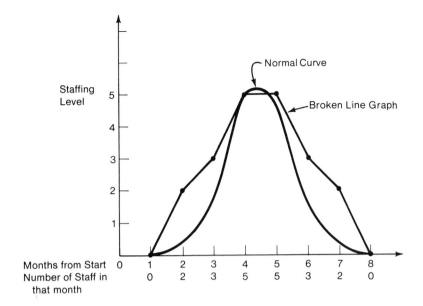

Figure 13-6b. The Normal or Bell-Shaped Curve and a Staffing Plan

stage, that is, the program specification stage, I like to carry over the experienced people into the programming specifications. It usually happens that there are systems analysts who are not only good at doing system analysis and system specification, but who are also good at doing programming specifications as well. These are the ones whom I carry over into the programming specification task.

It is never a good idea, however, to have programming specifications developed solely by systems analysts. The programmer's touch is essential. Therefore, a group of senior programmers comes into the programming specification task. Their involvement in the task is also a bell-shaped curve as shown in figure 13-6b.

When two tasks mesh, the result is an upward trend in staffing toward the time when the largest number of people will be working on the task. This event usually occurs when you are just finishing programming specifications. By this time, you are well into actual program coding.

Note that I do not normally carry junior staff over into the programming specification activity. For the most part, I consider this to be a task for senior people.

There is a similar overlap between the programming specification task and the program coding task. As the former ends and the latter begins, you: a) lose all of the systems analysts; b) acquire additional

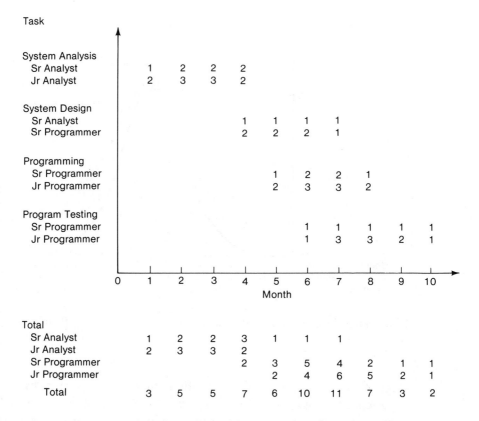

Total

	1	2	3	4	5	6	7	8	9	10
Sr Analyst	1	2	2	3	1	1	1			
Jr Analyst	2	3	3	2						
Sr Programmer				2	3	5	4	2	1	1
Jr Programmer					2	4	6	5	2	1
Total	3	5	5	7	6	10	11	7	3	2

Figure 13-7. First Iteration Staffing Chart

senior talent to take a leadership role in the programming task; c) employ many junior people for the time-consuming work of program coding.

Overlap Between Programming and Testing   I'm assuming that the program coding is going to follow structured programming principles and the program testing is going to follow structured testing principles. If so, programs are tested while they are being written. The kind of testing that will take place will be something like peer code review. I consider peer code reviews and the other various forms of static testing to be part of program coding. Then I leave the dynamic forms of program testing for the task which is literally called *testing.*

This distinction between static and dynamic testing activities follows that of Robert Glass and comes from his *Software Reliability Guidebook* (see bibliography). In the testing phase, you can release more of the senior talent because the testing work is very straightforward. In a well organized and well-run system development project, the tests were defined back in the system specification phase. Most of the work consists of verifying the reliability and validity of the system. Since the system has been developed according to structured design principles, it should be off to a very good start. However, some corrections and changes will call for senior talent. Therefore, some senior people should be retained.

13.1.8 Smoothed Staffing Chart

The next step is to combine all of the staffing numbers for each of the tasks. The first iteration will probably show uneven staffing (see figure 13-8). Most experienced managers will react very negatively to this kind

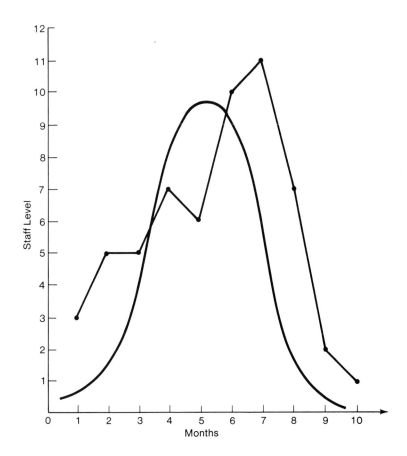

Figure 13-8. First Iteration Staffing Compared with Normal Curve

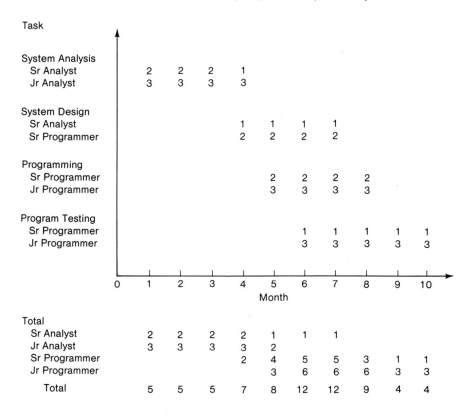

Task										
System Analysis										
Sr Analyst	2	2	2	1						
Jr Analyst	3	3	3	3						
System Design										
Sr Analyst				1	1	1	1			
Sr Programmer				2	2	2	2			
Programming										
Sr Programmer					2	2	2	2		
Jr Programmer					3	3	3	3		
Program Testing										
Sr Programmer						1	1	1	1	1
Jr Programmer						3	3	3	3	3

| Month | 0 | 1 | 2 | 3 | 4 | 5 | 6 | 7 | 8 | 9 | 10 |

Total										
Sr Analyst	2	2	2	2	1	1	1			
Jr Analyst	3	3	3	3	2					
Sr Programmer				2	4	5	5	3	1	1
Jr Programmer					3	6	6	6	3	3
Total	5	5	5	7	8	12	12	9	4	4

Figure 13-9. Final Staffing Plan

No.	*Step*
1	Estimate maximum and minimum strength for each task by labor categories using a system development staffing formula.
2	Allocate personnel across each task on a normal curve basis working from minima at each end to maxima at mid task.
3	Calculate staffing by categories for each time period across all tasks.
4	Reallocate each labor category to a normal curve, adding or subtracting small numbers as needed.
5	Calculate total of all labor categories.
6	Reallocate to achieve overall normal curve, adding or subtracting small numbers as necessary.

Figure 13-10. Staffing Chart Algorithm

of staffing pattern since it defies actual experience. The actual staffing pattern should look more like figure 13-6b. Therefore, some "smoothing" is required.

The smoothing consists of doing the task overlapping a little more effectively (see figure 13-9) and reducing some of the numbers by building up other numbers. This does not involve as much guess work as it seems to, if you use the steps outlined in figure 13-10.

What you are doing is combining two functions. One is the function of estimating the magnitude of the task and the management of the task from a data processing point of view; these are primarily technical considerations. Next you have the problem of management of the people as a team of individuals, and that calls for management experience. This is the data-smoothing activity.

13.2 ASSIGNING DOLLAR COSTS

Figure 13-11 represents the total budget for the project. Note that it is divided into monthly costs so that the project manager can monitor his costs very carefully. So can his superior.

A good data processing manager realizes two things about budgets. The first is that each of the figures in the budget represents something very important which has been very carefully thought out. The second is that if he wants to continue to be a good manager, he will bring in each of his projects within budget.

The next step is to produce the dollars budget shown in figure 13-11. Most data processing budgets are determined by the costs of labor. That is why you built the Gantt chart and the staffing plan first. Now you can convert the numbers of individuals into dollar costs and then add some reasonable estimates for the secondary costs which are dependent on the manpower costs. The secondary costs include the cost of computer time and associated support, travel, consumables, and, depending on the requirements of the company, the costs of overhead and general and administrative expenses.

13.2.1 Which Numbers to Use

The staffing chart (figure 13-9) identified four categories of people:

- senior systems analysts
- junior systems analysts

Month

	1	2	3	4	5	6	7	8	9	10	Total
Personnel											
Senior[1]	5,000	5,000	5,000	10,000	12,500	15,000	15,000	7,500	2,500	2,500	80,000
Junior	4,500	4,500	4,500	4,500	3,000	9,000	9,000	9,000	4,500	4,500	57,000
Overhead[2]	475	475	475	725	775	1,200	1,200	825	350	350	6,850
Total	9,975	9,975	9,975	15,225	16,275	25,200	25,200	17,325	7,350	7,350	143,850
Clerical Support	850	850	850	1,200	1,200	2,100	2,100	1,575	700	700	12,125
Travel[3]	500	500	500	500	500	500	500	500	500	500	5,000
Computer											
Time[4]						6,000	12,000	12,000	12,000	6,000	48,000
Media & Supplies @ 5%						300	600	600	600	300	2,400
Purchase[5]								1,500	1,500	1,500	4,500
Total						6,300	12,600	14,100	14,100	7,800	54,900
GRAND TOTAL	11,325	11,325	11,325	16,925	17,975	34,100	40,400	35,500	22,650	16,350	215,875

[1] Direct cost—(salary + benefits @ 20%) ÷ 12—Sr = $25,000/year, Jr = $15,000/year

[2] Desks, offices, heat, light, clerical support @ 5%

[3] 1 RT per month to remote site; all other travel local

[4] IBM 370/168 or IBM 3033 @ $300/hr. and $400 per hour respectively

[5] Minicomputer and RJE station @ $50,000 ÷ 40 months + 20% financing; transferred to production after 3 months

Figure 13-11. Project Budget

- senior programmers
- junior programmers.

It is impossible to give precise guidelines about how much to pay computer people. However, you do need dollars on your sample budget, so that you can see how the budget is derived. So without taking these numbers literally, make the following assumptions:

- Senior talent costs $25,000 per year in salary.
- Junior talent costs $15,000 per year in salary.

You may modify these numbers according to the prevalent salary figures in your area.

Next, convert the annual salary figures into monthly figures and then multiply by the number of people of each type in each month. Thus, you have gone from figure 13-9 to figure 13-11.

13.2.2 Direct Labor Costs

Some companies want their cost figures shown not just as salary costs, but as "direct labor" costs. A direct labor cost is the cost of an individual to the company. This cost figure includes not only salary but also sick leave and vacation time, bonuses, the cost of the benefits package, and any other costs directly related to salary, including the estimated raise in salary during the time of the project. For purposes of this budget, assume a figure which is 20 percent of the salary cost. This addition is shown in figure 13-11 as footnote 1.

13.2.3 Overhead Costs

Some companies also want the budget to include overhead costs. The bookkeeping practices of each company are different, but assume for illustration that the overhead expenses are going to be the per-person share of such non-technical support functions as the accounting office, the legal counsel's office, the president's office, certain secretaries, and perhaps heat, light, furniture, and office space rental. Let us add 5 percent of salary as this share. That is shown in figure 13-11 in the "Overhead" line and in footnote 2.

13.2.4 General and Administrative Costs

Some companies also include general and administrative costs in their project. Such costs are sometimes directly a function of salary, sometimes not. They include such things as the cost of borrowing money and estimates of legal fees. There is nothing to be gained by adding them in, so leave them out of this example.

13.2.5 Computer Costs

The next major cost is the cost of computer time. Today, probably no more than half of the new systems are developed on general purpose, large-scale computers where there is a system-usage cost algorithm that can be analyzed for cost-estimating purposes. The other systems will be developed on small, special purpose computers such as minicomputers or microcomputers. Some of these may be dedicated to the very project for which the development is being done.

For projects developed on large, general purpose computers, estimate the cost as follows: For each of the months in which the computer will be used estimate the number of hours of usage in that month and write that down. Next, multiply by the hourly rate. Sometimes the rates are dependent on job priority or shift. For your purposes, use a reasonable hourly rate and multiply this by the anticipated number of hours used in each month to arrive at the cost as shown in the "Time" line of figure 13-11 and in footnote 4.

At the opposite extreme, your firm may be purchasing equipment that is going to be used specifically for and dedicated to this project. As a normal rule of thumb for the monthly cost in such a case, take the total cost of the equipment and divide that by forty. This gives an approximate monthly rental figure. Next, because the company is purchasing the equipment, add twenty percent for the cost of financing. Typically, the equipment will not be installed until you are near to needing hands-on machine time. Therefore, the equipment cost begins to appear in the month that you begin doing dynamic testing.

Note that in figure 13-11 the purchased machine is not introduced until the eighth month of the ten-month project. What about the total cost of machine and its forty-month amortization? Why is it not reflected in the project cost? The reason is that the costs are considered part of the development cost only as long as the system is in a development mode. After the system is accepted and the system becomes operational, then the monthly cost of the equipment becomes an operating cost. At that point it shows up in someone else's budget—possibly the user's or perhaps the over-all budget of the data processing department. This fact is reflected in the "Purchase" line of figure 13-11 and in footnote 5.

13.2.6 Computer Related Costs

Every time a computer is used there are associated costs for such items as paper for the printer, printer ribbons, paper tape, and punched cards. These items are consumables and must be replaced continually.

There are other costs associated with the computer. They are the costs of the diskettes or "floppy disks," disk cartridges, magnetic tape cassettes, and other recording media. The unit cost of these items is relatively low. For all practical purposes, they can be lumped together with the consumables in computer media and supplies. A typical rule of thumb is that total related costs will be about five percent of the computer cost. This is reflected in the "Media & Supplies" line of figure 13-11.

13.2.7 Clerical Support Costs

In a book on writing for data processing professionals, it would be remiss to leave out the cost of documentation support. That is, the cost of typing, printing and copying. It is customary to call this the cost of clerical support. Say that the total clerical support cost with all benefits and overheads runs about ten dollars per hour. You will be documenting steadily during all of the tasks and the more people you have, if you manage properly, the more documentation you will be producing. Estimate one hour of clerical support for every ten hours of manpower. Using the "Total" row of the manning charts of figure 13-9 and this one-to-ten ratio at ten dollars an hour, you will come up with the costs shown in figure 13-12. These figures appear in figure 13-11 in the "Clerical Support" row.

13.2.8 Miscellaneous and Travel Costs

A typical project will have other costs as well. If these costs are not individually significant, they may be lumped under the miscellaneous category. For the sake of simplicity, restrict the miscellaneous costs to

	1	2	3	4	5	6	7	8	9	10
Labor Months	5	5	5	7	7	12	12	9	4	4
Labor Hours @ 172/mo	860	860	860	1204	1204	2112	2112	1584	704	704
Hours of Clerical Support @ 1 per 10 Labor hours	86.0	86.0	86.0	120.4	120.4	211.2	211.2	158.4	70.4	70.4
Cost of Clerical Support @ $10/hr	$860	$860	$860	$1204	$1204	$2112	$2112	$1584	$704	$704
Round to Nearest $25.00	850	850	850	1200	1200	2100	2100	1575	700	700

Figure 13-12. Sample Calculation of Clerical Support for Documentation

travel. Although a project may be performed entirely in plant, an occasional trip may be required to a distant user site or to acquire some information which cannot otherwise be obtained. For this example, estimate one trip every month, say half way across the country and back, at $300 per trip and expenses for two days at $100 per day. This comes to $500 every other month and is shown in figure 13-11 in the "Travel" line and in footnote 3.

13.3   MAKING YOUR BUDGETS BEST SELLERS

Packaging helps to sell budgets. Numbers should be reasonable. Spending categories should be sensible, and names of necessary items should be recognizable.

Keep a running budget yourself. Do it each month with pencil and paper because the accounting department's report will not be in the form you require and will not be current. Furthermore, that report shows actual expenditures but your budget will show committed funds. Spending commitments are what you need to remember when working within budget.

Use summary figures. Too much detail will either confuse and alienate the reader or else will cause him to worry about matters that are too detailed for discussion in management meetings. However, the figures should not be vague or misleading, and you should keep sound backup data for your summary figures.

13.4   REPORTING TO MANAGEMENT

Management wants to see the same measures that you are interested in, namely:

- funds expended
- revised spending plan
- manhours expended
- revised manpower plan
- tasks accomplished
- deliverables achieved

I recommend in your various reports to management that, wherever possible, you should reduce each item of information to a number. It sounds trite, but it works. Use dollars as your numbers wherever possible. Show dollars spent by month and by task. For your own sake, show the dollars committed right in with the dollars spent, even if the accounting department has not yet disbursed the committed funds. Show internal or "company" dollars right in with real dollars. Continually revise the anticipated expenditures as realistically as you can.

Always be realistic with dollar figures. If you must hedge, show a hedge account for your own reference. But restrain yourself from using it, if possible.

Why dollars? The most effective and safest decisions in business are those that are based on quantitative measurements, on numbers.

13.4.1 Directives and Project Decisions

The activities of management are decision or policy making, policy enforcement, and administration. The documents connected with the first two are called directives which are fully discussed in chapter 12.

Directives are not limited to administrative matters, but include project activities as well. The decisions which guide a project through to completion must be documented, as well as the procedures which are then developed to carry them out. An effective DP manager, knowing that people tend to forget or confuse project decisions, will see that project decisions are carefully recorded.

13.4.2 Administrative Matters

Administration is a fact of management life. Administrative matters must be taken care of even if they are a nuisance. DP management usually would much rather get on with technical and project management matters. On the bright side, there is always a form you can use. So, to get administrative matters taken care of swiftly, but carefully, make them part of a routine:

- Set up a system to file the forms.
- Avoid anything not requested. Administrative offices are highly routine shops; they react negatively to variances from the norm.
- Check for accuracy to avoid trouble.
- File on time.

13.5 HIGHLIGHTS

- Many data processing people feel that budgets are mysterious objects. Actually the budget is a combination of readily available data and professional judgment.
- Budgets may be simple or detailed; they may cover one year or any other time span.
- Use a Gantt chart to plot the tasks that must be done against the amount of time you have to do the project.
- Use a system development staffing formula and create a staffing chart which will show you how many people you need at each stage of your project.
- Your budget should take into account the cost of labor, overhead, administration, computers (and related costs), clerical support, and miscellaneous and travel.
- The documents which management produces in its policy making and enforcement functions are called directives. Project decisions should be carefully documented.
- Management's administrative function can be dealt with effectively by using forms wherever possible.

14

Archival Documents: Interim Reports and Writing for the Record

14.1 ROUTINE REPORTING

Some DP writing is necessarily of a very routine nature. Certain documents are written over and over again, perhaps on a weekly or even on a daily basis, with only minor changes. Examples include:

- performance monitoring reports
- test reports
- operations logs
- transaction logs
- financial reports.

14.1.1 Forms and Automation

When a document is rewritten periodically with no more changes than in parameter values, then it is time to consider converting that document into a form. If, in addition, the periodic changes are quantitative in nature and require arithmetic or algorithmic manipulation, then it is well to consider going a step further and automating that report.

Using a form saves you the hours of labor you otherwise would have to spend reinventing the wheel. A form has all the data identified so that nothing gets left out.

Human beings tend to make mistakes in arithmetic and are particularly bad at repetitive work. By contrast, a good computer-generated report capitalizes on what computers do particularly well, namely iterative calculation.

14.1.2   Performance Monitoring

Performance monitoring includes one or more of these three basic tasks:

- verifying that performance standards are being met
- identifying faults when they occur
- showing where systems can be improved.

A performance monitoring report should be designed to address specifically that function which is its objective (see figures 14-1 through 14-3). Raw data may be used if the measures can be expressed directly in such data (see figure 14-4). Otherwise, they must be converted for the reader in as straightforward a manner as possible. The simpler the measure the more credible it is (see figure 14-5).

14.1.3   Test Reports

From Robert L. Glass's *Software Reliability Guidebook,* © 1979, pp. 201–202. Reprinted by permission of Prentice-Hall, Inc., Englewood Cliffs, N.J.

> Test reports are . . . [extensions of] test procedure documents [which] sometimes have blank spaces to record results of test runs and critical test data which will demonstrate the expected performance. For convenience, the data to be recorded are usually grouped on separate data sheets appended to the procedural material. When all the blanks are filled in and signed off by the responsible individuals, they constitute the body of the test report document. Additional summary material and an explanation or interpretation of the test results may be prepared to accompany the data.

See figure 14-6.

SEQ. NUMBER	JOB START/STOP TIME	JOB NUMBER	ACCT NUMBER	TOT JOBS IN MEM.	K MEM.	TOTAL JOBS IN QUEUE	JOBS IN PRINT QUEUE	IN USE	
								DISKS	TAPES
21	070345.1	10118	93015001	6	120	23	3	10	5
22	070348.7	10119	83055007	7	150	22	3	12	5
21	070355.2	10118	93015001	6	120	22	4	09	5
17	081500.1	10110	58015003	5	105	22	2	08	0
23	081500.2	10120	55077002	6	115	21	2	11	0

Note: This format provides direct indication of multiprogramming, memory, disk, printer, tape, and input queue usage.

Figure 14-1. Performance Monitoring Report for Large Scale Multiprogrammed System—Printed at Console

JOB SEQUENCE NUMBER	START TIME	STOP TIME	JOB NUM- BER	ACCT NUMBER	USER PRI- ORITY	JOB CLASS	MAX KMEM	CPU SECS	DISKS	TAPES
21	070345.1	070355.2	10118	93015001	2	A	200	005.20	3	0
17	070030.5	081500.1	10110	58015003	2	B	150	150.20	1	5
22	076348.7	081631.9	10119	83055007	1	C	300	300.05	2	0
23	081500.2	082000.0	10120	55077002	1	C	100	121.01	3	0

Note: This format provides direct indication of memory usage, priority and job class, as well as CPU time, number of disks, and number of tapes used. These are the parameters needed for billing.

Figure 14-2. Performance Monitoring Report for Large Scale Multiprogrammed System—Printed from Accounting File

| | | | USED | | RESERVED |
DISK NUMBER	ACCT NUMBER	FILE NAME	NO. CYLINDERS	NO. TRACKS	NO. CYLINDERS
1001	93015001	PR001	10	3	20
	93015001	ER0001	5	15	10
	83055007	HIWY09	20	10	25
1002	58015003	BRDG95	100	5	110
	55077002	HACCT3	5	2	25

Note: This format provides direct indication of disk space allocation and usage. These are needed for billing.

Figure 14-3. Performance Monitoring Report for Large Scale System—Printed from Disk Volume Table of Contents

14.1.4 Operations Logs

Operations logs can be filled in using the outpourings of the operator's console and from such data gathering packages as the "Systems Management Facility" of IBM (see figure 14-7).

Management's wants from operations data are very simple:

- total number of jobs through the system
- total number of jobs by category
- average number of jobs in process simultaneously
- percentage of idle capacity by device
        memory
        cpu
        disk
        tape
        printer/reader
        communications line

The operations logs should satisfy these wants as directly as possible (see figure 14-8).

14.1.5 Transaction Records

Transaction records are application-dependent records showing what went into and what came out of the system. Statistics may be derived from them. The secret of keeping good transaction record documents is

JOB. SEQ. NO.	START TIME	STOP TIME	USER PRIORITY	JOB CLASS	MAX KMEM	CPM SECS	DISKS	TAPES	JOBS IN MEM	JOBS IN QUEUE
21	070345.1	070355.2	2	A	200	005.20	3	0	6	23
17	070030.5	081500.1	2	B	150	150.20	1	5	5	10
22	070348.7	081631.9	1	C	300	300.05	2	0	7	22
23	081500.2	082000.0	1	C	100	121.01	3	0	6	21

Figure 14-4. Performance Monitoring Report Presenting Raw Data—Printed from Accounting File

TIME PERIOD	NO. JOBS	AVG. ELAPSED TIME HHMMSS.SS	PRIORITIES			AVG. KMEM	MAX KMEM	MAX DISKS	MAX TAPES	AVG. CPU TIME HHMMSS.SS	IDLE TIME HHMMSS.SS	AVG. JOBS IN QUEUE	AVG. JOBS PRINT QUEUE
			1ST	2ND	3RD								
0400–0800	30	001630.42	4	6	10	188.55	1500	12	8	000035.17	034224.90	21.3	3.3
0800–1200	138	000500.05	55	80	3	108.15	1950	12	8	000041.12	022525.44	25.5	7.0

Figure 14-5. Performance Monitoring Report with Simple Measures Derived from Accounting File

TEST REPORT

Date Scheduled _____ Date Tested _____
System Name _____ Tester _____
Subsystem Name _____ Test Approved _____
Module Name _____ Date Approved _____

Description of Input Conditions _____

Description of Expected Results _____

Description of Actual Results _____

Errors Reported to _____ Date Reported _____
Test Repeat Date _____

Figure 14-6. General Purpose Software Test Report Form

to let the computer do the work of gathering and reporting on transactions (see figures 14-9 and 14-10).

14.1.6 Project Financials

These are the data which were described in the previous chapter. A simple crossfooting program is all that is required of the computer, with the provision for entering an extended (detailed) budget, and actual, committed, and projected spending.

This same capability can be used as well for reporting marketing data:

- actuals
- estimated values
- percent of capture
- totals.

RECORD TYPE	HEADER/RECORD	DATE PAGE	720117 1
02	0102 00681590 0072017F C2C2F4F5	* BB45	*
08	0108 0066D2E5 0072017F C2C2F4F5 002E 082300090802000D0808000E0808000F2008023020080231200802 3220080233200802342008023520080236	* KV BB45 * *	* * *
01	0101 0066D2E8 0072017F C2C2F4F5 0000602C 0066D2E8 00000000 00000000 00000000	* KY BB45 * KY	*
13	010D 0066D32F 0072017F C2C2F4F5 002E 00004000000140404040404040404040404040404040C1 01020000 00034040404040404040404040404040C1D1D4	* L BB45 * A * AJM	* .* *
10	010A 00672333 0072017F C2C2F4F5 4040404040404040 00000000 00000000 4040404040404040 0006 0801000C	* BB45 * *	.* .* *
05	0105 00677297 0072017F C2C2F4F5 C1C1D1E2F5F6C1F0 00672FFE 0072017F 0000000000000000 01 006769E5 0072017F 00000000 0000 06 00673036 0072017F 00 8000000 00 0801 C1 00 00000000000000000000000000 000000000000 2E D7C5D5C3C540D1F64040404040404040404040 000173 01 15 F7F6F0F1F0F1F3F1F6F2F0F2F7D5F0F2F2D7D9D6C4	* BB45 *AAJS56A0 * 5 * A * PENCE JW * 7601013162027NO22PROD	.* * * * * *
06	0106 006774D1 0072017F C2C2F4F5 C1C1D1F2F5F6C1F0 00672FFE 0072017F 0000000000000000 C1 00677408 0072017F 00000008 00 01 40404040 C3C5D5E3D9C1 D340 0000000000000000 00000000 00000000 00000000 000000 00 00000000 00000000 00 00	* J BB45 *AAJS56A0 A * CENTRA * *	* * *
05	0105 0067AE1F 0072017F C2C2F4F5 C1C1D1E2F5F6C2F0 00677F2F 0072017F 0000000000000000 01 00678238 0072017F 00000000 0000 06 00677F68 0072017F 00 8000000 00 0801 C1 00 00000000000000000000000000 000000000000 2E D7C5D5C3C540D1F64040404040404040404040 00031C 01 15 F7F6F0F1F0F1F3F1F6F2F0F2E7D5F0F2F2D7D9D6C4	* BB45 *AAJS56B0 * * A * PENCE JW * 761013162027NO22PROD	* * * * * *
06	0106 0067B073 0072017F C2C2F4F5 C1C1D1E2F5F6C2F0 00677F2F 0072017F 0000000000000000 C1 0067AF35 0072017F 00000008 00 01 40404040 C3C5D5E3D9C1 D340 0203010000000000 E3D54040 C8D54040 00000000 000000 00 C3D6D7F1 C6D3C1F1 04 C0	* BB45 *AAJS5680 A * CENTRA *L TN HN *..COP1..FLA1	* * * *
12	010C 0067B81A 0072017F C2C2F4F5 00009B2F 0067B7EF 0000051A 000005BF 00000002	* BB45 *	* *
03	0103 0068161A 0072017F C2C2F4F5	* BB45	*

Figure 14-7. Sample SMF Printout

Offsets		Name	Length	Format	Source	Description
0	0	SMF5FLG	1	binary	SVC 83	System indicator *Bit* *Meaning When Set* 0-5 Reserved 6 VS2 7 VS1
1	1	SMF5RTY	1	binary	internal	Record type
2	2	SMF5TME	4	binary	SVC 11 (Set by IEFSMFWI)	Time, in hundredths of a second, job terminated
6	6	SMF5DTE	4	packed	SVC 11 (Set by IEFSMFWI)	Date job terminated, in the form OOYYDDDF where F is the sign
10	A	SMF5SID	4	EBCDIC	JMRCPUID	System identification (taken from SID parameter)
14	E	SMF5JBN	8	EBCDIC	JMRJOB	Job name[1]
22	16	SMF5RST	4	binary	JMRENTRY	Time, in hundredths of a second, reader recognized the JOB card for this job[1]
26	1A	SMF5RSD	4	packed	JMREDATE	Date reader recognized the JOB card for this job, in the form 00YYDDDF where F is the sign[1]
30	1E	SMF5UIF	8	EBCDIC	JMRUSEID	User identification (taken from common exit parameter area)
38	26	SMF5NST	1	binary	LCTSNUMB	Number of steps in the job
39	27	SMF5JIT	4	binary	JCTJMRJT (Set by IEFSMFIE)	Time, in hundredths of a second, initiator selected the job
43	2B	SMF5JID	4	packed	JCTJMRJD (Set by IEFSMFIE)	Date initiator selected the job, in the form 00YYDDDF where F is the sign
47	2F	SMF5NCI	4	binary	JMRJOBIN	Number of card-image records in instream DD DATA and DD* data sets read by the reader for the job. (This number does not include records from associated data sets.)

[1] The job name and the time and date that the reader recognized the JOB card for this job constitute the job log identification.

Figure 14-7. (cont.)

SEQ. NUMBER	JOB START/STOP TIME	JOB NUMBER	ACCT NUMBER	TOT JOBS IN MEM.	K MEM.	TOTAL JOBS IN QUEUE	JOBS IN PRINT QUEUE	IN USE	
								DISKS	TAPES
21	070345.1	10118	93015001	6	1200	23	3	10	5
22	070348.7	10119	83055007	7	1500	22	3	12	5
21	070355.2	10118	93015001	6	1200	22	4	09	5
17	081500.1	10110	58015003	5	1050	22	2	08	0
23	081500.2	10120	55077002	6	1150	21	2	11	0

Note: This format provides direct indication of multiprogramming, memory, disk, printer, tape, and input queue usage.

Figure 14-8. Operations Log with Disk and Tape Usage Plus Number of Simultaneous Jobs

DAILY TRANSACTIONS LOG

TIME OF DAY REC'D	SOURCE OFFICE	DESTINATION OFFICE	PRIORITY	LENGTH
10:31:17	PAOLA	ARMONK	1	115
10:40:05	ARMONK	MINNEAPOLIS	1	109
10:41:13	PAOLA	MINNEAPOLIS	5	1552
10:42:23	ROCHESTER	EL SEGUNDO	1	125

Figure 14-9. Representative Transaction Log for a Message Switching System

NUMBER OF MESSAGES RECEIVED (By Priority)

TIME INTERVAL	1	2	3	4	5	AVG MSG LENGTH
0000–0100	0	0	0	0	1	500
0100–0200	0	0	0	0	0	0
0200–0300	0	0	0	0	1	352
0300–0400	0	0	0	0	2	267
0400–0500	0	0	0	0	2	323
0500–0600	0	0	0	0	2	220
0600–0700	0	0	0	0	12	198
0700–0800	0	1	0	0	15	190
0800–0900	22	5	0	0	18	120
0900–1000	30	30	0	0	18	120
1000–1100	51	30	0	1	22	100
1100–1200	73	20	0	2	15	81
1200–1300	5	17	1	0	10	111
1300–1400	24	18	0	1	12	101
1400–1500	33	18	0	2	15	113
1500–1600	48	20	2	0	15	125
1600–1700	15	5	0	0	11	198
1700–1800	21	1	0	0	10	199
1800–1900	1	1	0	0	9	245
1900–2000	0	0	0	0	9	315
2000–2100	0	0	0	0	10	385
2100–2200	0	0	0	0	4	400
2200–2300	0	0	0	0	3	422
2300–0000	0	0	0	0	1	551

Figure 14-10. Representative Statistical Report Prepared from Transaction Log

14.2 HISTORICAL OR ARCHIVAL DOCUMENTS

In addition to the forward-looking documents of data processing—project development, marketing, and management—there is a distinctly different set of documents to be considered. This is the set of historical or achival documents. These documents are written either to show what has been accomplished or to show how the provisions of an earlier plan have been carried out. These documents that you write "for the record" fall into two types: active and passive.

14.2.1 Active Documents

The *active* documents are those which are in frequent or constant use. These include the following:

- test results associated with test plans
- trouble reports—such as those operators, users, or maintenance personnel submit
- repair (maintenance) logs—showing what troubles, either routine or unusual, have been attended to
- maintenance guides—documents used by programmers to keep software operational

14.2.2 Passive Documents

Active documents are written because they are needed as part of day-to-day work. *Passive* documents, on the other hand, are those documents which are written primarily to be filed away. Sometimes they may be required by law or by company policy. They include the following:

- project summaries or histories
- special reports on the system
- journal articles

14.2.3   Advantages of Active Documents

Of these two types of documents, the active documents tend to be well-written and to improve with time. Because people are using them, their layouts are revised and their contents are added to or modified as needs evolve.

Passive documents, on the other hand, tend to be poorly written. They receive insufficient attention to begin with, being ad hoc by nature rather than part of some evolution. They reflect haphazard "made do" workmanship because no one is expected to review them seriously. They are considered administrative documents rather than technical ones since they are not in the mainstream of computer people's work.

14.2.4   Handling Passive Documents

As a professional writer you should want your passive documents to be every bit as well-written as your active documents. You can accomplish this by converting the passive documents into active documents. You achieve that conversion by revising the plan of deliverables.

At the beginning of the project, look ahead to see what passive documents are coming up. Try to anticipate their contents and ask yourself, for each document, when something similar is likely to be developed, but in an active context. Rearrange the schedule, if necessary, so that the active version is produced before the passive document is needed. Then cut and paste from all such sources to produce the passive one.

14.3   ARCHIVAL RECORDS

Certain DP documents tend to have lasting usefulness while others have only a short life. Those with long lives tend to be kept current because they deal with something that is a changing entity. These long lived, dynamic documents include the following:

- studies
- systems specifications
- maintenance guides
- run books
- user manuals

Because these documents last so long, they should be developed with special care. Write so that the document is self contained, so that the reader will need the minimum of crossreference to other documents.

System maintenance documents are good examples of archival documents. They include the following:

- data base management guide—like an operator's guide, but for the data base administrator. It shows the cycle of data collection, correction, validation, and destruction.
- program maintenance guide—used by the programmers to keep software functioning.
- hardware preventive maintenance guide—a reference like the manufacturer's checklist, but for special purpose equipment maintained by the user shop.

Since these maintenance documents can get out of date very quickly, use top down methods when writing them so that changed portions can be plugged in at the right level of abstraction and with the minimum of impact on the rest of the documentation. The responsible organization should review and test the maintenance documents periodically using team testing techniques.

14.4   HIGHLIGHTS

- Many DP documents are written over and over again with only minor changes. These documents should be converted into forms or be automated.
- Archival documents are written "for the record." They show what has already been accomplished.
- Active archival documents are those which are in constant use. Passive ones are written primarily to be filed away.
- The secret to making passive documents as well-written as active ones is to revise the document delivery plan so as to convert your passive documents into active ones.

PART D

Promotional Writing

This kind of writing is produced by computer people who participate in marketing activities. Their objective is to promote (sell) their products. They write proposals, newsletters, flyers, and resumes.

15

Promotional Documents: Newsletters, Brochures, Proposals

When the computer professional writes for the purpose of convincing someone to buy something, he is writing a promotional document. The most well-known promotional document is probably the proposal. There are others as well. For example, there are brochures, product announcements, newsletters, and bulletins.

The budget which a manager prepares for his department or project is also a promotional document to be "sold" to top management. The budget is an instrument that the manager uses to promote his own ideas about how he will manage his department.

The very first technical document of your professional life had a promotional purpose. It was your *resume*. In a resume you describe yourself to another person with the intention of getting that person to procure your services.

15.1.1 Basic Ingredients in Marketing

Strictly speaking, there are four ingredients in marketing: first, creation of a need; second, identification of a need; third, showing that one's product fulfills that need; fourth, identifying oneself with one's product.

A total of three relationships must be established: the relationship of *felt need* to *named need,* the relationship of *named need* to *named product,* and finally the relationship of the *named product* to the *firm* (see figure 15-1).

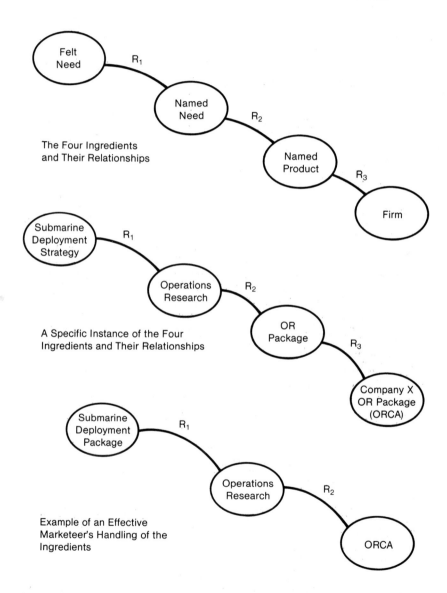

Figure 15-1. Ingredients and Relationships in Marketing

Obviously, there are many possible solutions for any customer problem. However, an effective marketeer does not want to make this clear to his reader. That is, he does not want to be completely objective in his selling, nor is he normally expected to be so. He wants to create the impression that there is one and only one solution to the problem. He wants that solution to be the same as his product in the mind of the customer.

15.1.2 The Challenge of Marketing Documents

A good marketing document must inform without *giving away* or *giving up*. In other words, it must not be so detailed as to permit someone else to steal your idea and do equally as good a job. On the other hand, it must be sufficiently detailed that you keep your reader's interest.

A marketing document must *not* give away your competitive edge. If you are writing a technical proposal in which the techniques are the key elements, the proposal should not give so much technical information that a competitor can reconstruct the product or service at less cost than you incurred or in less time.

If the technology is well-known, as would be the case if you were selling raw machine time, then you should focus the document on any extras that you supply such as express overnight service. Do not show how your price advantage, if any, is achieved. Typically in computer time selling, the price advantage lies in a cost algorithm based on anticipated job mixes.

Marketing documents must provide enough information to convince the reader that the product will do the job, that it is the best such product for the job, and that it is obtainable at a good price. The product should not be too cheap because buyers are suspicious of cheap products. Computer systems buyers are no exception.

15.1.3 Basic Steps in Promotional Writing

Every promotional document follows the general marketing principles:

- It must create a need.
- It must identify the need.
- It must fulfill that need.

The document must first convince the reader that he has a problem that needs solving or that he needs to buy something. For example, if you are trying to sell a new data entry device, you must first of all convince the reader that he needs a data entry device. You may do this by emphasizing some of the crises and disasters that could affect the reader because he does not have a data entry capability.

Next the promotional document must identify that need. You do this by giving the thing you are trying to sell a name. For example, you might say that the reader needs DATATAB. This is a name that I made up, and I hope that it does not match anything available in the industry. Giving something a name has a tremendous promotional marketing advantage. Assume the person who reads the document has purchasing authority. He can ask his subordinates, "Do we have a DATATAB?" If the answer is "no," the next question is likely to be, "Why don't we have one?"

The final step is to show that the company or the individual writing the promotional document can supply the product in question. This is normally just a simple matter of identifying the company with the product and perhaps adding some additional attractions.

15.2   NEWSLETTERS AND BULLETINS

Both newsletters and bulletins are tip-of-the-iceberg documents for their readers, the user community. These documents are intended to give a small amount of information that is of immediate interest to their readers so that the readers know what to follow up or what to avoid. They herald changes in the order of things for their audiences.

The principal difference between newsletters and bulletins is that newsletters are produced periodically whereas bulletins are produced ad hoc, usually when a sufficient backlog of urgent news has developed.

There is one other difference. Since there is not always enough news to fill out a newsletter, the superfluous space is often used for promotional information about the computer center or computer organization that it represents. For example, an issue may contain an editorial by the computer systems manager, or a profile of a recently hired technical specialist, or a reprint of a policy on computer access after hours.

There are three keys to effectiveness for documents of this type. *Keep them short and timely, make them useful,* and *keep them interesting* (see figures 15-2a through 15-3).

THE KENTUCKY REGISTER

PUBLISHED   BY   THE   UNIVERSITY   OF   KENTUCKY   COMPUTING   CENTER

McVey Hall, Lexington, Kentucky 40506   *Area Code 606 Phone 258-2914*

March 1981   Volume 14, Issue 7

XEDIT To Replace EDGAR on May 10

Martin B. Solomon & Dave Elbon

XEDIT, a new IBM CMS full-screen editor now available on the IBM 370, will replace EDGAR on Sunday, May 10, 1981. XEDIT is flexible and easy to use. It contains powerful commands, tailoring features, a macro facility to create new edit commands, and a HELP facility to explain each command.

XEDIT supports 3270-type terminals (Telex 277, IBM 3277, Memorex 1377) in full-screen mode, and ASCII terminals (Televideo, Silent 700, DECwriter, etc.) in line-at-a-time mode. Consequently, people who make use of both types of terminals can use the same editor for both.

EDGAR, XEDIT's predecessor, will become unavailable on Sunday, May 10. Conversion from EDGAR to XEDIT is not difficult, but also not completely trivial. To help users with conversion, our CJS help sessions include information on XEDIT, and the **UKCC CJS User's Guide** contains a detailed section on XEDIT. This manual is available with the MANUAL command in CJS and at the University Bookstore in the Student Center (Lexington campus). The IBM manual for XEDIT (**System Product Editor User's Guide**) may also be purchased at the University Bookstore for $6.60.

Beginning May 10, EDGAR will no longer be available, and the EDGAR command will call XEDIT in EDGAR compatibility mode. This mode of operation is described in the **UKCC CJS Reference** manual (also known as the **CP and CMS Command Reference**), available with the MANUAL command in CJS. Handouts on the EDGAR compatibility mode and on converting to XEDIT are available outside the Consulting Room, 110 McVey Hall.

We recommend that all CJS users switch to XEDIT before May 10, as the EDGAR compatibility mode is expensive to use and has several unpleasant restrictions. If you would like to try the compatibility mode before May 10, you may use the EDGARC command.

The present CMS editor (EDIT) will continue to be available until IBM withdraws it; we expect that to happen within the next year.

Serious Hardware Problem

Selwyn Zerof

The University of Kentucky Computing Center had a very unusual problem with the IBM 370-165 computer recently. The two packed decimal add instructions, AP (add packed) and ZAP (zero add packed), would sometimes subtract rather than add the second operand. This probably (we are not certain) began on Tuesday, February 24, and was fixed the morning of Friday, February 27. This problem gave no indication of failure such as a machine check, and could only be detected by bad results such as negative subscripts. The failure did not occur every time these instructions were executed.

The packed decimal instructions are used heavily by COBOL programs and may be used by some PL/I and assembly programs. FORTRAN programs would not be affected.

Figure 15-2a. Example of Computer Systems Newsletter—Front Page, *The Kentucky Register*, March 1981. Reprinted with permission.

Online Account Balance Updating Error Discovered

Bill Sallee

From February 1 through February 25, 1981, a software error caused all jobs which normally run at the 70 percent rate to deduct an incorrect amount from the online account balance. This included all jobs which ran on deferred project numbers. The error applied only to the CPU time portion of the charge and not to the lines or EXCP charge. These jobs deducted the full rate for CPU time and the 70 percent rate for lines and EXCPs. The job cost printed on the HASP trailer page was correct but the accounting record for the job was incorrectly updated. Therefore, some account balances might have gone negative in error. The accounting records for all affected jobs and the account balances were corrected on March 8 to reflect the proper balances.

Rules for DEC-10 Users

Clarke Thacher

Usage of the DECsystem-10 at the University of Kentucky this semester is very heavy, and it will get much heavier as the semester progresses. We have sixteen ports available to the DEC-10 which must be shared by all University of Kentucky users.

In order to assure that the system can be used by everyone who needs it for class work, the following procedures will be in effect from from **9:00 a.m. to midnight, Monday through Sunday.** These hours are extended during periods of heavy usage, such as at the end of the semester. At all times, users of the DEC-10 should be considerate of other users of the system, and give priority to those people who must use the system.

1. Usage of the DEC-10 will be limited to projects required by a university class, research projects which are under the direct supervision of faculty members, faculty or staff research and development, and necessary system administrative functions.
2. Terminal sessions will be limited to one hour. This means that you should plan your terminal sessions in advance and be prepared. Even if you do not see anyone waiting to use a terminal, sign off and disconnect the terminal to give people in other locations a chance to get a port.
3. Absolutely no game playing! Most uses of RWATCH-type programs can be considered game playing. The only exception to this rule is if you can prove that the game playing is required for a class.
4. Only one terminal per person at a time will be allowed.
5. The DEC-10 is not to be used as a substitute for a CB radio. The SEND command should only be used for short messages necessary for completing your work on the DEC-10, not for long conversations. This means that there is no reason for you to change your LOGIN name to a "handle."

Failure to follow these rules can result in loss of computing privileges and possible disciplinary action.

Attention: Users With Long-Running Computer Jobs

Martin B. Solomon

Computing utilization continues to increase at the University of Kentucky. Since jobs are scheduled for execution based upon resource requirements (smallest resource requirements first), very large jobs are being delayed for long periods of time. Recently some jobs with 20-minute CPU estimates were not executed for up to four days. Such jobs actually require three to four hours to execute.

A better strategy involves breaking large jobs into smaller parts, not only because the parts will be run more frequently, but because errors in such large jobs will require much longer to fix. A recent job with a 20-minute CPU estimate waited 40 hours to execute, only to find an error that occurred in the first two seconds.

Some jobs have been submitted with 100-minute CPU estimates. Such jobs, if run to completion, might require 10-15 actual elapsed hours in the computer. Since the IBM 370-165 averages a failure every three to four days, such long-running jobs are likely to be running when the computer fails. If so, they would then be required to start again from the beginning, delaying them for another day or more.

During busy weeks, the Computing Center may be able to run very large jobs on weekends only.

End of Semester Reminders

During April and early May, the Computing Center will be extremely busy. Please try to complete your computing work for the semester as early as possible. The crowded conditions in the Users' Rooms (106 and 111 McVey Hall) and the possible delay in turnaround time may cause problems for users who wait until the last minute to complete projects.

Please be considerate of other users and staff members who are also rushing to meet end-of-semester deadlines. When possible, use Class X on the Hands-On Reader to minimize turnaround time. Time will also be saved if several persons read their cards on the reader, rather than one person at a time.

It is not necessary to remain logged on while waiting for a submitted job to run, especially when the workload is heavy. Submit your job to your reader or to print 'CENTRAL' and return later for the results, thus allowing others to use the terminal.

If you are leaving at the end of the semester, please release any tapes borrowed from the Computing Center. Also, remove card boxes that you have stored in room 111 or in the basement of McVey Hall.

Check your disk rental space and save money by deleting data sets that are no longer needed. Data sets not needed for the summer can be copied to tape and then deleted from disk; if they are needed later, they can be restored to disk.

All regular and deferred computing dollar allocations at the Computing Center and all DECsystem-10 project numbers issued by UK will expire on June 30 and must be renewed for the 1981-82 fiscal year. The May 1981 issue of **The Kentucky Register** will contain more information on account renewals.

Figure 15-2b. Example of Computer Systems Newsletter—Page Two, *The Kentucky Register,* March 1981. Reprinted with permission.

UKCC Holiday Schedule

Computer Operations, the Data Center, and the Users' Rooms (106 and 111 McVey Hall) at the University of Kentucky Computing Center will close for Christmas at 9:00 p.m. on Wednesday, December 24, and reopen at 9:00 a.m. on Friday, December 26. They will remain open until 9:00 p.m. on Wednesday, December 31, when they will close for New Year's Day. They will reopen at 9:00 a.m. on Friday, January 2, when the Computing Center resumes its normal operating schedule.

The Computing Center Main Office (72 McVey Hall), the Consulting Room (110 McVey Hall), and the Microcomputer Room (107 McVey Hall) will close at 4:30 p.m. on December 24. On January 2 the Main Office will reopen at 8:00 a.m., and the Consulting and Microcomputer Rooms will reopen at 9:00 a.m. Users who plan to work on computing projects during the holidays should check their project allocations and submit requests for additional allocations or new projects no later than Tuesday, December 23; after December 23, no additional project allocations will be processed until January 2, 1981.

Figure 15-3. Example of Computer Systems Bulletin—*The Kentucky Register*, December 1980. Reprinted with permission.

15.3 BROCHURES

Figure 15-4 shows the brochure for a class we give in Advanced Programming Techniques. Note that the brochure begins by establishing a need. Then note how the brochure then gives this need a name.

Note also how the brochure shows that the need will be satisfied. This is done in the most authoritative way possible, by showing exactly what will be taught in the course. Finally, the brochure indicates the qualifications of the people who are doing the instructing.

15.4 PROPOSALS

The proposal is the document which tells the reader what he will get if he does business with you. In the proposal you say what you and your company will provide.

In data processing there are proposals for computer systems, for

Advanced Programming Techniques

Purpose:

Until recently, advanced programming techniques focused exclusively on execution speed and core size. Things have changed during the past decade. Hardware has become faster, more reliable, more versatile, and cheaper. The same cannot be said for software. Today a state-of-the-art seminar on advanced programming techniques must address such issues as reliability measures and design control, as well as execution speed and core size, plus data structure manipulation techniques for today's larger data bases.

This seminar discusses structured programming, top down design, data structuring, testing techniques, and debugging techniques. It shows their relation to project development objectives, project control and cost control. This seminar **emphasizes those techniques which have been shown to be effective in today's business and scientific applications.**

Who Should Attend:

Programmers, analysts, designers, managers, engineers, scientists, business professionals—anyone who needs to produce, evaluate, or maintain state-of-the-art software, and to achieve a comprehensive understanding of today's programming techniques.

Program:

What is Programming?
  Terminology
  History
  Central Issues
  State of the Art
The Design Process
  The Design and Testing Spectrum
  Overview of the Design Process
    Module External Design
    Module Logic Design
  Structured Design
    Module Strength
    Module Coupling
    Levels of Abstraction
    Black Box-White Box Techniques
  Composite Design
    Module Decomposition Techniques
  Top Down Design
  Structured Programming
    Definition
    Fundamentals
    Stepwise Refinement
    Pseudo Code
    Chief Programmer Team
  Programming Style
  Defensive Programming
Testing Strategies
  Peer Code Reviews
  Test Case Design
  Higher Order Testing
  Walk Throughs
  Black Box-White Box Techniques
Debugging Strategies
  Debugging Tools
  Induction Techniques
  Deduction Techniques
  Common Bugs and Errors
Table Driven Systems

Data Structures
  Linear Structures
    Lists
    Stacks
    Queues
    Deques
  Non-Linear Structures
    Trees
    Graphs
Data Handling Techniques
  Sorting
  Searching
  List Processing
  String Processing
Module Relationships
  Coroutines
  Recursive Routines
  Re-entrant Routines
Program and System Optimization
  Hardware and Software Considerations
  Microefficiencies
  Macroefficiencies
  Checklists and Guidelines
Graphic Aids
  ANSI Flowcharts
  Structure Charts
  Data Flow Diagrams
  Decision Tables
  HIPO
  Warnier-Orr Charts
  Jackson Diagrams
  Nassi-Chapin Charts

Seminar Leaders:

EDWARD V. BERARD is a consultant in business, scientific, social science and educational systems. His experience includes management, systems design and documentation, very large data bases, networking systems, code optimization, mathematical modeling, numerical analysis, benchmarking, graphics, and computer science education.

WILLIAM D. SKEES, President of Skees Associates, Inc., is an internationally known consultant to management in automation and the computer sciences.

Dates and Locations:

Jan. 26-28	**Atlanta**	
	Sheraton Atlanta	
	404/881-6000	
Feb. 23-25	**Washington, D.C.**	
	Holiday Inn-Old Town Alexandria	
	703/549-6080	
Mar. 3-5	**Phoenix**	
	Del Webb's Townehouse	
	602/279-9811	
Apr. 21-23	**New York**	
	New York Sheraton	
	212/247-8410	
May 27-29	**Washington, D.C.**	
	Holiday Inn Old Town Alexandria	
	703/549-6080	
June 15-17	**Denver**	
	Regency Inn	
	303/433-6131	

Figure 15-4. Brochure for Advanced Programming Techniques Class

computer services—both labor services and service bureau services—for supplies, for new systems, and for research and development (R&D). Other proposal terms are listed in figure 15-5.

15.4.1 Research and Development Proposals

The research and development (R&D) proposal is the most elaborate. It covers all the subjects that would be covered in any of the other proposals, so I have chosen it as the model for proposals in this chapter.

A research and development proposal is a document that tells how you and your firm propose to solve a particular problem. A good R&D proposal will identify the problem, tell how you are going to tackle the problem, and delineate the time schedule and the deliverables which are part of the work that you will do. It will tell who is in charge, and how much the work will cost.

The well-written R&D proposal will also tell what is expected of the customer in carrying out this work. After all, a proposal is really a preliminary form of a contract and a contract is a document which binds two parties in an agreement. Hence it is frequently necessary in the proposal to show not only the role of the proposing firm, but also the role and the responsibilities of the customer.

Frequently the R&D proposal is adopted as a contract agreement in its entirety. In such cases the more carefully the responsibilities of each party are described, the better control document the proposal will be. In my experience good contracts are those in which each party understands his role.

15.4.2 The Cost Proposal

A proposal is normally divided into two parts—the technical proposal and the cost proposal. The latter is usually very brief, sometimes containing only a page of data. A typical cost proposal for a fixed price contract may have only one figure on it and, perhaps, some qualifying statements outlining the proposer's liabilities in case of nonperformance. It may also state the penalties that accrue to the customer if he does not do his part of the work.

There are more elaborate cost proposals for firm fixed price with multiple deliverables, for time and materials, and for cost plus fixed fee. There are some variations in the cost plus fixed fee (CPFF)—the cost plus incentive fee and the cost plus award fee. Examples of all these different types of cost proposals are shown in figures 15-6 through 15-10.

RFQ—request for (price) quotation
RFP—request for proposal
CPFF—cost plus fixed fee
CPIF—cost plus incentive fee
CPAF—cost plus award fee
T&M—time and materials
FFP—firm fixed price

Figure 15-5. Proposal and Solicitation Terms

Your Company Inc.

Warehouse Inventory Control System

                                         Price $100,000

Figure 15-6. Firm Fixed Price (FFP) Bid Anticipating One Lump Sum Payment

---

Your Company Inc.
Warehouse Inventory Control System
Payment Schedule

Requirements Study	$ 15,000
System Design	45,000
Programming, Testing & Delivery	40,000
Total	$100,000

Payment due upon receipt of deliverable

Figure 15-7. Progress Payment Bid

```
┌─────────────────────────────────────────────┐
│              Your Company Inc.                │
│      Warehouse Inventory Control System       │
│       Schedule of Deliverables & Payments     │
│    1. Requirements Study Report   $ 15,000    │
│    2. System Specification          20,000    │
│    3. Programming Specification     25,000    │
│    4. Program Listings              20,000    │
│    5. Final Test Report             10,000    │
│    6. Installation Report            2,500    │
│    7. User Manual                    5,000    │
│    8. Operator's Guide               2,500    │
│                                    ────────   │
│                       Total     $100,000      │
│                                               │
│  Payment due upon receipt of deliverable      │
└─────────────────────────────────────────────┘
```

Figure 15-8. Fixed Price Per Deliverable Bid

```
┌─────────────────────────────────────────────┐
│              Your Company Inc.                │
│      Warehouse Inventory Control System       │
│      Fixed Price Level of Effort   $100,000   │
└─────────────────────────────────────────────┘
```

Figure 15-9. Fixed Price Level of Effort Bid

```
┌─────────────────────────────────────────────┐
│              Your Company Inc.                │
│      Warehouse Inventory Control System       │
│                                               │
│                       Price   $100,000        │
│                                               │
│  Invoices to be submitted monthly. Payment    │
│  due upon receipt of invoice.                 │
└─────────────────────────────────────────────┘
```

Figure 15-10. Firm Fixed Price with Monthly Payments

15.4.3   The Ethics of R&D Proposals

In the following sections I will tell you how to write good proposals. I will not only show you how a proposal should be organized and what its contents are, I will also show you what I think is ethically incumbent upon the proposer to include in his proposal. For example, in a fixed price proposal it is possible to say something to the following effect: "We will perform a study for $100,000." Personally I feel this is unethical if the proposal does not say what the customer is going to get for this $100,000.

A more thorough proposal would say something like this: "We will conduct a study and produce a final report, consisting of not fewer than 200 pages, for $100,000." Here, at least, the proposer is saying what the customer is going to get for his $100,000. Even at this point it is possible to be unethical. For example, you could provide a proposal of blank paper or, what is more likely, a study report consisting of pure nonsense.

In this book, however, I am teaching you to write proposals that are sound not only technically, but also ethically.

15.4.4   Good Customer Relations

There is another reason for being very explicit about what you propose to deliver for the money you are paid. It makes the customer aware of what he is going to get.

There is a saying among contract computer professionals that *the worst kind of customer is a dumb customer.* Thus, it is in your interest to convert him into a smart customer by keeping him aware of what you are doing. There is another saying that *you never want to surprise your customers.* Both the *tasks and the deliverables* should be spelled out in the proposal.

Even with fixed price proposals, it is a good idea to attach a price to each deliverable. Then if, for any reason, the contract needs to be modified, extended, or otherwise renegotiated, it is always possible to get a reasonable update of the cost by reviewing the list of deliverables that have been provided to date. Also, from a purely cash flow point of view, it is better to get payments as the contract goes along rather than wait to the end and get a single lump sum payment. A variation of this approach is called "progress payments," but a good progress payment schedule will attach a particular payment to a tangible piece of progress, which to me means a document.

15.4.5   Payment Schedules

With time and materials (T&M) contracts and cost plus fixed fee (CPFF) contracts, payments are normally made in response to monthly invoices, unless some other arrangement has been requested and agreed upon (see figures 15-6 through 15-10).

15.5   GENERAL PROPOSAL STRUCTURE

The general contents, not necessarily in this order, of the technical proposal are as follows:

- Executive Summary
- Introduction
- Understanding of the Problem
- Technical Approach
- Management Approach
- Deliverables
- Individual Qualifications
- Corporate Qualifications

This chapter contains parts of a proposal to one of my firm's customers. This was a successful proposal, and it is written basically in accordance with the above outline, but with some differences.

Writing a proposal is like writing music or painting with oils. You must first *know the rules* before you can *break the rules.*

There are some differences between the above outline and the sample proposal. The sample proposal can, however, be used very effectively as a reference during the following discussion.

Figures 15-11 and 15-12 show the title page and table of contents of the sample proposal.

15.5.1   Executive Summary

This is a frontispiece for a proposal and should be provided only if the introduction, technical, understanding, and management sections total more than fifty pages. The sample proposal does not contain an executive summary.

As with all executive summaries, the proposal summary should be a true summary, not a reproduction of other parts of the proposal. It should contain not more than three pages.

A RECORDS MANAGEMENT TRAINING PROGRAM
FOR THREE LEVELS OF MANAGEMENT—
TOP MANAGEMENT, MIDDLE MANAGEMENT
AND FIRST LINE SUPERVISORS

SUBMITTED TO:
The Office of Records Management
National Archives Records Service
AUGUST 19, 19XX

Figure 15-11. Sample Proposal Title Page

TABLE OF CONTENTS

Figure 15-12. Sample Proposal Table of Contents

The contents of the executive summary should come from the introduction, the understanding, the technical proposal, and the management approach. It should be written in as interesting and lively a manner as possible, because it will be read by people without the time or inclination to read the more detailed parts of the proposal.

15.5.2 Introduction

The introduction contains a brief background statement on the nature of the problem and a brief summary about what the company proposes to do (see figures 15-13a through 15-13f). This section should be written as if the intended reader has no prior knowledge at all of the proposed effort. Indeed, there may be many readers who fit into this category, for example, the boss of the customer as well as the chief accountant, the legal counsel, and the procurement officer of the company.

The introduction should start off with a statement of the problem (see figure 15-13b). For example, if you are proposing to automate a warehouse, you might begin something like this: "In the last two years, the central warehouse facility of XYZ Corporation has developed a six-month backlog of customer orders. The XYZ Company has determined that the only way to get caught up with, and to stay abreast of, the orders is to automate its inventory control operations. Our company has written the following proposal to determine the feasibility of automating inventory control in the warehouse, to design a system that will do the job, and to develop that system using the company's existing facilities."

I. INTRODUCTION

Every organization in the federal government, whether
department, office, bureau, or branch, has one particular
thing in common with all the rest--they all generate
records. To the extent that each organization originates,
distributes, reproduces, files, and processes the records
which it produces or acquires, the organization is
engaged in what administrators call records management.

Records management is an integral part of able, efficient
management, yet few organizations, whether inside or
outside the federal government, make effective use of
records management principles. Few organizations use
the techniques of sound records management to improve
office efficiency, to reduce forms processing time,
or to enhance the quality of interpersonal communications.

Moreover, it is a rare organization that a) recognizes
the existence of records management as one facet of
management, separable in concept but integral to the task
of management, and b) utilizes records management concepts
in any conscious and deliberate way in order to achieve
specific management objectives.

The National Archives Records Service's Office of Records
Management is the federal government's center of records
management expertise. The Office of Records Management
(ORM) is chartered by the Federal Records Management
Amendment of 1976 to promote management efficiency
through developing and promulgating standards and guidelines
in records management.

Figure 15-13a. Sample Proposal Introduction

Next the introduction should have a section giving some *more details about the problem* (see figures 15-13b and 15-13c). The introduction
should then *summarize your approach.* It should *give a brief statement of
the management essentials, such as the schedule and deliverables.* It is appropriate in the introduction to *say a little bit about the proposer's particular qualifications* to do this job.

Sometimes the introduction closes with *a highlights section,* that is, a
section which tells what are the unique and outstanding features of this
particular proposal. For example, you might have just done a first-rate
inventory control system for someone else, and can use exactly the same
people with no relearning costs, or perhaps your company is proposing
to use a canned package that can be readily installed on the customer's
facilities. Any really special feature that the reader should know about
can be placed in the highlights section.

In order to carry out its mission ORM provides its records management expertise to other agencies of the federal government through publication of the standards which it develops and through the evaluation and control of government forms. ORM also provides technical assistance directly to personnel of other agencies through audits and on site agency studies. The latter functions are performed when needs are highly visible and the agency's problems are particularly acute. Such activities impose a severe drain on the Office's professional staff resources; and the demand is such that ORM has much more such "business" than it can handle with its existing human resources.

statement of the problem

The long term solution to the problem is the function of providing training to agencies so that the agencies can improve their own records management through internal programs of self help, built upon the technical and managerial skills they have acquired through the courses of the Office of Records Management.

more details about the problem

Here again the resources of the Office are severely strained to provide training at the appropriate level, at the proper depth, and to the proper extent for each client agency. The training programs conducted by ORM must be adaptable to the particular audience's needs. This means intensive and extensive attention of the Office's professionals on an individual basis in each agency. In other words the presence of a qualified Office of Records Management professional is mandatory. Still, it is not practical to design a special course for each agency.

Moreover, the courses which constitute the Records Management Training Program must be directed within each agency at three different levels of management---top management, middle management, and first line supervisors.

Figure 15-13b. Sample Proposal Introduction (cont.)

If you do not need a highlights section, leave it out because it may raise the question of whether there are "lowlights" in the proposal. The introduction should be brief, professional, and competent sounding; then the *technical approach, management approach,* and *understanding* sections should speak for themselves.

15.5.3 Understanding of the Problem

In this section, the proposal writing team must demonstrate its knowledge of the problem to be solved. For example, in a warehouse inventory control system, it would be appropriate to give facts and figures

This is not to say that the three courses which make
up the program would be totally different from one another.
Many components of the courses would be common to all.
(Peter F. Drucker's most recent large work, "Management---
Tasks, Responsibilities, and Practices" lays heavy stress
on the concerns and responsibilities common to all three
levels). Still management's decreasing involvement with
details and increasing involvement in policy=making and
conceptualization as the individual moves up the ladder
and indeed, the manager's dwindling amounts of time
which can be allotted to coursework must both be reflected
in the Records Management Training Program.

A thorough, detailed records management course for
first line supervisors---individuals who are working
professionals---must be short enough not to impact
their workload but long enough to cover the essential
technical material. A reasonable time for them would
be about 8 hours.

Moving up the hierarchy, middle and top management
officials have less time and less need for the mechanics
and techniques of records handling as increasingly greater
amounts of their time and attention are taken up by
policy matters. For them, sessions of 4 hours, and 1
hour, respectively, would more accurately reflect their
available time and the pressures of executive priorities.

The two longer sessions, the 8=hour first line management
course and the 4=hour middle management course, will
utilize proportionally more comprehensive notes and each
will emphasize certain areas of management effectiveness
through records management.

A particularly effective means of organizing the three
courses into related themes and of maintaining a central
message would be the use of an audio visual aid which
would be common to all three courses.

Figure 15-13c. Sample Proposal Introduction (cont.)

about the situation that confronts the customer in his warehouse, if
those facts and figures are available. Such information establishes the
problem in the context of the customer's own company. In the sample
proposal, this section has been incorporated into the introduction (see
figures 15-13c and 15-13d).

To paint a picture in exact detail about the customer's own dilem-
mas is not in itself sufficient. You should broaden the discussion to
include all you know about the problem in general. In the case of the
warehouse inventory control system, you would move from a discus-

This audio visual (AV) aid would permit all three courses
to build up from the same management foundation. Properly
constructed the AV aid would accomplish the following
objectives:

- introduce the NARS Office of Records Management
- tell the records management story in an interesting
  way
- define records management in its integral relationship
  with all of management
- motivate the various level managers to improve their
  effectiveness through good records management
  practices
- describe and explain basic, effective records
  management elements and functions
- illustrate the means by which sound records
  management programs can be put into practice
  within the agencies' own offices

Skees Associates Inc. is uniquely qualified to perform the
extensive analysis and client interviews prerequisite to developing
the course, writing the mandatory several hundred pages
of student handout material, and filming the audio visual
aid. We have developed courses in related fields of management
using the professional skills required in the above tasks
and, most significantly, we have recently developed a
similar course in records management for one of our clients
(please refer to the Corporate Qualifications chapter for
a description of the course).

Skees Associates Inc. is a management consulting firm. As a
contractor in the Washington D.C. area, we have extensive
credentials in professional management; our employees are
professionals who are highly respected in the management
sciences and in the field of information science.

Figure 15-13d. Sample Proposal Introduction (cont.)

sion of the client's own warehouse problem to the common characteristics of all warehouses which deal with this kind of inventory.

It is appropriate to inject some theoretical considerations. For example, in warehousing, the economics of bulk shipping and storing, shelf-life, optimum order quantity and optimum shipping quantity, economic re-order point, and other measures and formulae of inventory control can be discussed.

Tension and Climax. A good proposal should build up a certain amount of tension just as a good novel does. In finishing up the *under-*

```
Our staff has prepared and presented courses in modern
management to the federal government and to the general
public.  With our audio visual resources as well,
Skees Associates Inc. is in a position to provide all
the professional capabilities required for this undertaking
and has the resources to complete the work effort
in a timely manner at a very modest cost to the government.

Our senior consultant on this project has written a
number of books on management which have been published
under the sponsorship of the American Management Association.

We have the technical skills to develop a total program
concept for the three records management courses and the
audio visual aid which will establish the common thread
among them.  Our research staff has the experience
and professionalism to interview past and potential
client agencies, and to develop and analyze the necessary
survey questionnaire for determination of client learning
requirements.

We will combine these learning requirements with the
teaching objectives of NARS instructors through interviews
in the Office of Records Management in order to generate
the most effective profile for the training program's
course material.

Together with our affiliate corporation, Applied Management
Systems Inc. of Gaithersburg, Maryland, we have a
corporate history of careful and painstaking craftsmanship
in development of management=level training courses.
Our seminars and professional training courses are
presented on a regular basis in the Washington D.C. area
for such sponsors as the George Washington University, and
throughout the United States as well as abroad.  Our
clients include such companies as the New York Telephone
Co. and such agencies as the State Department's Agency
of International Development (AID).
```

Figure 15-13e. Sample Proposal Introduction (cont.)

standing of the problem chapter, you should point out some of the things that can go wrong when the new system is built.

For example, you might mention the possibility of the firm's coming to rely on the automated system and being immobilized if the computer goes down. You might also mention the dangers in letting the computer exercise absolute control over inventory. A system that combines seasonal and nonseasonal merchandise in the same inventory might turn out to be completely unresponsive to market requirements.

I will leave it to your imagination to think of even more catastrophic

> Skees Associates Inc. and its affiliate, Applied Management
> Systems Inc., have a record of successful and noteworthy
> contracts with federal government and commercial clients.
> The professionalism for which we are recognized and our
> sound approach to projects of this type are reflected
> in the task plan contained in the following Scope of Work.

Figure 15-13f. Sample Proposal Introduction (cont.)

things to suggest in your proposal. My point is simply that this is the place to create tension in the minds of your audience, so that they are anxious to look into the *technical approach* section to find out how your company is going to handle these dire possibilities.

15.5.4   Technical Approach

This section is called "Scope of Work" in the sample proposal (see figures 15-14a through 15-14h). It describes the how-to of the proposal.

There are two things to be provided in the *technical approach* chapter. The first is a description of the methodology to be followed. In the case of scientific activities, such as simulation, it is appropriate to talk about the mathematics which will be used and how the model will be developed using those mathematics. In some proposals it is not possible to distinguish the general theoretical approach from the technical tasks. The descriptions of these tasks constitute the second item in the technical approach.

Suppose in the warehouse example that the inventory control system is going to be an on-line system. Shipments which are received are entered into the database. Orders are placed against the database from on-line terminals.

Suppose further that the decisions about what merchandise to reorder and in what quantities to do so are made by the computer, subject to human audit and review. Assume that the computer makes its decisions based on forecasts and that the forecasts are not simple formulae, but the result of a simulation of the warehouse inventory situation. In other words, you are assuming that the warehouse inventory control system contains within it a model of the warehouse in operation.

This model is central to the decision-making activities. It is fed by orders that are placed by human beings in the real world. The model extrapolates from the pattern of these orders to several weeks or months

II.   SCOPE OF WORK

Skees Associates Inc. proposes to perform the following
tasks for the National Archives Records Service's
Office of Records Management.

Task 1.   Orientation

Skees Associates Inc. (SAI) personnel will meet with
designated key officials of NARS to discuss general
policy of the Office of Records Management (ORM) and
the specific objectives of the Office with respect to
the project and the Records Management Training Program.

SAI professionals will review the relevant enabling
legislation such as the Records Management Amendment
of 1976. They will discuss that legislation and NARS
policy with the contract monitor and other NARS officials
in order to more fully understand and appreciate the
charter and training goals of the Office of Records
Management.

Task 2.   NARS Interviews

Skees Associates Inc. staff will interview Office of
Records Management instructors currently engaged in
training. We will talk with such other NARS personnel
as may be designated by the ORM contract monitor,
including those who have participated in earlier ORM
records management programs of instruction.

Figure 15-14a. Sample Proposal Technical Approach

into the future in order to predict what should be on hand at any given
time period (see figure 15-15).

In this situation, the *technical approach* chapter can be divided con-
veniently into two subsections. The first subsection will consist of a
description of the proposed system with all its features. It will describe
the terminals which will be at the users' work stations and the transactions that will take place at the terminals. It will describe the relationship between the various transaction processes and the data base. It will
describe the role of the computer model in the order placing process and
in the decision making process.

The second subsection will consist of a list of the various tasks to be
performed. With each task will be a brief description of that task.

Task Identification   The tasks could be listed in simple chronological

From these interviews we will identify the objectives
of the training program in records management and we
will determine the critical problems as well as the
most important facts, functions, and elements of good
records management as perceived by the instructors.
We will take special note of their recommendations
for emphasis and course content.

SAI staff will also examine and familiarize themselves
with the ongoing workshop and training programs of
NARS with the objective of maintaining compatibility
in the Records Management Training Program with other
courses in the spectrum of ORM training activities.

Task 3. Client Agency Interviews

SAI staff will interview potential clients for NARS
training programs from representative agencies. In
consultation with the contract monitor we will also
talk with selected attendees of other NARS training
courses.

We will identify the needs for office records handling
improvements as they are reported and envisioned by
the agencies' individual managers at their various
levels of management. We will also identify those
training presentations which have been most effective
and most useful in earlier courses.

Task 4. Development of Client Agency Questionnaire

Acting upon the information we have received from our
interviews and with the guidance of the contract monitor,
we will identify client populations and develop a
questionnaire for submittal to several selected agencies.
This questionnaire will be the vehicle for a survey
which will identify the concerns and needs of management

Figure 15-14b. Sample Proposal Technical Approach (cont.)

order. However, most well-managed projects have several tasks running
at a given time and some tasks will operate in parallel (see figures 15-16
and 15-17b). Therefore, it is preferable for the tasks to be numbered and
then listed in numerical order. For example, the task breakdown in the
warehouse application might be as follows:

- Task 1—review of the firm's warehousing operations
- Task 2—analysis of the warehouse operations
- Task 3—data base design
- Task 4—warehouse model draft design

with respect to handling and scheduling of reports, forms, correspondence and directives.

The questionnaire will address the primary elements of records management---directives, forms, reports, correspondence, mail handling and duplication. The survey resulting from the questionnaire will be used in the data analysis of the following task.

Task 5.   Analysis of Client Agency Questionnaire

Questionnaires returned from the agencies will be analyzed by Skees Associates Inc. staff. A profile will be drawn up of the real and preceived needs of the three general levels of management---first line supervision, middle management, and top level management.

The analysis will be performed along the classical lines of the elements and functions of records management--- standards development and promulgation, evaluation, reports, correspondence, directives, forms, copying and mailhandling. The supporting areas of micrographics, automated data processing, and word processing will be incorporated into the analysis, together with the learning objectives which had emerged from the earlier interview sessions.

Task 6.   Development of the Training Program Concept

Based on our analysis of the returns from the various agencies, our interviews with NARS personnel and with representatives of other agencies, Skees Associates Inc. will develop a concept for a training program in records management that can be packaged and presented in three different courses, one for each of the three general levels of management.

Figure 15-14c. Sample Proposal Technical Approach (cont.)

- Task 5—system concept
- Task 6—detailed system design
- Task 7—programming specifications development
- Task 8—programming
- Task 9—system testing
- Task 10—user education
- Task 11—data base loading
- Task 12—parallel operation
- Task 13—system refinement
- Task 14—system operation performance review

The concept will include the use of a single audio
visual aid---filmstrip and phonograph record, or slide
show and cassette recording---which can be utilized
in each of the three courses.

This concept will identify those practices of records
management which can be most effectively conveyed
through the combined media of the course handouts,
classroom instruction and audio visuals. It will
include a basic introduction to the underlying principles
and objectives of scientific records management as
reflected in good business practice.

The concept will address each area of the client population
and the extent to which they will benefit from the
combined handout and audio visual material. It will
provide the means to satisfy the objective of promoting
general management awareness of records management through
discussion of records management in business and government
management terms.

In addition to providing an overview of the way the course
material will be handled, the concept will describe the
usage that will be made of the audio visual accompaniment---
introductory, concluding presentation, interrupted for
discussion---and will recommend the tone and approach
of the two media. It will indicate the recommended
treatment---light, pedantic, unified, topical, and so on.

The course handouts will most likely be recommended to
follow well developed models developed by Skees Associates Inc.
and NARS for similar courses. The concept for the audio
visual component will include a recommended medium,
such as film strip or slides, based on course content,
NARS audio visual equipment resources, resources of the
client organizations and the anticipated size of each
class of attendees.

Figure 15-14d. Sample Proposal Technical Approach (cont.)

Task Naming and Task Description For each of these task names,
a brief paragraph or two should be written to describe the work that
will be performed in that task. If the task cannot be described in a paragraph or two, perhaps it really should be broken into two or more
subtasks.

Each task name should be so explicit that a person familiar with the
project can recognize from the name what is going to be accomplished
in that task. If you cannot come up with a task name that has a verb and
a noun in it, your task may be too broad and need to be broken up into
subtasks.

Task 7. Outlines of Course Handouts

After reviewing and consulting with the Office of Records
Management on NARS's comments on the Training Course
Concept, Skees Associates Inc. will develop course
outlines for each of the three training courses. In
the interest of cost savings for the government, and
in the interest of developing a unified program of
training, we will strive to achieve a maximum overlap
in the use of practices, concepts, objectives and,
where possible, explanatory material among the three
courses. (Please refer to the Corporate Qualifications
chapter for an example of course outlines developed
by Skees Associates Inc.)

Task 8. Course Handouts

Using the comments of the NARS Office of Records Management
staff on the outlines of Task 7, Skees Associates Inc.
will develop full scale handouts for training students,
filling in the details suggested by the outlines. At
this time two versions will be produced for each course---
a student text and an instructor's manual.

These course handouts will be proportional in size and
level of detail to the anticipated duration of each of
the three courses. For example, the top level management
course will be one hour long and consist of approximately
30 pages of student material. Middle management's
course, for a 4-hour seminar, will be approximately
75 pages, and the first line supervisor's, for the
all day session,will run to about 125 pages.

In our experience these are reasonable-length packages.
At present our two day seminars run about 200 pages of
handouts and the three day seminars total about 300
pages with an optional 100 pages of additional homework
reading.

Figure 15-14e. Sample Proposal Technical Approach (cont.)

15.5.5 Sample Task Description

A typical task description might be as follows:

> *Parallel Operation* In this task the system will be op-
> erated in a live mode. Every transaction that arises during
> this time period will be put through the new system. At
> the same time, however, the transaction will be handled in
> the old manual manner as well. The results will be com-
> pared and notations made for future system improve-

The course handouts will be delivered to the National
Archives Records Service's Office of Records Management
for final review and revision. Clerical support for
incorporating the Office's revisions into the final
draft will be provided by Skees Associates Inc.

Task 9. Audio Visuals Planning

After obtaining the NARS comments and guidance on the
Training Program Concept, Skees Associates Inc. will
review the projected requirements of the audio visual
aid and establish the parameters of use of the material---
size of anticipated audiences, viewing-listening accomo-
dations, updatability (implying a static or modular
medium), access to equipment, impact on scheduled equipment,
expertise of operators, and operating training requirements.

Task 10. Preliminary Treatment and Storyboard Development

With the NARS guidance from the Training Program Concept
and the parameters established in Task 9, we will
develop a preliminary script and a "shot list". These
will reflect the training concepts and implement the
learning objectives of Task 6.

We will work the script into a complete narrative, suitable
for recording by a professional announcer. The storyboard's
accompanying illustrations will be paced and modified
as necessary, requiring possible modifications of the
narrative as well, for a well integrated presentation.

The graphics requiring professional artwork and onsite
camera work will be roughed out for the artist. Colors
and other unifying factors will be worked in.

Figure 15-14f. Sample Proposal Technical Approach (cont.)

ments. During this phase the system will be considered to
be in a test mode. That is, the system may be shut off or
started up as necessary to check on its operation. Also any
orders generated by the system may be overridden by the
system manager.

The parallel operation mode will continue until (a) the
system manager has declared the system to be acceptable
or (b) he has decided that extensive revision must be done
before the task can be meaningfully continued or (c) the
end of two weeks' parallel operation is reached—
whichever comes first. At the end of this task the observations about the parallel operation will be collected into a
single report and recommendations will be made for (a)

Task 11. Graphic Production and Voice Recording

Artwork identified in the preceding task will be developed
by professional artists under SAI supervision. Scenes
on location and scenes requiring studio layouts will
be prepared and lighting arrangements coordinated
with photographers and other graphic arts professionals.
Filming and sound recording will be performed under
SAI supervision.

Task 12. Final Audio Visual Production

The filmed material and the narrative will be edited,
synchronized, titled and processed for final copy in
the audio visual lab under SAI supervision, in accordance
with guidance previously established in consultation
with NARS Office of Records Management as a result
of their review of Task 6.

Task 13. Delivery of the Finished Product and Simulated
          Training

In this task, Skees Associates Inc. will present to the
government two copies of the handouts for the three
training courses-^--each course handout consisting of
a student text and an instructor's manual---and a
master copy of the audio visual aid.

We will then conduct a training course with designated
NARS Office of Records Management staff members as
students. The course which we will conduct will be
the longest of the three, the supervisor's course, so
as to give the Office staff the maximum exposure to the
new material.

This simulated training session will also serve to
familiarize the staff with the use of the audio visual
aid in the context of the course setting.

Figure 15-14g. Sample Proposal Technical Approach (cont.)

modifications that must be made immediately and (b)
other modifications which are important but which can
wait until the refinement phase.

15.5.6 Management Approach

This is the section in which the businessmen in the client's company
will be most interested (see figures 15-17a through 15-17e). It contains

Task 14. Project Summary and Final Report

Skees Associates Inc. will provide a brief history of
all the project tasks and a summary of the SAI team's
activities and experiences in carrying out the work
of this contract effort. Particular stress will be
placed on needs and requirements as expressed and
identified by the interviewees at the other agencies
and upon the learning objectives which they represent.

Any learning objectives, as well as client agency or
NARS Office of Records Management needs, which were
identified during the project, but which were determined
to be outside the scope of this effort, will be described
to the government in this report. Such records may
be of assistance to the Office in ascertaining the
usefulness of future NARS Office of Records Management
training programs.

Also we will include in the final report any findings
of a general nature which represent opportunities
for cost savings and expediting the research and development
of other NARS courses in the future.

We propose to conduct the preceding tasks in accordance
with the following Management Plan.

Figure 15-14h. Sample Proposal Technical Approach (cont.)

the timetable within which each of the tasks will be completed and
identifies the organization of the team that will be doing the job. *It shows
what the day-to-day responsibilities* of each of the team members are. *It
describes the liaison* that will exist between the proposing company and
the client's organization.

Timetable   Normally a timetable is presented in the form of a Gantt
chart as shown in figure 15-17b. It is important to call the reader's
attention to anything that is unusual or of particular interest about the
schedule.

If two tasks overlap in a special way or run in parallel for some
reason, this fact should be pointed out and the explanation given. For
example, testing should begin as soon as there are programs to test even
if not all the programming is completed.

This presupposes the availability of a good test plan. It is always
wise to point out to the reader that the testing can begin before programming is finished because readers are not typically aware of the

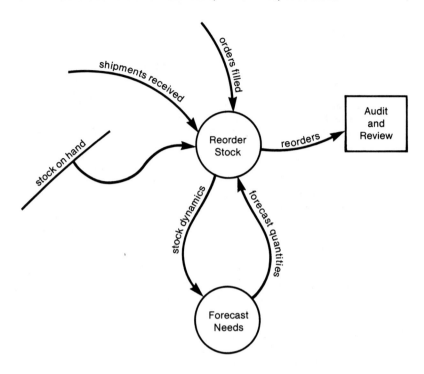

Figure 15-15. Inventory Control System Containing Forecasting Model

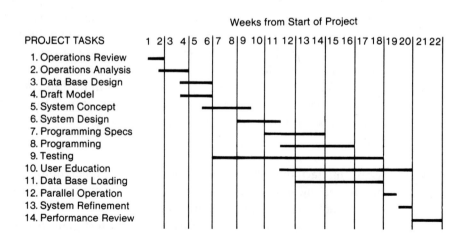

Figure 15-16. Project Schedule for Warehouse System

III. MANAGEMENT PLAN

Project Schedule
  (see figure 1.)
Project Team Organization
  (see figure 2.)
Areas of Responsibility
  Project Manager—William D. Skees, President of Skees Associates Inc.
  Mr. Skees will have overall responsibility for the project and for the
  technical accuracy and quality of all deliverables. As a technical
  contributor as well, he will conduct the initial NARS and client
  agency interviews, analyze the learning objectives, and manage
  the development of the training program concept.

Figure 15-17a. Sample Proposal Management Approach

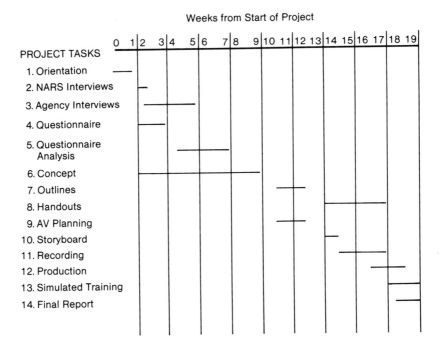

Figure 15-17b. Sample Proposal Management Approach (cont.)

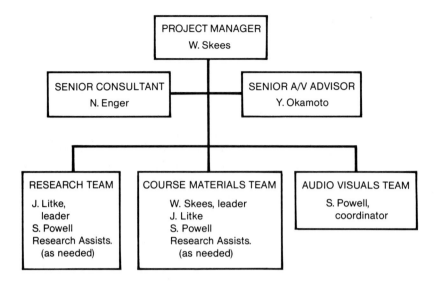

Figure 15-17c. Sample Proposal Management Approach (cont.)

great flexibility there is in the programming/testing activities and they are usually not aware of good structured programming and structured testing principles.

In addition, many readers are not aware of the importance of having a test plan. They assume that the test is driven by the programs rather than the other way around. This is a holdover from the days of the 1960's before the importance of program reliability began to be recognized.

A project may need to be finished by a certain date for some reason external to the project, such as a scheduled abandonment of the old warehouse and occupation of a new and modern warehouse. This type of contingency should be explained in this section also.

Organization Chart   Present an organization chart (see figure 15-17c). Reviewers like to see them so they know who is the key person, who are the key subordinates, and what the correct titles are.

The chart also shows whether the group has been divided into teams and subteams and, if so, who reports to whom. It shows which team is going to be working on which tasks.

It is important not only for the client but also for the author of the proposal to know what the management scheme is going to be. The material in the proposal should not just be for the client's benefit; all these things are important for the people who are doing the work too.

Senior Consultant - Norman L. Enger, President of
Applied Management Systems, Inc. Mr.
Enger will develop the agency questionnaire,
meet with key NARS personnel and participate
in selected agency interviews. He will
have primary responsibility for analysis
of the questionnaire and for the
design analysis of the training program
concept. He will also provide senior
guidance in development of the course
outlines and the course handout material.

Senior Audio Visual Advisor - Yoichi R. Okamoto. Mr.
Okamoto will be responsible for the quality
of the audio visual presentation —
tone, pace, appearance, message and
impact. He will also perform some of
the photographic tasks for the audio visual
aid which will be common to all three
courses.

Research Analyst - Joan Litke, Management Specialist.
Ms. Litke will participate in the formulation
of the questionnaire and will lead the data
analysis effort. She will also participate
in all documentation tasks, and in most
SAI-government interview sessions. She
will utilize her extensive experience in
management studies and organizational
procedures in the development of the three
courses' handout materials.

Technical Writer - Susan F. Powell, Technical Advisor
and Media Specialist. Ms. Powell will
participate in the data gathering activities
of the project tasks. During those tasks
devoted to audio visual production she
will serve as coordinator between the
management analysts' team and the audio
visual artists and technicians.

Figure 15-17d. Sample Proposal Management Approach (cont.)

15.5.7   Individual Qualifications

By the time he reaches the staff qualifications section, the reader of your proposal knows what you plan to do if you win the contract and how you plan to go about it. Now the reader wants to know which people are going to do the work and what their particular qualifications are. This section of the proposal provides that information. It contains the resumes of the individuals who will be assigned to the project.

Other Skees Associates Inc. Personnel - In a project
    of this type, with its severe time constraints,
    there may arise from time to time the need to
    provide additional manpower for short periods
    of time, in order to handle peak workloads
    in such areas as questionnaire analysis and
    development of student text handouts and
    instructor's manuals from the approved outlines
    of the three courses. In such cases we anticipate
    the possible use of other Skees Associates Inc.
    professionals in the management sciences.
    These staff members will be utilized at all
    times in a manner consistent with the interests
    of the government, being fully qualified, properly
    briefed, and 100% productive, available to
    the project team strictly on an as needed basis.

Other Management Sciences and Clerical Resource Personnel
    For the purposes of this project as we have often
    done in the past, Skees Associates Inc. has teamed
    with Applied Management Systems Inc. of Gaithersburg,
    Maryland. Mr. Norman L. Enger, our proposed
    senior consultant, is the president of Applied
    Management Systems Inc. (AMS). This arrangement
    has the particular advantage that the combined
    clerical and administrative resources of the two
    companies, SAI and AMS, will be available to the
    project team, headed by Mr. Skees.

Audio Visual Production Personnel - In developing the
    audio visual training aid deliverable described
    in the Scope of Work, Skees Associates Inc. will
    utilize the services of one or more of the firms
    which are identified in the Corporate Qualifications
    chapter and with whom our staff have worked on
    other joint projects.

Figure 15-17e. Sample Proposal Management Approach (cont.)

Commitment of Individuals   In some projects it will not be possible
to identify ahead of time exactly which individuals will be working on
the project. This frequently happens with contracts which are advertised months in advance of the actual award data. Obviously it would
not be possible for a vendor to have his people sitting around all that
time waiting for the contract to be awarded.

It is expected, however, that the key personnel in the project will be
those proposed. In other words, the most important positions should be
as advertised in the proposal. This is most important with R&D type
work because in this type of work something is going to be done that

has never been done exactly that way before. Success is highly dependent on the capabilities of the individuals who will do the work.

Unpredictable Levels of Effort   In some contracts, such as time and
materials (T&M) contracts, it may be impossible to predict ahead of time
how many people will be required. In such cases, it is not possible to
identify all the individuals who would be ultimately working on each
task. Sometimes neither party knows until a week or so before a particular task commences.

If such is the case, you should provide at proposal time resumes of
all the people who are qualified to do the work. Then include a statement to the effect that the people who are to do the work will be selected
from among those whose resumes are provided. Typical wording is as
follows:

> Company X intends to provide the services of the individ-
> uals identified in this proposal to accomplish the contract
> tasks. If for any reason a proposed individual cannot be
> made available for a particular task, Company X will pro-
> vide another individual of equal or higher qualifications.

Changes in Personnel   In the natural course of things people leave
companies and new people come on board. Thus it may happen that
between the time the proposal is submitted and the time the contract is
awarded, significant changes have occurred in the staffing for the contract. This cannot be helped. Neither the seasoned vendor nor the seasoned procurement officer will be flustered by this situation. However,
it is always possible that one party or the other may be inexperienced.
The best way to avoid any unpleasant reactions is to include a statement
like the above.

15.5.8 Corporate Qualifications

This section describes the capabilities of the firm as represented by
previous experience. Use the same device as in the "individual qualifications" section—the slanted resume. A slanted resume emphasizes the
aspects of an individual's work experience that are immediately relevant to the project (see section 15.7.1). In this case, however, the slanted
resume is a resume of the company and of the company's experience on
a particular project. It is called a statement of corporate qualifications.

Again, assume that you are proposing an inventory control system
and that you wish to describe previous inventory control system development efforts of your firm. You must check the company's files and

bring out all the contracts that developed or dealt with inventory control systems.

Project titles may not give the necessary information. You may need to look closely at each project description or else rely on your own memory. For example, a project may be called the ACME Project, indicating simply that the work was done for the ACME Corporation even though the major project effort may have been to develop an order filling capability to which inventory control was a subordinate part.

Rewrite the project description to highlight the inventory control features and deemphasize the rest of the project.

Here the ethics must be examined closely. I object most strongly, and I think any professional would, to the notion of fabricating inventory control experience when the corporation has none. However, corporations, like individual people, have rich and varied backgrounds. The corporation may well have developed a very important and significant inventory control system in order to build the order filling capability on the ACME Project. However, the inventory control system may not have been identified as such because the marketing thrust of the effort was with order filling.

Nobody is going to come up and ask you if in doing project X you had inventory control experience. It's your job to look analytically at project X and ask yourself if there was some experience in it that can be exploited for this particular proposal.

15.6 PROPOSAL STRATEGY

The overriding strategy in most straightforward proposals is to *feature the things specifically sought in the request for proposal (RFP)*. After all you must assume that customers know what they're looking for. But *give them better than what they asked for,* either at no extra cost, or as an option, if the improvement has to be priced separately. If they ask for the impossible, offer something that is possible and tell them why it is better than what they wanted.

15.6.1 Postbid Strategy

Usually if proposals go into a second round elimination, the vendors are asked if they want to modify their proposal. Typically this means an invitation to lower the price. Do *not* change the technical content of your proposal as you might be ruled out of the bidding. You may add a new feature, but the only safe course is a simple price reduction.

15.6.2 Harsh Realities of Proposals

Some RFPs call for "God and Motherhood." That is, they ask the preparer, not to use his technical skills and imagination, but to provide something very cut and dried, such as programmer hours or raw machine time.

In such situations you may be tempted to skip the management section, thinking, "Well everyone knows the programmers will work under a senior programmer. Why should we spell it out in the proposal?"

Disregard the temptation, and go ahead and say the things that everyone knows. Your real opportunity in this situation comes from dressing up the mundane facts. For example, show the form and explain the procedure whereby the senior programmer assigns work to his subordinates and evaluates their programming efforts. Remember the most mundane facts look interesting when properly presented.

15.7 RÉSUMÉS

Résumés should always be honest and accurately reflect the qualifications and experience of the individuals proposed. The usual contents of a résumé are shown in figure 15-18. A sample résumé is shown in figure 15-19.

15.7.1 Slanted Résumés

You may *slant* a résumé to emphasize the particular experience that your customer wants to know about. This is not misrepresenting. This is *changing the emphasis* of a document.

Human beings are very complex individuals with very rich backgrounds. Say that for the inventory control system, COBOL programmers are needed. Perhaps an individual proposed for this inventory control system was previously listed in a proposal to a different client as being a FORTRAN programmer. If the individual in question is qualified both as a FORTRAN programmer and as a COBOL programmer, then it is perfectly ethical and appropriate to bid him on one

- NAME—written as the person signs his name
  For example, John D. Doe
- CLASSIFICATION—usually the position held or position proposed or applied for, as Project Manager
- ACADEMIC CREDENTIALS—usually all degrees and associated work, with highest attainment listed first, as
  - M.A.—University of Illinois
  - Post graduate—Universities of Wisconsin & Kentucky, American University, Catholic University

  If the individual holds an M.A. or PhD, then the baccalaureate degree is not mentioned unless it came from a prestigious school such as Harvard or Yale.
- YEARS   ⎫ Repeated for each
- POSITION   ⎪ *relevant* position, in
- EMPLOYER   ⎬ reverse chronological
- DESCRIPTION OF RESPONSIBILITIES   ⎭ order

  Example 1965–1967 Manager of Operating Systems— University of Kentucky

  Responsible for maintenance and enhancement of the IBM 7040 and IBM 360 Operating Systems, applications library, and teleprocessing subsystem. Also managed data center, keypunch section, and computer operations
- PUBLICATIONS—any relevant articles or books written

  Example *Computer Software for Data Communications*, Lifetime Learning, 1981.
- LANGUAGES—all computer languages known, if position sought is programming

  Examples FORTRAN, COBOL, BASIC, PL/I, Algol, MAD, ALC, IITRAN, SPS, Symbol/Metasymbol, COMPASS

Figure 15-18. Contents of a Résumé

job as a FORTRAN programmer while bidding him on a second job as a COBOL programmer.

Likewise, you may propose an individual as the potential manager of the inventory control system development team by virtue of his ex-

JOHN J. DOE   Senior Programmer Analyst

Education: Fordham University 1967–1971
            AB, mathematics
            Cornell University 1972–1974
            MS, computer science

1978– present   Martin-Marietta—Group Leader. Designs and develops computer systems from specifications supplied by operating divisions. Leads team of programmers and analysts using data base management software on large scale IBM equipment.

1974–1978   Boeing Computer Corporation—Senior Programmer. Member of team developing large scale simulations for customers. —Programmer. Member of team converting systems from large scale CDC computers to IBM and Amdahl mainframes.

1971–1972   Boeing Computer Corporation—Programmer. Programmed and tested modules of customer manufacturing control system.

Computers: IBM 360, 370, 3300, 4300; CDC 6600, CYBER 170, 172

Languages: ALC, BAL, COMPASS, FORTRAN, COBOL, PL/I

Figure 15-19. Sample Résumé

tensive experience in inventory control. On an earlier job he may have been bid to do simulations because of his extensive simulations experience. In fact this same individual may have developed the inventory control simulation model in a previous job and done that work in FORTRAN. He can carry over the same simulations and inventory control experience into this new proposed effort.

His COBOL experience may have dated from earlier years before he got into inventory control. Perhaps he was supporting an accounting office which would be directly relevant to inventory control and warehouse bookkeeping.

Figures 15-20a and 15-20b show two different résumés for the same individual. Both of them can be honest and accurate. One of them emphasizes the individual's scientific experience, while the other emphasizes his business experience.

JOHN J. DOE   Senior Programmer Analyst

Education: Fordham University 1967–1971
AB, mathematics
Cornell University 1972–1974
MS, computer science

1978– present   Martin-Marietta—Group Leader. Designs and develops computer systems from specifications supplied by operating divisions. Led team of programmers and analysts in developing a financial reporting subsystem using data base management software on large scale IBM equipment.

1974– 1978   Boeing Computer Corporation—Senior Programmer. Member of team developing large scale simulations for customers. —Programmer. Member of team converting systems from large scale CDC computers to IBM and Amdahl mainframes.

1971– 1972   Boeing Computer Corporation—Programmer. Programmed and tested modules of customer manufacturing control system.

Computers: IBM 360, 370, 3300, 4300; CDC 6600, CYBER 170, 172

Languages: ALC, BAL, COMPASS, FORTRAN, COBOL, PL/I

Figure 15-20a. Sample Résumé with Business Slant

15.8   BIOGRAPHICAL STATEMENTS

It is common nowadays to see bios (small biographical statements) in informal documents such as marketing brochures. For an example of such a brochure and biographical statement see figure 15-4.

In such a document the emphasis is on brevity and pointedness; in other words, everything, including the bio, should be aimed directly at the brochure's objective. Everything in the bio in figure 15-4 has a direct bearing on the instructor's programming background and his teaching ability.

JOHN J. DOE Senior Programmer Analyst

Education: Fordham University 1967–1971
AB, mathematics

Cornell University 1972–1974
MS, computer science

1978–present Martin-Marietta—Group Leader. Designs and develops computer systems from specifications supplied by operating divisions. Led team of programmers and analysts in developing stress analysis models. Implemented large scale stress scenarios using data base management techniques.

1974–1978 Boeing Computer Corporation—Senior Programmer. Member of team developing large scale simulations for customers. —Programmer. Member of team converting systems from large scale CDC computers to IBM and Amdahl mainframes.

1971–1972 Boeing Computer Corporation—Programmer. Programmed and tested modules of customer manufacturing control system, including simulation of engine performance.

Computers: IBM 360, 370, 3300, 4300; CDC 6600, CYBER 170, 172

Languages: ALC, BAL, COMPASS, FORTRAN, COBOL, PL/I

Figure 15-20b. Sample Résumé with Scientific Slant

15.9 HIGHLIGHTS

- Promotional documents are written to convince someone to buy something. The best-known promotional document is the proposal.

- Promotional documents must create a need, identify that need, and show how you propose to satisfy that need.

- The proposal tells the reader what he will receive if he does business with you. A well-written proposal can function as a contract.

- Be as explicit as possible when writing proposals. Both tasks and deliverables should be spelled out.

- A proposal should include the following sections: Executive Summary (if the proposal is lengthy), Introduction, Understanding of the Problem, Technical Approach, Management Approach, Deliverables, Individual Qualifications, and Corporate Qualifications.

- The Individual Qualifications section includes résumés of the people who will be working on the project. These may be slanted to highlight the relevant experience of the individual.

Bibliography

Documentation Standards

Enger, Norman L. *Documentation Standards for Computer Systems.* Fairfax Station, Va.: Technology Press, 1976. Forms with emphasis on their use in system documentation.

———. *Management Standards for Developing Information Systems.* New York: American Management Associations, 1976. Good ideas on data collection forms with emphasis on management considerations.

Rubin, Martin L., ed. *Documentation Standards and Procedures for Online Systems.* New York: Van Nostrand Reinhold, 1979. Documentation, including forms and procedures, for online systems.

Tausworthe, Robert C. *Standardized Development of Computer Software, Part II Standards.* Englewood Cliffs, N.J.: Prentice-Hall, 1979. A lengthy set of notes about a certain instance of documentation.

Wooldridge, Susan. *Systems and Programming Standards.* New York: Petrocelli/Charter, 1977. Good ideas on data collection forms; oriented towards card and tape systems.

Estimating Computer Project Costs

Brandon, Dick H. *Data Processing Organization and Manpower Planning.* New York: Petrocelli/Charter, 1974. Worth a quick reading on staffing philosophy.

Brooks, Frederick P. Jr. *The Mythical Man-Month: Essays in Software Engineering.* Reading, Mass.: Addison-Wesley, 1975.

287

Putnam, Larry. "Estimating Software Costs." *Datamation,* September 1979, 189–98.

Wofsey, Marvin M. *Management of Automatic Data Processing Systems.* Washington, D.C.: Thompson Book Co., 1968. Similar to Dick Brandon's book.

Management—Effective Practice

Del Regno, Nancy. "Managing Executive Time." *Travelhost,* 24 May, 1981. A view of time as an irreplaceable resource; practical suggestions on making the best use of time (not DP oriented).

Townsend, Robert C. *Up the Organization.* Greenwich, Conn.: Fawcett, 1978.

Programming—Effective Practice

Kernighan, Brian W., and Plaugher, P. J. *The Elements of Programming Style.* 2nd ed. New York: McGraw-Hill, 1978.

Ledgard, Henry F. *Programming Proverbs.* Rochelle Park, N.J.: Hayden, 1975.

————. *Programming Proverbs for Fortran Programmers.* Rochelle Park, N.J.: Hayden, 1975.

Ledgard, Henry F., and Chmuva, Louis J. Jr. *COBOL with Style: Programming Proverbs.* Rochelle Park, N.J.: Hayden, 1976.

Proposals

Paxson, William C. *The Business Writing Handbook.* New York: Bantam Books, 1981. Good summary; contains brief but useful chapter on proposals, RFPs, packaging with examples of a construction/engineering proposal and a study proposal.

Quality Assurance

Glass, Robert L. *Software Reliability Guidebook.* Englewood Cliffs, N.J.: Prentice-Hall, 1979. A comprehensive and analytic catalogue of contemporary system testing methods.

Myers, Glenford J. *The Art of Software Testing.* New York: John Wiley and Sons, 1979. An important book about the real objectives of testing and what testing can accomplish.

Résumés

Biegeleisen, J. I. *Job Résumés.* New York: Grosset & Dunlap, 1976. Layouts of sample résumés, steps in gathering and organizing input material.

Brennan, L. D.; Strand, S.; and Gruber, E. G. *Résumés for Better Jobs.* New York: Monarch Press, 1973. Similar to Biegeleisen's book.

Faux, Marian. *The Complete Résumé Guide.* New York: Monarch Press, 1980. Includes worksheets. Special sections for those over forty and for handicapped.

Lewis, Adele. *How to Write Better Résumés.* New York: Barron's Educational Series, 1977. Same as Marian Faux' plus section on identifying the right employer.

Jackson, Tom. *The Perfect Résumé.* Garden City, N.Y.: Anchor Books, 1981. Sections on college graduates and on women re-entering the job market.

System Analysis

DeMarco, Tom. *Structured Analysis and System Specification.* New York: Yourdon, 1978. Highly readable explanation of structured analysis with lots of examples.

Gane, Chris, and Sarson, Trish. *Structured Systems Analysis: Tools and Techniques.* Englewood Cliffs, N.J.: Prentice-Hall, 1979. Equivalent to Tom DeMarco's book but more rigorous, with different graphics.

Katzan, Harry Jr. *Systems Design and Documentation.* New York: Van Nostrand Reinhold, 1976. A lucid treatment of HIPO.

Myers, Glenford J. *Composite/Structured Design.* New York: Van Nostrand Reinhold, 1978. A developed philosophy of structured design.

———. *Reliable Software through Composite Design.* New York: Petrocelli/Charter, 1975. An introduction to structured design principles.

Writing—Communication

Bates, Jefferson D. *Writing with Precision.* Washington, D.C.: Acropolis Books, 1978. A very practical writing guide, aimed primarily at creative writing.

Department of the Air Force. *Guide for Air Force Writing.* Washington, D.C.: Government Printing Office, 1960. $1.75. Contains detailed treatment of fog index.

Gunning, Robert. *Technique of Clear Writing.* Rev. ed. New York: McGraw-Hill, 1968.

Holcombe, Marya W., and Stein, Judith K. *Writing for Decision Makers.* Belmont Ca.: Lifetime Learning Publications, 1981. Techniques for turning out well-planned, well-worded, and timely memoranda and reports.

"Plain Letters for Managers." A training course in good writing practice, available to federal, state, and local government employees. Contact: General Services Administration; GSA Training Center; Washington, D.C. 20406.

Sheppard, Mona. *Plain Letters: the Secret of Successful Business Writing.* New York: Simon & Schuster, 1960.

Smith, Randi Sigmund. *Written Communication for Data Processing.* New York: Van Nostrand Reinhold, 1976.

Winett, Ruth Schiff. A series of twelve articles on better writing which appeared in *Computerworld* from 1 October 1979 through 17 December 1979.

Writing—Handbooks and Manuals

Dorris, L., and Miller, B. M. *Complete Secretary's Handbook.* 4th ed. Englewood Cliffs, N.J.: Prentice-Hall, 1977. Similar to Eckersley-Johnson handbook but in brighter style.

Eckersley-Johnson, A. L., ed. *Webster's Secretarial Handbook.* Springfield, Mass.: G. & C. Merriam, 1976. Word usage, correspondence style including salutations and closings, many other things.

Hutchinson, Lois Irene. *Standard Handbook for Secretaries.* New York: McGraw-Hill, 1979. Similar to Eckersley-Johnson, but in less lively format.

Mallery, Richard D. *Grammar, Rhetoric and Composition.* New York: Barnes & Noble, 1967. Ideas on writing, good usage, and effective expression.

The McGraw-Hill Author's Book. New York: McGraw-Hill, 1968. Recommendations on how to prepare manuscript.

Prentice-Hall Author's Guide. Englewood Cliffs, N.J.: Prentice-Hall, 1975. Similar to the McGraw-Hill book.

Strunk, William Jr., and White, E. B. *The Elements of Style.* 3rd ed. New York: Macmillan, 1979. A brief, classic guide to writers' style.

Turabian, Kate L. *A Manual for Writers of Term Papers, Theses, and Dissertations.* 4th ed. Chicago: University of Chicago Press, 1973. Similar to the publishers' guides, but aimed at academic reading audiences.

Ziegler, Isabelle. *The Creative Writer's Handbook.* 2d ed. New York: Barnes & Noble, 1975. A guide to making writing interesting enough for publication.

Writing—Spelling

Ellis, Kaethe. *The Word Book.* Boston: Houghton Mifflin, 1976. List of 40,000 words spelled and divided.

Leslie, Louis A. *20,000 Words.* 7th ed. New York: McGraw-Hill, 1977. Pocket-sized list in dictionary sequence, similar to Kaethe Ellis' book, but with fewer words.

Miller, Shirley M. *Webster's New World Speller/Divider.* New York: Simon & Schuster, 1971. Similar to the others but with 33,000 words.

Index

Note: Numbers in **boldface type** (for example, **2.1.2**) refer to section numbers. The other numbers (for example, 12, 13) refer to page numbers.